GREAT SINGERS ON GREAT SINGING

Jerome Hines

GREAT SINGERS ON GREAT SINGING

Doubleday & Company, Inc.
Garden City, New York
1982

Library of Congress Cataloging in Publication Data
Hines, Jerome, 1921-
    Great singers on great singing.
    1. Singing.   2. Singers—Interviews.   I. Title.
ML1460.H46   784.9′3   AACR2
ISBN 0-385-14638-8
Library of Congress Catalog Card Number: 81-43280
Copyright © 1982 by Jerome Hines
Printed in the United States of America
First Edition

Acknowledgments

FRANCIS ROBINSON, I cannot, and will not, speak of you in the past tense. You are one of the most faithful friends I have had in my entire career. I thank you for sending me to Ken McCormick of Doubleday, making this book a possibility. I thank you, also, for offering to write the preface for me, despite the fact that unforeseen commitments have rendered that impossible. But the spirit was there, and still is through this book itself. I hope your faith in me is justified and that you are happy with this work.

Lucia Evangelista Hines, you are a sweetheart. Among those who labored to get this tome to press, you deserve star billing. Forgive me for the countless times I drove you to distraction with so many questions, but you are the Italian in our family. Although I speeka you language pretty good, I needed you help a much. When I recall those interviews with great Italian artists stalking about the room, gesticulating (that's hard to catch on a cassette tape), waxing so enthusiastic that their thoughts flowed in a torrent . . . Too fast! Too fast for my Anglo-Saxon mentality! Thank you, love, for those long, frustrating hours of transcribing from cassette to paper. Love and kisses from me.

Harold Grabau, you were a joy to work with. Thank you for the excellent biographies. And thank you, Cy Rogers, for trying to teach me, in one easy lesson, where to put my commas.

Thank you, Louise Gault and Ken McCormick, for pulling me through these three trying years of my first major writing assignment.

Last, but far from least, thank you, my talented colleagues, who so graciously gave of your time and know-how, patiently respond-

6

Acknowledgments

ing to the barrage of questions I fielded to you in those interviews. You are great, you are smart, and you are most dear to me. Also, you are the book.

Gratefully,

Jerry Hines

Contents

Warning

*This book may be injurious
to your vocal health*

—Cornell MacNeil

Preface

You may have derived a chuckle from Cornell MacNeil's dire warning on the opening page of this book, but it bears serious consideration. The truth of the matter is that to learn to sing from a book alone is an utter impossibility. If you, the reader, are in any way deluded into believing that perusing these pages will reveal secrets that will miraculously transform you into a vocal superstar, you had best return this book and get your money back. Indeed, you should even reconsider whether you are really cut out to be an opera singer at all.

A successful operatic career requires much more than a fine natural voice. It calls for a good, clear intellect, dogged determination, and a great capacity for self-denial. Many people have the misconception that opera singers as a whole do not have to be very bright. As a result of conducting the interviews compiled in this book, I have been forced to the conclusion that singers who have achieved long and successful careers are very intelligent people as a whole. They may not be intellectuals in the academic sense, but I found them to be just *plain smart* and, contrary to common opinion, they know very clearly what they are doing when they sing.

Most of the interviewees had difficulty at first in verbalizing their universe of vocal experience. This does not mean they don't understand it; it means they are accustomed to thinking about it in the non-verbal language of kinesthetic sensation. As a result, they tend to describe their private little world of vocalism by gestures, shaping of the hands and fingers to represent laryngeal and pharyngeal configurations, or using arms and elbows to demonstrate use of the diaphragm. Some even resort to pencil and paper, drawing diagrams to project their esoteric mechanisms of vocal production.

Many times their pristine intellects manifest themselves in unortho-dox ways, but that basic intelligence always shines forth.

I have encountered many students with good natural material, some the proud possessors of an academic background, who still do not have, mentally, what it takes to put it all together and make it work. Such students will inevitably be *ruined* by any and every teacher with whom they come in contact, and usually the teacher will get the blame (not to imply that all teachers are blameless). These students simply do not have the mental endowment sufficient to handle the complexities of the operatic voice and career. Princi-pally, these are the ones who will be harmed by reading this book. They will not be able to resolve the semantic confusion that arises from seemingly conflicting statements made by famous singers. They will not be capable of translating the verbal imagery in this book into their own private vocabulary of bodily sensation. And, just as important, they will not be able to adjust to the iron-willed discipline needed to forge a successful career.

As obvious as they may be, the limitations on learning to sing by reading a book should be spelled out. What should one expect to derive from a book on vocal technique? I, for one, have found these three years of interviews a truly enriching experience. Many of my dormant, half-formed concepts have found their completion in these dialogues with my colleagues. Sometimes I was pleasantly surprised by a completely new and fresh idea. I must admit that I was puzzled on occasion by seemingly conflicting views held by re-spected artists. And yet those views cannot be offhandedly rejected by saying that these artists don't really know what they are doing when they sing. This, I feel, is a very superficial attitude.

Apropos of this, I would like to make one observation. If, for ex-ample, a singer says he does not believe in *placement* of the voice, it is simply possible that he, having a naturally excellent placement from the beginning, has never felt the necessity of considering it. Most every great singer had certain things about the voice that were *naturally* there from the beginning . . . things that he or she never had to learn (of course, this will differ from person to per-son). Later in the career, if one of these *natural* functions of the singer should break down, the artist would surely have to struggle to survive. Indeed, if he lacked sufficient basic intelligence and emotional stability, it could mean the end of a career. I know of whence I speak, since forty-one years of opera singing has presented me my share of crises, and no one is exempt.

Another feature of this book that might cause trouble is that it might be considered too important a facet in a young student's quest for technique. There are several important factors that must be melded together to produce a proper method of singing. The first is hearing and imitating. I almost hesitate to use the word imitating, since it is generally so maligned by the pedagogues. So much is made, and rightfully so, of directing students to discover their own voices without imitating someone else that we tend to forget the importance of the ability to imitate. Most male students could no more conceive of the idea of *covering* without first hearing it than a man blind from birth could conceive of the color green. The sound has to be registered in the imagination and then reproduced.

As the singer tries to reproduce a certain kind of sound, he is introduced to the second factor. There must be another pair of *trained* ears. It is pretty generally acknowledged that we singers do not hear ourselves as others do. Of course, the teacher must have good ears, ears that know when the sound is right and wrong. This leads to a series of observations . . . yes, no, better, and worse. But this teacher-pupil relationship is critical, and it depends on the pupil's ingenuity as much as the teacher's. The pupil must have a facile mind that will lead him to experiment with his own inner vocal equipment, but that mind must always be subject to his teacher's critical judgment. The student must also have the ability to monitor his internal sensations so, when the teacher says he has done something right, he will be able to recall what he did and be able to repeat it.

A third factor enters when this approach is not sufficient; the teacher must now employ *imagery*. This book cannot make sounds for you to imitate, nor can it listen to you sing and make observations, but it can provide you with a wealth of imagery of such diversity that one cannot help but find many things that communicate.

Preface

In addition to this, one will find much fruitful information regarding the discipline that singers must follow if they want to remain on top in their careers.

Yes, this book may be injurious to your vocal health if you take it as your sole guide to the development of your voice. If it is used in the stead of a good teacher, there will be real trouble. A student studying this book alone, without the guidance of someone more experienced, would soon collapse in confusion due to the diversity of opinions to be found within these covers. Well, any professional singer will eventually have to face such conflicting opinions at some time in his career, and have the wisdom to select those which work for him. Perhaps the sooner one faces up to this challenge the better.

I would also like to remind the reader that, although we are all somewhat different, we do all have the same fundamental anatomy. There exist certain basics in technique which are common to all singers. Attempt, when reading this book, to follow the fine thread of logic that is woven into the methods of all great singers. Often differences between things they say are not so much contradictions as a matter of semantics. Remember, although we are different, we are not alien to each other.

Also, if you hear another singer doing something you cannot do, don't sell yourself short by assuming it is just a freak voice doing things unattainable by you. Within reason, you can probably do almost anything your colleagues can. Otherwise you will end up being the prisoner of your own attitudes and your growth will be stunted.

A final word on the peripheral aids to which many singers cling so fervently. It is a common sight, when one enters a singer's dressing room, to see good luck charms, dolls, icons, etc. Some form of security blanket is usually in evidence with most artists. I am not going to comment on the validity of superstition or religion (my religious stand is well documented), but I am reminded of a particular performance when my opera agent, Jim Sardos, entered the dressing room of a famous singer. There were more good luck charms on the makeup table than there was makeup. His penetrating remark was, "That only helps if you know how to sing." 𝄐

GREAT SINGERS ON GREAT SINGING

Licia Albanese

Licia Albanese was one of the Metropolitan Opera's most admired singers for twenty-five years, from her debut in 1940 as Puccini's Madama Butterfly to her retirement in the 1960s. During that time she sang more than one thousand performances at the Met in a large number of lyric soprano roles ranging from Mozart to Verdi. Miss Albanese was born in Bari, Italy, and made her operatic debut as Butterfly in Parma in 1934. During her Met years, she also took part in two historic opera broadcasts with Arturo Toscanini and the NBC Symphony Orchestra, in the leading roles of Puccini's LA BOHÈME *and Verdi's* LA TRAVIATA. *Miss Albanese is a U.S. citizen and currently leads an active life as a teacher in New York City.* 🎵

I BROWSED through two large rooms of the Albanese-Gimma Park Avenue apartment as I waited for Licia to appear. It was resplendent with beautiful works of art, memorabilia of an illustrious career and countless paintings and photographs of the great personages of yesterday and today whose lives have touched Licia's. Many years were spanned in this glittering collection, a vast heritage of the past and present. Happy is the person who cherishes the precious lessons of the past and lives vigorously in the present. Such a one bears a heritage that augurs well for a prosperous future.

Among the celebrity photos were some cardinals and three Popes. The Popes brought to mind the title Pontifex, or "Bridge Builder," and Licia Albanese is surely a bridge builder in her own right. Her brilliant career was capped by twenty-five years as a reigning diva at the Metropolitan Opera House, and today she is vigorously living in the present sharing her wonderful heritage with dozens of promising pupils. Her experience is a graceful bridge spanning the years of Toscanini's era and today's.

Licia Albanese

Cups and saucers for coffee time had been set in hospitable anticipation of my arrival and I prepared my excuses as Licia entered the room, since I no longer drink coffee . . . "These lips are so pure" . . . actually, I've been a fanatical health nut for five years.

Licia was most understanding, and we passed a few pleasant moments as she filled me in on her busy routine of music committees and teaching. Finally we got around to the interview.

"I always sang when I was a child," she began. "My mother sang, my aunt sang, my three brothers and three sisters sang. We sang all the time. We had no piano but my brothers played and sang jazz. We sang in the kitchen and every room in the house. Growing up in Bari, we didn't have many places to go or much to do, so we entertained our friends singing and playing in our home."

"At what age did you begin to study voice?" I asked.

"I was twelve. We all studied with the same teacher, Rosetta di Leone. She taught all the children in the family, including me, using the Concone books for scales. We trained two times a day, first in the morning and then in the afternoon.

"She did not teach us technical things like open throat, support, or placement. Instead she taught us *sfumatura, smorzato,* and musical style. She did not say to 'put your tongue flat' and that sort of thing. We just sang! Maybe it was the sun and the climate. Or maybe it was Concone and learning to sing with long breath.

"When I was fourteen Rosetta sent me to the Conservatory of San Pietro a Marella, where I studied with the tenor Emmanuele de Rosa. We continued with the Concone books, again without training with the use of technical terms. He took a group of his best students, including me, and we performed in various localities in the area just as I do today with my own pupils.

"Then my last teacher was Giuseppina Baldassare, who was the greatest Butterfly of her time. She taught me all the verismo operas and she taught me to act, too. In those days it was different. We carried our own costumes and all of our own props with us. If you are an actor, you learn to create the opera . . . not to do the same thing every time, not the same dress . . . Now everybody's the same," she concluded unhappily.

"With whom did you study after that, Licia?"

Licia Albanese

"In 1934 I made my debut in Parma singing Butterfly. From then on I found a good school in the theater singing with great singers . . . Caniglia, Schipa, Gigli, Cigna, Lauri-Volpi . . . they gave me my schooling, and in my day conductors were voice teachers, too. 'Put the note this way . . . sing so-so . . . do the expression like this! They were all teachers, Toscanini, Sir Thomas Beecham, Mannuzzi, Barbirolli.

"When we were engaged by the Metropolitan, we came every night to Box B to hear and learn . . . also how to walk on stage when performing. We learned on the stage with the great singers. They should never take great artists from the stage; they teach the younger ones from their vast experience."

"What can you tell me about your technique?" I asked.

"An artist should have nine lives like a cat," she began. "One for the use of the hands, one for walking on stage, one for acting, one for expression on the face, one for memory for words, one for musicality, and so on.

"Now things like open throat, like yawning, larynx down . . . When I was younger I never thought in this way, but I began thinking this way more than twenty years ago. I have discovered how I used to sing. What did I do? Now I lift up the palate and open the throat . . . especially for the high notes. When you sing high notes, you must open the mouth and the throat and also open the jaw more. But you must not do this so much that you lose the expression on the face. When you sing about being in love you must have love on your face. When you are angry you must have an angry face. If you say 'I love you' and make a face like a devil . . . it is no good.

"Expression and quality of voice go with the meaning of the words. You see, I think in terms of qualities. I feel I can see the tone. You have to treat one note with velvet cloth, another taffeta, another chiffon. I think very much in terms of texture."

"Let's be more specific about the mechanics of how you used to sing," I said. "What are your views on breathing?"

"If you have long phrases you must breathe deeply," she replied. "Lift the chest a little from the back, mostly by lifting the head expressively . . . as when you're shocked . . ." She took in a quick breath, lifting her head with a vibrant expression on her face, and simultaneously raised her arms up and out from her body in a graceful, theatrical sweep. How often I have seen her start a phrase in this manner on the stage, and it is a beautiful sight to behold.

"You see," she went on, "you inhale with this motion, breathing deeply, but you make it part of your acting . . . whether it's just with one arm, or just the head.

"If you have a short phrase, you don't take a breath. When you have a lot of emotion," Licia added, "you must use more breath! When I breathe I use everything. If you inhale using the tummy alone and pull it in to sing . . . you will not have a long career . . . I think. You start to lose the support."

"What do you mean by *support?*" I asked.

"If you push down with the chest and abdomen," she replied, "where do you get the breath? I tried this years ago. For me it did not work. Expand down and push up to sing . . . you just don't get a good breath.

"You should leave your belly in, expand your chest and back, and you should use your hands and arms in an upward sweep to get a full breath. It is a taller feeling and pulls the shoulders back to a good posture."

"Let's go on to *open throat,*" I said. "Earlier you mentioned in conjunction with it that you lift the soft palate."

"Yes," she said.

"What about the larynx? Does it enter in?"

"Yes," she said, feeling her voice box as she tried a note, "it goes down. It's like yawning. The sound should be round . . . beautiful."

"And now, what about placement?"

"Some people put it in the nose," she said with a grimace. "That's wrong. It comes from the breath . . . the sound is on the breath. The breath comes with the words and is the support of the phrases. If the breath lets down, the phrase comes down. Everything is controlled by the breath. The sound must be high. Don't let the breath go down with the pitch. If the note [pitch] goes down you have to keep the same round, high quality. I think here," she said, indicating the mask area of the cheeks, "but the sound should come out . . . go through the mask . . . brilliant and alive.

Licia Albanese

"Students seem to sleep when they sing. The sound that is up and round is alive . . . awake. You shouldn't sing keeping the breath inside the mouth or nose. You have to put it out like when you speak. Everything in the mask . . . round . . . beautiful . . . listen for the beauty."

Observing her face as she spoke, I was prompted to ask, "You don't use your lips when you sing, do you?"

"I don't use so much the lips," she said, overpronouncing with the mouth. "My teacher"—I assumed she meant Baldassare—"had good diction, but used no lips. Good vowels are made in the throat, not in the mouth!"

"What do you feel is the function of the tongue in singing?" I inquired.

"The great baritone DeLuca once told me, 'The tongue of the artist is the antenna.' I believe if the quality is beautiful, leave the tongue alone. If you push a spoon on the tongue, or push the tongue against the teeth, how can you sing? You can adjust your quality. You sing with expression, love, warmth, and your voice becomes more beautiful. If the sound is right, don't touch the tongue."

"Did you use your chest voice?"

"Not too much. It's dangerous and vulgar. If you do use it, you must use it with much expression. Sometimes you use it as a defense when you're in bad voice, but you can cover it up with beautiful expression."

"Then you've never had to face the problem of the *passaggio* [passage] from the chest voice to the head voice?"

"No," was her answer.

"How about any *passaggio* you might find higher up, say, around the second E and F above middle C?" I asked. "How does one go about smoothing that out?"

"The *maschera* [mask] helps a lot in bridging the *passaggio*. You shouldn't move [in the throat] too much going through the *passaggio*. Use much legato between the notes . . . don't let the throat change too much. Hold the position [in the throat]."

"I guess that covers it, Licia. Anything to add about your vocal habits?"

"Well, I sang every day. I believe in that . . . Saturdays and

Sundays included. I constantly used scales . . . about a half hour every day."

"And now you are busier than ever, passing a wonderful heritage on to this generation. I wish you many fruitful years in your new work of dedication, *bridge building*."

John Alexander

John Alexander is an American-born and -trained lyric tenor. His debut was as Faust in Gounod's opera in 1952 in Cincinnati. A long association with the Metropolitan Opera began on December 19, 1961, when he sang the role of Ferrando in Così Fan Tutte. *His versatility and superior musicianship have been of great service to the Met, where his roles have included Pollione in* Norma, *Hoffmann in* Tales of Hoffmann, *and Belmonte in* Die Entführung aus dem Serail. 𝄞

By the time John Alexander debuted at the Met, he was already well known for his excellent singing and stage presence through performances at the New York City Opera. His has been a long and solid career, and a recent cover story on John in *Opera News* dubbed him "The Rock of Gibraltar," and rightfully so.

He has most successfully survived all the major pitfalls that threaten every leading singer, although we thought we had lost him about three seasons ago when he underwent open-heart surgery. There were complications and he was rushed back to the operating room; his life hung in the balance, and many of us despaired of ever seeing him again on the opera stage, or anywhere, for that matter. But it was not long before his indomitable faith and determination had him back before the footlights.

As we performed together in the 1981 season, I marveled at his remarkable stamina and youthful sound. Here was a singer who really knew what he was doing, and I hastened to secure an interview. But it took an entire year to find a mutually satisfactory time, which turned out to be in the middle of a Met broadcast. I conducted this interview in knee breeches and a powdered white wig.

"John," I began, "we don't have much time, so let's do away with your bio. I'm more interested in how you do it, rather than how you got here. Let's start right off with your breathing technique."

"Jerry, the first thing in good breathing is to put yourself in a comfortable singing position."

"And just what constitutes a comfortable singing position?" I asked.

"Without the chest raised abnormally high," he said, "or collapsed."

"Let's discuss support, or its Italian equivalent, *appoggio?*" I suggested.

"If you can have a sensation of wearing a belt, then imagine that the relationship between the belt and the belly is one of tightening a bit. As you exhale, you try to maintain that pressure between the belt and your belly, without allowing your chest to collapse. That, of course, forces you to use the very low muscles."

"When you take the breath, is it through the mouth or the nose?"

"It is important," he emphasized, "on inhaling, to use *all* available openings, namely the nose *and* the mouth simultaneously.

"The biggest problem in singing is complex explanations by teachers, which tend to create more problems than they solve. For me, good singing is tone riding on breath. Breathing is a matter of timing. When you prepare to sing, you take your maximum amount of breath, and as you approach that maximum amount, you must time it so you can immediately begin to expel it and sing. You must not take the breath and hold it. It is a rhythmic thing. There must be a freedom of sound and no tension at all above the belly. The best technique is achieved by the most relaxation. There must be absolutely no tension in the throat, the jaw, the shoulders, or the chest. For example, if you have to bring your shoulders forward to sing, this is tension. Muscles which are tight and rigid are not free to work properly.

"Now, when we speak of dropping the jaw, we must allow the jaw to drop freely; we must not force it open. Good singing is tone riding on the breath, completely unimpeded by any tension of the tongue or jaw."

"Now, what is your impression of *open throat?*" I asked.

John Alexander

"Open throat is a matter of relaxation. I think it is the consequence of a relaxed state.

"We should sing as we speak. I feel almost all vocal problems can be solved by shaping the singing technique to conform to the speaking technique. Singing is simply sustained speech."

"Well," I mused, "I have often heard it stated the other way around, that one should learn to speak as he sings."

"Wrong, Jerry! They should sing as they speak!"

"But John," I protested, "suppose the singer does not speak correctly in the first place?"

"Normally one's speaking voice is produced correctly,* unless one is trying to fabricate a special image of himself . . . It is important not to be a phony, but to be natural. You have heard basses speaking with a deep unnatural tone . . ."

"Trying to prove they are basses," I ventured, "when it is sufficient to merely be what you are. If you are by nature a bass, there is no need to try to sound bassy. The key word is 'be,' *not* 'try'!"

"One of the greatest enemies of good singing is the recording," he added. "We listen to recordings and admire what we hear, and try to imitate it. And this is very bad. Voices are like fingerprints; there are no two alike in the world. God gave each of us our own unique sound, and if we can build on that, then we have built on a firm foundation. If, instead, we build on what we like to hear, or what we admire, we build on sand.

"I think everyone should sing as lyrically as possible with what God has given them."

"Now let's move on to the subject of placement," I suggested.

"I think the tone should be as high and far forward as possible," he said. "Placing it very high means 'nothing below the upper lip, and nothing behind the front teeth.'"

"Is there any variation in the position of the placement with different parts of one's range?" I asked.

"Jerry, if you sing 'Sparafucil' and do it . . ." He made like a bass singing the end of the duet between Rigoletto and Sparafucile. As

---

* But my point is that this is not always so: this is the abnormal case.

he sang the low note on "-cil" he dropped his tongue deep in his throat, changing the color of his vocal production to a foggy bass sound in contrast to the clear upper notes that preceded it. "If you try for sound on the low note, rather than speaking it on pitch, it will be a less perfect tone."

"Let's move on to the problem of *passaggio,* or passage in the voice," I said.

"The less we think about *passaggio,* the better off we are," he said firmly. "What we must strive for is an even scale from top to bottom. If you try for the forward placement as you ascend the scale, you will naturally compensate for the pitch. The higher you go, the more forward it must go. But you must also strive to keep the vowels pure."

"But John, as a male singer goes up the scale on an *awe,* there comes a point where the color of the vowel must change, it cannot remain a pure *awe.* It tends first to *oh* and then to *oo.*"

"That's true, but we must strive for the pure *awe,* and then nature will take care of the adjustment you described. The danger lies in artificially coloring the vowel to compensate for pitch, rather than keeping the voice forward and letting the pitch compensate for the vowel. Some singers also compensate when singing an *ee* vowel by going to *ih.* As a result the brilliance is lost. I feel this is less than desirable."

"Those singers," I said, "advocate a feeling of more space in the throat as they proceed to the high notes. I assume you disagree with that, or do you also think of giving more space on the high notes?"

"No," he answered. "I try to keep it the same in my throat at all times. I try to keep as much space as possible, but always the same throughout the entire range of my voice."

"Let's pinpoint the use of this word 'space,' John. Where is this space we're speaking of?"

"When I say, 'as much space as possible,' that means the same thing to me as 'relaxed,' a relaxed openness. The key to this is the mouth: if we try to spread the mouth, that is what happens to the tone, it too is spread. In conclusion, when we think of space, we should think of vertical space rather than horizontal space."

John Alexander

"And," I observed, "that fits in with what you mentioned in passing a while ago of dropping the jaw freely, not forcing it open.

"John, I know you're in a hurry to catch a train . . . I see you anxiously glancing at your watch . . . and I very much appreciate the time you've given me, but just one more question and I'll let you go . . . how about the use of the lips in forming the vowels?"

"I think the lips absolutely should be used in the formation of the vowels. You can't sing an *oh* in an *ah* position. If you try to sing an *eh* in an *ah* position, you're in trouble. If you would look at yourself in the mirror, you should try to have, in essence, the same vowel formation with the lips in singing as in speaking."

He rose to his feet and cast an anxious glance at his watch.

"Sorry, Jerry, I've got to run," and run he did. And so did I, because I almost missed my curtain call. That just began the running: I had to catch a plane to Miami to begin rehearsing for *Nabucco*.

Such is the singer's life, and I have to complicate mine by writing a book? But don't waste any sympathy on me; by these interviews I'm getting free voice lessons from all of my great colleagues. And don't waste any sympathy on John Alexander, either: he's the Rock of Gibraltar all right.

Martina Arroyo

Martina Arroyo is a native of New York City. Her debut took place when she was very young, in 1958 in a Carnegie Hall performance of Pizzetti's Murder in the Cathedral. *The same year she won the Metropolitan Opera Auditions and was given a contract for small roles at the Met. For several seasons she sang the usual Rhinemaidens, Celestial Voices, etc. Miss Arroyo then left New York to sing in Europe, where she developed her artistry and gained experience in opera and in contemporary music. She achieved "overnight" success on her return to the Met in the leading role of Aïda, substituting for an indisposed Birgit Nilsson on short notice. Miss Arroyo's large but flexible soprano voice is ideally suited for Verdi, and over the years she has given outstanding performances in operas such as* Il Trovatore, Don Carlos, Aïda, *and* Ernani. *In addition, her appearances on "The Tonight Show" have made her voice and her warm personality familiar to millions of American TV viewers.*

I am sure Martina Arroyo has had as many problems during the course of her career and personal life as anyone else, but there are no scars showing. I have crossed paths with this delightful soprano in opera houses, out in the street, and in hotel lobbies in both this country and Europe, and I have always seen that same cheerful, friendly glow radiating from her cherubic face. I knew that my interview in her New York apartment would be a warm, pleasant contrast to the icy winter wind blowing in from the East River that day. I never wear an overcoat in the winter, and after hiking six blocks from the nearest parking lot I was ready for some warmth in my bones.

When Martina greeted me at the door, her enthusiasm was not in the least dampened by an obvious case of the sniffles.

Martina Arroyo

"Don't tell me you've got a cold?"

"Nndough," was the stuffy reply. "Hay feeber."

"You too!" I exclaimed. "I almost blew my debut in Buenos Aires with hay fever and asthma in 1952. Fortunately I got over it just in time."

I will not bore the reader with our five minutes of commiseration on the vagaries of being allergic types. But even that discussion was in a pleasantly humorous vein.

"I remember when you debuted at the Met as the 'Angelic Voice' in Don Carlos," I began. "It was *truly* an angelic voice singing a devilishly high and hard part. Everyone felt that a new star had arrived."

As we talked further I found that Martina's angelic voice was first heard in church when she was a child. Later, at fourteen years of age, she began formal vocal study. During her high school years, because of her outstanding gift she was allowed to attend the opera workshop at Hunter College, but only to listen, not to participate as a student.

Martina has had only one teacher throughout her career, Marinka Gurewich. When she began studying with her, she had no intention of being an opera singer; rather she was planning on a career as a schoolteacher.

"What," I asked, "was Madame Gurewich's technique based upon?"

"Oh, lots of vocalises, but no particular book or method. Only what I needed. Marinka Gurewich always approaches a pupil according to her needs. I always had an easy top from the beginning, so we worked a lot on my middle and lower voice."

"Do you fundamentally use scales when studying or warming up?"

"Absolutely," she said. "I always do scales before singing, even for rehearsals. I just can't get up and sing cold. I also can't drink and sing."

"I never did drink," I said, "but we've a lot of colleagues who can't sing without taking a drink to calm their nerves. But I wonder if it really sounds any better to the audience?" Changing the subject, "How often do you recommend using the voice?"

"I try to vocalize every day," she said. "The voice gets stiff if not used. I always sing around the house, it's part of my life. I sing hymns with my family all the time."

"Martina, what do you do specifically to prepare your voice for a performance?"

"I vocalize until my voice is ready for what I have to do. It depends on whether I'm tired or not. If I've been performing regularly, my voice warms up more easily. I do like to get out in the fresh air and walk before a performance."

"Can you be more specific about the vocal discipline?"

"Well, I use all kinds of scales and arpeggios designed for the conditions—fast scales, octaves—everything. I use certain scales according to the opera I am learning or singing at the moment—scales designed according to the hard passages.

"If I'm in bad voice, I begin with the simplest scales, three or five tones up and down on la, la, la. I sing very simply until the voice begins to move. I never start ambitiously, but wait until the voice is flexible. Sometimes I stop in the middle of a scale and go back to a simpler one and then return when ready.

"I always start vocalizing in the middle voice and then go up to the high. Especially on the day of a performance I take it easy at first on the high voice until it is ready."

"What does *chest voice* mean to you?" I asked.

"I have no chest voice!"

"Really?" I said, surprised.

"It's true. I can't even fake it. I use a bit of opening when I sing down, but I have never had a strong lower voice, by nature. I have pushed, trying to find it."

"You said *pushed*. What does pushing mean to you?"

"Just more pressure than necessary. Using muscles you don't need. But if you support low you don't force or push."

"Now you used the term *support*. What do you mean by that?" I asked.

"It's an intake of breath that is straight down with no movement of the chest involved. You take the breath low and keep it low. But as you do this you must think high in placement. You never start the tone from underneath, always from above.

Martina Arroyo

"You see, pitch is mental as well as physical. Mentally you must be as high as you are physically. The voice starts in the mind, not in the body.

"When you take this deep breath, there should be a yawning feeling which opens the throat before singing. That doesn't mean it should look or feel unnatural. Singing is natural . . . the face loose . . . no showing of teeth.

"There is a slight exception to this in my case. I have a thick upper lip, which interferes with my production of the *ah* vowel, so for this vowel only I slightly lift my upper lip."

"You mentioned a yawning feeling," I said. "Can you elaborate on this?"

"I mean *yawning down,* which gives the open throat. A yawn down is total involvement of the torso . . . straight down. *That* is *support!* Once you have taken the breath straight down, you must keep it straight down. But thinking down does not mean forcing or pushing down. It's relaxing down."

"Now let's talk about pianissimo singing and its technique. How do you approach that?"

"I always use the entire voice, even when singing softly. The center of the tone must always be there. I'm talking of singing pianissimo with the complete sound, not volume. Crescendo is simply giving more with the whole body. The increase starts with the mind and the body does it. Of course, giving more breath is involved. Now, your nerves always get involved in actual performance and you do not always have complete control. The nerves wipe out about twenty percent, but that still leaves you eighty percent control from an instinctive retaining of technique."

"Are there differences in approach between high notes and low notes?"

"I believe in matching them both in quality and placement. *There* is the discrepancy . . . that *low C* and *high C* are not exactly in the same place, but mentally you should be in the same place. You should stay mentally high throughout the entire scale."

"More specifically," I continued, "what difference do you feel between low and high notes?"

"I feel more space in the very high. That doesn't mean you start small or closed on the low. As I go up, I think deeper in my breath support. That opens my throat more, but without forcing it open. High notes should be at *maximum natural.* You understand what I mean?"

"I think the term *maximum natural* is self-explanatory and a good choice of words," I concurred.

"You know," she went on, "at the age of twenty, singing is natural. At thirty, forty, and fifty you should keep what you have because you should know what you're doing technically. This is difficult in a career because all conditions affect the voice: travel, diet, weather, emotions, etc. One must always keep on studying to meet the challenges. And I continue to study with my original teacher. It's so important to have another ear outside of your own."

"Truly," I said, "it is easy to get off the track, and you need someone else who knows your voice well."

"That's right," Martina said with glowing eyes. "Singers are no longer afraid to admit they have problems. The new breed of opera singers are much more interested in being people and being approachable—rather than being untouched on pedestals. There is much more openness between singers now.

"Thank God I have other normal interests. I don't live for my vocal cords. Naturally, that doesn't mean I don't take care of my voice, just that I'm not obsessed by it. You see, I don't have to be adored by the world and yet not loved by any one single person. Of course I like applause and success, but . . ."

Obviously, Martina has found a beautiful blending of successful career and wisdom of the heart. I believe I saw more fully the *raison d'être* of Martina's warm, generous nature when, before leaving, I was taken to a bedroom doorway and introduced to a gentle but strong-looking woman in a wheelchair, who greeted me warmly. Martina and her mother do not look alike, but they both have that same cheerful, friendly glow radiating from their eyes.

It wasn't as cold walking back to the parking lot as it had seemed two and a half hours before.

Kurt Baum

Kurt Baum was born in Czechoslovakia and made his debut in Cologne. For many seasons, Mr. Baum was a mainstay of the Metropolitan Opera. From his debut there as the Italian Singer in Strauss's DER ROSENKAVALIER *his tenor was acclaimed for its strength and its forceful, clear high notes. Among his roles were Manrico in Verdi's* IL TROVATORE, *Radames in the same composer's* AÏDA, *and Enzo in Ponchielli's* LA GIOCONDA. *Currently Mr. Baum lives in New York City, and incredibly, in his eighties is still active as a singer.* 🎶

"THIS summer I sang ten concerts in Stockholm and Germany," he said cheerfully.

Not that ten concerts would be considered a prodigious feat for most singers, but this came from Kurt Baum, who was now eighty years young. I was impressed, but even more so a few moments after when he sang a Neapolitan song for me, ending with a dazzling B natural.

"Not that the voice is better at eighty," he went on, "but it is steady and well preserved."

Steady was the word. There was not even a hint of the wobble or tremor in his voice that are the usual products of aging.

Although Kurt had sung as a child in school and church choruses, when he went to Italy to study with the great lyric tenor Scolari, he didn't know if he was a bass, baritone, or tenor. When he sang scales for the maestro ranging up to a high D, it became obvious what his voice category was.

He worked with Scolari singing scales from the García books. The maestro sang for Kurt and demonstrated.

"The most important thing for me was to have a good ear for

what the maestro was doing. A student with a good ear for sound can learn faster from his maestro's singing than from someone else who explains. After using the ear the maestro explains if there's difficulty."

"What," I asked, "are the most important factors in singing?"

"There are five vowels . . . *ah, eh, ee, oh, oo.* I'm a vowel singer. Vowels, consonants, and good speaking, in any language, are the main cause of producing good singing.

"When I couldn't imitate my maestro, he explained that the vowel must be in its place. The question was . . . 'What is *the* place?' The maestro said, 'Drink the sound . . . drink the vowel.' But what is that? It is a certain sensation on the inner, lower palate produced by drinking the sound, or the breath and . . . almost . . . the vowel, but not too much back down. If you breathe in gently it will be okay.

"The vowel goes here," he said, pointing to the hinge of the jaw, "not down below there or the sound will be *ingollato* [throaty]."

"We really seem to be talking about placement, and I would like to come back to that. But first let us talk about breathing and support," I said.

"Breathing is the life of your voice," Kurt said. "Breathing is all of it . . . for a long career." (Who could be better qualified for discussing longevity of voice?)

"Now, I am strictly a mouth breather," he continued.

"How about some teachers who insist one should breathe through the nose before each phrase?"

"No!" was his authoritative reply. "The nose is only there to avoid germs. If you take air *gently* through the mouth, you have an open throat. With a heavy breath you tighten the throat. No gasping . . . ever! Breathing should be like a massage on the vocal cords, and you take the breath according to the phrase, but *never* use a sharp or heavy attack . . . it *has* to be *gentle.*"

"And then . . . support?" I prompted.

"There are two kinds. Some singers have the tendency to use the 'going to the bathroom' feeling. Gigli used this, but I don't agree with it. It's too painful . . . it takes too much time during breathing.

Kurt Baum

"With my method the breath is taken by the lower abdomen, but *not too low!* It is also taken around the ribs and back as you raise the body to a wonderful posture . . . but always in such a way that the breath is used gently and kindly on the vocal cords.

"In the low register the breath escapes more. That is right! Let the breath come through, blow out, so the cords are not pressurized in the low register. On the higher voice you switch . . . the *slancio* . . . if you like. The same amount of *gentle* breathing you use in the lower register should be used in the higher register, only you raise the diaphragm . . . the upper rib cage . . . before singing.

"When you sing low notes," he clarified his statement, "the *pipe* from the larynx down is longer. When you sing high notes, the *pipe* is shorter.

"But," he warned sternly, "the differences in the *pipe*—or position of the diaphragm—are small, *gentle* changes! Don't *push* on the diaphragm. Everything has to be *gentle*." (*Gentle* seemed to be Kurt's favorite word, and this should be carefully considered.)

"Now, Kurt, how about an open throat?"

"An open throat? Well, Italians are born with it . . . by their language."

"How about a lowered larynx?" I asked.

"I am sorry, I refuse even to talk about lowering the larynx, or else it all becomes too mechanical. Besides, I don't feel too much that it goes down. It comes from breathing gently and drinking the vowel. The gentle attack is important. It is like a fountain with a ball on top. If the fountain is turned on too suddenly, the ball will fall off. It must be supported . . . turned on . . . used . . . *gently*. [That word again.] But above all, you should feel nothing in the throat when you sing."

"It all keeps coming back to the way the breath is used," I said.

"But breath can be overdone, too. You have to try to sing on a minimum of breath. Remember the ball on the fountain."

"And now, Kurt, let's discuss *placement*."

"Placement was a useful concept for a singer like me, who developed the voice from not so natural a basis."

"Doesn't 'drink the sound' apply more to placement than breathing?" I broke in. "It gives me a feeling of placing the tone a little farther back. You mentioned the hinge of the jaw," I observed.

"Don't say *back*," he protested. "The sound begins in the lower and upper palate in the back, but the *resonance* you feel in the front . . . going through the cheeks . . . pointing to the bridge of the nose . . . yet not in the *nose*."

"If the sound begins in the lower and upper palate," I said, "how do you project it . . . or put it in the mask?"

"You don't *put* the voice in the mask. The voice is like an organ; you pump air through a pipe. The voice goes by itself, bouncing off the back of the palate."

"But you said point the voice 'to the bridge of the nose.'"

"That is an illusion, but you feel it buzzing up there, you can't get it by tensions. It comes normally when you use the breath properly."

"And *gently*," I added.

Kurt smiled. "To put the whole thing together is a sensitivity that some people have, and some people don't. You have to be a genius to be a great singer. There are about ten in the world at a time."

"And during your time you were one of the ten?"

"Of course," he acknowledged with *gentle* modesty.

"As you go up a scale from the low to the high voice, is there any change in the throat?" I asked.

"Yes. As you go up, instead of feeling the voice going straight up into the head, you have a feeling of curving it forward . . . the breath stream bends in back of the nose, aiming at the bridge of the nose.

"But now I have to give a singing lesson—"

"One quick question," I cut in. "Do you use your lips in forming the vowels when you sing?"

The answer was no.

I left, wishing the interview could have been longer, but Kurt at eighty is a very busy man. I am sure many of my readers, knowing Kurt's voice from his performances or recordings, would have preferred that I had questioned him more in depth as to how he got those fabulous high notes: he was called "The King of the High C."

Kurt Baum

But I think it is obvious from his background that he didn't *get* them . . . he *had* them. Perhaps the most important question to consider is: how did he *keep* them? In my humble opinion, the clue lies in the word *gently*. This means a concentrated soul and heart, emotion and patience.

Kurt is currently working on his own book on how to sing after eighty.

Nico Castel

Nico Castel sings more than one hundred character tenor roles. Born in Portugal, Mr. Castel made his debut as Fenton in FAL-STAFF in Santa Fe, New Mexico, in 1958. For many years he sang with the New York City Opera, then made his Metropolitan Opera debut on March 30, 1970, as Don Basilio in LE NOZZE DI FIGARO. Since then he has been an invaluable member of the Met company. 🎶

"Nico," I began, "the *comprimario* is considered a bit-part player, but I find it hard to apply such a term to an unusually fine artist like you. That little walk-on you did in the *Carmelites* recently was fascinating as a character. How do you react to the term *comprimario?*"

"*Comprimario* means 'someone who sings *with* a primary singer,' and it's a term invented by Italians for primarily Italian opera. I don't like to use *comprimario*. I prefer to use the term *character tenor;* it encompasses a range of roles that transcend the Italian repertoire, and some of the best character tenor parts are in the German, French, and Russian repertoires. Take a role like Shuisky, or Mime, or the Magician in *The Consul,* by Menotti . . ."

"Italian repertoire has very few good character tenor parts. Why?"

"I think basically it has to do with the Italians' preoccupation with melody and *bel canto* . . . to give the big chunks of music to the singers who are pouring out the big sounds."

"How did you start singing?"

"I was working for a company in Venezuela that imported whiskey. One of my fellow workers said I could not work for the company and not try some whiskey, so he gave me a glass of Johnnie Walker Red. I downed it in one draught and became very drunk and I began to sing. One fellow said, 'Nico, you have a good voice, you ought to have it trained,' and that's how I began. So I've had a wonderful predilection for Johnnie Walker Red ever since."

"I also understand you have a wonderful predilection for languages," I said.

"I served as an interpreter in the U.S. Army in Europe . . . in German and French. Language is my second love. My father is a linguist, he speaks eleven languages: we correspond in German, because I spoke German when I was very young. My governess was German."

"What are your other languages?"

"Italian and Spanish."

"Besides Portuguese, of course," I added. "Before you began your career, did you do any other kind of work?"

"Yes," he said. "I sold toilets for American Standard all over Latin America. But I was in the lobby of a hotel in San Salvador and I heard the 'Intermezzo' from *Cavalleria Rusticana,* which moved me to tears. I decided if music had such an effect upon me, I really didn't want to sell toilets for the rest of my life."

"So your opera career did not go down the drain," I observed. "How did you break through in New York?"

"I won the 'Joy in Singing' contest. They were awarding a Town Hall recital as a prize. After that I was hired for the Santa Fe Opera. Next I did twelve seasons with the City Opera, and then came to the Met in the '69–'70 season."

"What is the most interesting character tenor role you have ever done?"

"The most challenging of all is the Magician in *The Consul.* That is a nightmare. The challenge is not vocal. You have to actually perform magic tricks on the stage. On certain beats, on certain measures, you must produce pigeons, a flaming arrow, handkerchiefs, canes . . . you have to make a watch disappear.

"I was having lunch with Tommy Schippers and some other singers in Buenos Aires, and he said, 'I'm going to do *The Consul* for Gian-Carlo next summer in Spoleto.' As he was talking to the others, I took some rolls from the table, and I put my handkerchief over them, and I said, 'Now you see it, now you don't,' and I dropped them between my legs. I did this about three times *sotto voce*, and all of a sudden Tommy jumped up and said, 'Nico, you're auditioning!' This was in May. Comes October and Schippers hires me to do the Magician in Spoleto.

"When I learned the role, I hired a magician through a magic shop in Times Square. I showed him the score and said, 'I need a magic trick here, and I need a magic trick here' . . . Of course, certain tricks were specified, like a rocket . . . the rocket was a magic wand with flash paper in there.

"He showed me a wonderful trick with an appearing and disappearing cane; he showed me how to palm a ball and make it disappear, and how to make it appear in back of your ear, or take it out of a lady's bosom. So I spent six months with this guy, and by the time I got to Italy to do my rehearsals, I *was* a magician. As a matter of fact, I do it for birthday parties for my daughter.

"I once asked Tommy Schippers if he really hired me on the strength of that crazy audition. He said, 'Absolutely! Anybody who could audition for me in such a charming manner must be very good.'"

"Have you ever done Shuisky in *Boris?*" I asked. "To do it, one has to be a good singer and a consummate actor as well."

"When I first did Shuisky it was in San Diego and Houston. I was studying at the time with a Russian lady, and she said, 'My dearrr, when you do Shuisky you must come in strrroking yourrr bearrd. The public must know that you're evil.' But the director conceived Shuisky without a beard, so I wasn't strrroking anything."

"Did you study acting?"

"No, I never studied acting formally."

"Do you learn by watching opera performances?"

"In the opera you don't learn much about acting, but in the theater you do. I remember going to the Comédie Française and learning a lot about baroque-style acting, that wonderful florid French style of Molière. That came in very handy in Massenet's *Manon.*

"When I did Shuisky, I had recently seen Eisenstein's *Ivan the Terrible,* with all the boyars crouching under those low ceilings and rolling their eyeballs. It was wonderful. That's the feeling you want, everybody looking over their shoulders, rolling their eyes . . . strrroking their beards!" That provoked a good laugh.

"Do you find any difficulty in keeping your voice in condition as a character tenor? After all, with the characterization . . . coloring the voice to fit the part . . ."

"I do not characterize my voice to the point where I distort it. The moment I distort my voice, it goes out of focus, and it's bad for my larynx. I learned that from the very beginning when I was studying with an Italian teacher. I said, 'Shall I sing Goro as people are used to hearing Goro sung, with a whiny, nasal tone?' He said, 'No, sing it with your normal voice. The coloration comes with the expression of the words, with the acting of the body and the dynamics, without having to distort your voice. You wouldn't last.'

"So I keep up my voice. I have a vocal coach with whom I work when I am in New York."

"Do you vocalize the day of a performance?"

"Absolutely! I have been paid dearly for being careless . . . for going on cold. I developed an edema . . . it was Monostatos in *Magic Flute* . . . I came in furious, and I hit the vocal cords just a little too hard . . . they weren't properly warmed up, and they swelled up on me. I got hoarse, and spent the next forty-five minutes in the dressing room, just massaging them with soft vocalises. That scared me. I'll never go out without being warmed up. If you have an act to rest between scenes, when you go out again warm up again."

"Now," I said, "back to languages."

"Languages are very important, diction especially. You want to sound authentic as possible when you sing in a foreign language for people who understand it."

"You've had much experience in teaching," I observed.

"I am an associate professor of music and music education at NYU and Queens College, and have been teaching a diction and language course for singers at the West Side Y for the last five semesters. It's Spanish, French, German, and Italian and we deal with problems inherent in all different languages; examples: double consonants and single consonants, open vowels in French, fricatives in German . . ."

Nico Castel

"Excuse me," I said, risking a show of ignorance, "*what* is a *fricative?*"

"In German," he said, "the vowel fricatives and the palatal fricatives . . . the *kha* and *shi* sounds. [According to Webster's New World Dictionary: fricative: pronounced by forcing the breath . . . through a narrow slit formed at some point in the mouth, as f, v, z, n, a fricative consonant.] *Bilabial* in Spanish . . ."

"Wait," I broke in, "let's back up to simple fricatives."

"In German," he said, "there is the palatal fricative, which is formed by the upper hard palate and the upper part of your tongue, which is the *ich* sound."

"Some people make it *ish,*" I said, "and my German teacher at UCLA pronounced it in the back of the throat." I demonstrated it with my guttural best.

"That's Austrian," he remonstrated.

"We were taught to do it that way; it was gospel at UCLA."

"No, no. That's formed with the velum."

"The velum?" (Well, back to the dictionary.)

"The soft palate," he explained. "The velum . . . back in your mouth . . . as in *Dach* [German] . . . you know, that kind of sound which is often used in Spanish."

"Are there other major problems in German?" I asked.

"The mixed vowels like *ö* and *ü,* the umlauts, that's a problem for people who don't know how to mix the vowels."

Fearing he might catch me on something even worse than a fricative, I decided to get on safer ground with my second language, Italian. I should be an expert . . . my wife is Italian.

"What did you mean when you mentioned open and closed vowels in Italian?" I was on safe ground, as Italian is a relatively simple language with only five vowels (none mixed; i.e., no umlauts) and definitely sparing on fricatives.

"Italian has, of course, seven vowel sounds." (Oh no, I was in trouble again.) "You have words like *pesca* [pronounced pe*y*sska, where *ey* sounds like the vowel in the English word *late,* but with no trace of diphthong to an *ee* sound] and *pesca* [pronounced pe*hs*ska, where *eh* should sound like the vowel in the word *let*], and one means 'fishing' and one means 'a peach.' You have *venti* [ve*y*ntee], which means 'twenty,' and *venti* [ve*h*ntee], which means 'winds,' and you pronounce them differently, but it's a subtle difference."

"All right, Nico, I do recall hearing a difference in the use of this vowel in my experience, especially in the case of *e* as *and*, and *è* as *is*. The first is pronounced *ey* and the second is *eh*. You win. But is there another vowel which has these open and closed sounds? I don't recall any."

"*Poi* [pronounced p*aw*ee] is more open. The *o* is almost to an *awe*, but not so with *voi* [pronounced vo*h*ee, with no diphthong to *oo*], it's closed."

"What would you say is the most difficult problem for an American trying to pronounce Italian?" I asked.

"Americans tend to weaken vowels," he responded. "Don Puhsquale . . . *puh* . . . *puh* . . . No! P*ah*squale.

"Riguhletto . . . NO! *Reegohleytto*." (He also emphasized the double *t*.)

"The Italian double consonants are also problematic for Americans," I said. "How do you teach those?"

"You shorten the vowel preceding it. *Pero* [pey*r*o] . . . *perro* [pe*h*rrro]. In *pero* the *e* vowel was long. In *perro* the *e* vowel was short."

"You're leaving out one point," I said, recalling my first agonizing years when I struggled to make authentic-sounding Italian double consonants. "You *are* shortening the vowel, but you are also remaining longer on the consonant. With the single *r*, it is rolled, or touched, only once. With the double *r*, it is rolled two or more times. With the double *t*, you remain on the *t*, with the tip of the tongue glued for an instant to the front of the hard palate (just above the teeth).

"As you said," I continued, "words differing only by a single or double consonant have entirely different meanings. Sometimes it means the difference between a commonly used word and a very dirty word, which would cause hysterics in a public performance. I have heard it happen.

"Are there any general language problems for singers?" I asked.

"There's a difference between spoken language and sung language," Nico said. "You've got to give sung language *space*."

"I have always been told to Italianize my French vowels a bit," I said, "so they can be a bit more open-throated, but not enough to distort them. What other problems are there in singing French?"

"You have to learn how to mix a vowel. If a singer learns to say *eu* (as in French) he's in business, otherwise his French becomes really provincial Italian."

"The nasal vowels are also a problem in French, regarding good vocal technique," I ventured.

"When you sing a nasal vowel, you don't really sing through your nose. You basically sing on the vowel," he continued, "without nasalization. 'Ton amour' . . . you're basically singing *oh* [in *ton*]." He sang an *oh* that was related in sound to *awe*, the open-throated Italian *ah*. You can't sing *ton* . . . [he did it on a nasal vowel] . . . that would be too much."

"You only supplied the nasalization at the end of the *oh* vowel as a cutoff," I observed.

"Yes! At the *end.*"

"Like a diphthong," I said.

"Then you don't have to sing through your nose." This was a completely new idea to me. The interview had thus far been most profitable.

"One more point," I said, "regarding the German language. The vowels are not really the same as in Italian."

"They're more closed," he said. "*E* [as in *Schwert*] is almost like an *ee* sound. *O* [as in *roth*] is almost like an *oo.*"

After this, Nico and I discussed other subjects such as makeup and styles of composers, and we could have gone on endlessly. All in all it was a very stimulating conversation. Such detail in language fascinates me, but might not have the same effect on artists who do everything in a very natural way with a certain disdain for intellectualizing. I decided to try out some of the results of this interview on Lucia, my Italian wife and diva. As I finished my first draft of the interview, I took it upstairs to our bedroom. Lucia was in the bathroom cleaning her face.

"Lulu-bird," I said, "I found Nico's interview quite intriguing. I am sure those with analytic minds will like it, but perhaps you wouldn't." The look in her eyes told me that combat was engaged.

"How many vowels are there in Italian?"

"Five," she said, as if humoring a child.

"Ha!" I exulted. "That shows you don't know *fagioli* [beans] about Italian. There are seven vowels in your language." Her frigid silence demanded that I continue. "Now, take the Italian words *poi* and *voi;* the vowel *o* is pronounced differently in these two words."

"It ees not! They are pronounced the same!"

"Oh no," I insisted. "You see, the letter *v* is a fricative in Italian, and . . ."

"What ees theese freecateev?" she demanded.

"Well, according to Webster, it is a sound produced by forcing air through a slit formed by the tongue and some part of the mouth."

She did not seem impressed.

"Look," I continued, "*o* in *poi* is an open sound, and *o* in *voi* is a closed sound."

"No, they are both the same. He is wrong!"

"But Nico is a professor!"

"And I am an Italian!"

"He teaches fricatives at the university!"

"And now," she retorted, "I teach you a new *fricativa Italiana* . . ."

It was a sound produced by forcing air through a slit formed by her tongue and lips . . .

She's more intellectual than I thought. A Bronx cheer is a fricative in any language.*

* I am happy to report that Lucia and Nico met face to face soon after and ended up in full accord without recourse to *"fricative Italiane."*

Morton Cooper, Ph.D.

In the mid-1960s, when I was suffering from a severe vocal problem, I consulted Dr. Morton Cooper, who was a most successful speech therapist in Westwood, California. The short time I spent with him provided insights that were very important to my vocal recovery. Thus I felt he should be given his own chapter in this book, as it may prove to be of great value to some other operatic colleagues who may find themselves in similar difficulty. 🎝

THE speaking voice of the singer is seldom trained and often misused and inefficient. Why should a singer be concerned with the *speaking* voice? Misuse and abuse of the speaking voice may negatively influence and affect, if not destroy, the singing voice. Vocal misuse of the speaking voice is everywhere. It is seldom recognized as a problem. Singers are aware of singing-voice quality and the aesthetic and efficient aspect of singing. They know that the singing voice should be clear, comfortable, and durable, but most singers have little if any awareness of what is efficient or inefficient, let alone what is aesthetic, in regard to the speaking voice. Singers, therefore, accept whatever speaking-voice quality they have as normal, whereas that voice may be habitual but not natural. They train the singing voice, and develop that instrument, and leave the speaking voice to fend for itself, often untutored and untrained.

How do you know you have vocal misuse and abuse of your speaking voice? A simple means of identifying vocal misuse and abuse is by negative vocal symptoms. Negative vocal symptoms may be visual, auditory, or sensory. Visual negative vocal symptoms may include inflammation or edema of the vocal cords, bowed vocal cords, or growths on the vocal cords, such as nodules, polyps,

Morton Cooper, Ph.D.

or contact ulcer granuloma. These symptoms may be seen by a laryngologist during a laryngeal examination.

Some individuals may not experience visual symptoms, but they may have auditory or sensory symptoms, or both. Auditory negative vocal symptoms are those heard by the speaker and perhaps by the listener. Auditory symptoms may include acute or chronic hoarseness; a limited or reduced vocal range; an inability to talk at will and at length in variable situations; repeated loss of voice or laryngitis; tone change from a clear voice to a breathy, raspy, squeaky, foggy, or rough voice; voice skips or breaks; and an inability to be heard clearly and easily throughout the day; as well as many other symptoms.

Sensory negative vocal symptoms are those experienced by the individual. These may include repeated throat clearing without relief; progressive vocal fatigue or "tired voice" following brief or extended vocal usage; acute or chronic pain in or about the larynx; a feeling of a foreign substance or "lump" in the throat; repeated sore throats; a tickling, tearing, or burning sensation in the throat; a feeling that talking is an effort; tension or tightness in the throat; frequent mucus formation; prominent swelling of veins or arteries in the throat during speaking.

Negative vocal symptoms are usually cumulative and progressive, so that inflammation or thickening of the vocal cords may eventuate into growths on the vocal cords. There is also a strong indication in the literature that continued vocal misuse and abuse may contribute to premalignant as well as to malignant growths of the vocal cords.

What are vocal misuse and abuse of the speaking voice? Vocal abuse of the speaking voice occurs from excessive yelling at sports events, continual talking against or above noise at parties, on planes, in cars, or on buses, and competing with the loud sound of radios and television. Competing with noise sooner or later can create abuse and misuse of the speaking voice as well as of the singing voice. Vocal misuse of the speaking voice may occur in one or more of the areas of pitch, tone focus, quality, breath support, volume, and rate.

In every speaking voice there is an optimal pitch that affords the most amount of sound for the least amount of effort. Each individual also has a habitual pitch, which is the pitch he or she uses. If the optimal and habitual pitches are the same, the individual does not have a pitch problem. If the habitual pitch is higher or lower than the optimal pitch, vocal misuse is occurring. When there is a marked difference between the pitch and tone focus of the speaking and singing voices, one or both voices are not being used properly.

Tone focus of the speaking voice involves three major resonance areas of the throat: nasopharynx (upper throat or nose area), oropharynx (middle throat or mouth area), and laryngopharynx (lower throat or laryngeal area). Correct tone focus of the speaking voice should involve balanced oral-nasal resonance with some laryngeal resonance. If the speaking voice has proper tone focus and pitch range, there will be a natural buzz or ring in the "mask," which is the area that includes the bridge of the nose extending down to and around the lips. Emphasis upon lower throat resonance can easily create pathology of the speaking voice. Excessive upper throat or nasal resonance may cause an unaesthetic sound but does not contribute to pathology of the vocal cords.

Quality is affected by pitch, tone focus, breath support, and the condition of the vocal cords. Good quality may be described as a tone that is clear, natural, and "open." Some misused voice qualities are hoarseness, harshness, breathiness, and nasality.

Correct breath support should be controlled from the midsection. This type of breathing is also known as diaphragmatic, abdominal, medial, or central breath support. Incorrect breath support involves upper chest or clavicular breathing. Singers may have excellent breath support for the singing voice; however, in most cases, there is little, if any, carry-over of good breath support from the singing voice to the speaking voice.

Speaking-voice volume should be appropriate to the situation. Misused volume is too loud, too soft, or inappropriate. Volume is affected by pitch, tone focus, quality, and breath support.

The rate of speech should also be appropriate and easily intelligible. Incorrect rate is too fast, too slow, or inappropriate.

What causes vocal misuse and abuse of the speaking voice? One of the main causes is the vocal image, which is an individual's conception of what his voice should or should not sound like. If his vocal image agrees with his vocal ability, he has a correct vocal identity. If his vocal image is inappropriate for his vocal abilities, he is misusing his speaking voice.

The vocal image (vocal likes and dislikes) is formed by the family, by friends and associates, by the mass media, and by self-needs and desires. The vocal image may be formed consciously or unconsciously. If a young man identifies with his father and tries to emulate the father's voice, depending upon his individual vocal abilities he may or may not be misusing the voice. A young lady who dislikes her sister's or her mother's voice may attempt to use a different voice and in so doing misuse her natural or real voice.

The mass media of television, theater, and movies have for years placed a premium on low-pitched, sexy, sultry voices for women and low-pitched, macho, authoritarian voices for men. Newspapers, books, and magazines even describe the voices of personalities in these terms, indicating that voices like these are desirable attributes. These sultry or macho voice types can often be achieved without vocal misuse through competent voice direction; vocal misuse occurs when these voices are achieved by using an incorrect tone focus and pitch.

Vocal misuse of the speaking voice is often due to lack of training of the speaking voice. Even singers who are totally aware of the need for training of the singing voice are basically unaware of a similar need for the speaking voice. Other causes of vocal misuse are poor vocal hygiene, incorrect vocal training, and poor vocal models or styles. A singer, in trying to imitate a particular singer or specific style, may use a range and style unsuitable for his or her vocal abilities.

What are the physical, emotional, and psychological situations that can contribute to the misuse or inefficiency of the speaking voice? Psychological factors, such as a poor vocal image or identity, can begin or continue vocal misuse. Emotional factors, such as depression, anxiety, and mental tension, can be major influences in controlling and affecting the speaking voice. Physical factors, such as exhaustion or physical fatigue from demanding schedules and tours, or a cold or upper respiratory infection, can begin a voice problem. Trying to protect the speaking voice by pampering the voice, such as speaking softer or near-whispering with a raised or lowered pitch level, when an individual has a cold or is fatigued, may contribute to a wrong vocal pattern.

A misused speaking voice may affect the personality of the individual. Any problem with the speaking voice can cause a personality change or a vocal neurosis. A vocal neurosis is an extreme concern with the voice to the extent that the voice, rather than speech content, becomes the dominant concern of communication. Because talking is effortful and perhaps painful, an outgoing person may become withdrawn and depressed. The individual feels cut off and isolated from others and anxious within himself. Singers, especially, may become depressed over problems with the singing voice which are a direct result of the misused speaking voice. The negative effect that the misused speaking voice is having on the singing voice may cause the singer to fault his or her singing technique or singing coach. Our clinical experience indicates that many problems with the singing voice were due to problems with the speaking voice and not with singing techniques or singing instructors.

Jerome Hines, author of this book, is one singer who illustrates this point. (Mr. Hines has been kind enough to allow me in this paper to describe his problems with his speaking voice and his vocal recovery some fifteen years ago with my help, using direct vocal rehabilitation.) As Jerome Hines explained: "I was doing a lot of public speaking and public speaking wasn't very good for me. In fact, I found that speaking for forty-five minutes could be much worse on me than, let's say, singing concerts on two or three consecutive days. Naturally, when one particular set of muscles gets overtired from speaking, it's going to affect the singing, too."

What can be done to change the misused speaking voice of the singer? Direct vocal rehabilitation has been successful in treating singers for about twenty years. Direct vocal rehabilitation is changing, as is necessary, the pitch, tone focus, quality, breath support, volume, and rate of the speaking voice. It includes resolving the vocal image through vocal psychotherapy; minimizing, if not eliminating, vocal abuse; and establishing the use of the new voice through biofeedback techniques.

Morton Cooper, Ph.D.

The success of direct vocal rehabilitation depends upon the trained ear as well as the knowledge, training, and experience of the voice clinician. The voice clinician or voice pathologist must be able to hear the correct voice and guide the individual to this voice. Often the correct voice can be produced within the first therapy session.

When the patient comes in for vocal rehabilitation, a vocal case history, including a negative vocal symptom sheet, is taken, a laryngological report is requested and later reviewed with the patient, and the patient's speaking and singing voices are recorded on a tape recorder and on the Bell and Howell Language Master cards. These recordings allow for comparisons during the process of therapy and at the conclusion of the rehabilitation program.

The first step in vocal rehabilitation is to locate and identify the optimal pitch level and range and the correct, balanced tone focus. A simple method for finding the correct pitch and tone focus is the "um-hum" technique. The patient is asked to say "um-hum" spontaneously and sincerely as though he were agreeing with someone. (Saying "hello" and "really" in the same easy and spontaneous manner produces other ways to indicate pitch and tone focus.) If these key words are said with the correct pitch and tone focus, there should be a buzz or ring in the mask area.

Several total body techniques have been evolved that are quick and direct, and almost always give the correct pitch and tone focus. The first is to have the patient stand up with arms at his side. He is then directed to bend over from the waist, relaxed, but not bending his knees, allowing his arms to fall forward toward the floor, and the head to fall downward. While in this position, the patient sustains a hum or "oh." The patient is directed to hum or vocalize louder (or softer) until the correct sound is produced. This position breaks the tension, or the body armor, as well as the vocal image.

Another approach is to direct the patient to hum while the clinician presses on the midsection in a staccato fashion. This approach may well bring out the real voice. This technique may be used when the patient is bent over or in an upright position.

Still another body technique is to press in on the sides at the waist in a staccato fashion, quickly, while the patient is humming

Morton Cooper, Ph.D.

or vocalizing a sustained "ah" or "oh." This approach may also be used with the patient upright or bent over.

One other approach is to manipulate the laryngeal and hyoid area gently and quickly while the speaker hums. This is done manually with the speaker standing or sitting.

All of these approaches or techniques and variations on them simply open the throat area and allow the real or natural voice to come out, making the individual aware that another voice—a natural voice—other than the one he or she normally uses really exists.

The natural voice is quickly and easily identified. The problem is the establishment and use of this new voice by the patient, who must learn to hear the sound of the new voice, and to learn to get the kinesthetic feel of the new voice. This is now done by biofeedback techniques. The patient can see the pitch of the new voice on the Voice Mirror (an instrument that shows the pitch of voice with lights). The patient can hear the new voice on a Bell and Howell Language Master, a recording device that gives instant replay. The ear of the therapist remains the key to the entire process of identifying, establishing, and developing the new voice. The patient is the key to the use and final carry-over of the new voice.

Usually in singers, breath support for the singing voice is excellent. This correct breath support and control must be transferred to the speaking voice. All too often, midsection breath support is lacking for the speaking voice in singers and must be developed.

The quality of voice is nearly always altered and improved with the change in pitch and tone focus. Midsection breath control also improves the quality.

Because of the new pitch and tone focus, the volume usually appears louder (and sometimes is comparatively louder) to the individual, and he feels he is shouting when his volume is normal and natural. This phenomenon appears to be almost universal.

As the new voice develops, the rate may become faster or slower. This rate change is temporary.

The new voice often creates a vocal identity crisis. The individual feels the new voice is strange, artificial, phony, and "not me." Accepting and using the new vocal identity are the most important psychological and emotional attributes in the establishment of the new voice. Vocal psychotherapy is almost always an essential part of direct vocal rehabilitation.

Good vocal hygiene is a necessity for minimizing vocal abuse and for continued vocal health. A correct, efficient speaking voice allows for easy and flexible volume and good carrying quality so that the voice can be heard without pressure, tension, or forcing. Individuals can be taught how to use the voice efficiently in noisy environments.

Changing the speaking voice has been found to be unusually successful in rehabilitating the impaired singing voice. The major problems are lack of awareness and detection of misused speaking voices and lack of a sophisticated understanding of the relationship between the singing and speaking voices. Physicians and singing teachers seldom notice or hear misuse and abuse of the speaking voice. How can they be more aware of this? They can detect problems with the speaking voice from the negative sensory and auditory vocal symptoms that the singer describes. As Jerome Hines pointed out, his speaking voice fatigued his singing voice before he began singing. In his case, a laryngologist, Dr. Julius Samuels, recognized vocal misuse of the speaking voice and referred him for vocal rehabilitation.

How long does vocal rehabilitation take? Depending on the cooperation of the individual, the ability to hear and use the new voice, the severity of the voice problem, willingness to accept the new vocal identity, and the speed with which the new voice can be established, vocal rehabilitation takes anywhere from a few sessions to a year or more. Mr. Hines responded immediately and was seen for only four or five sessions.

Unfortunately, the usual approach for a voice problem is palliative, that is, antibiotics, pills, vocal rest, steam, hormones, to name a few. Some of these approaches may temporarily relieve the problem, but they are not permanent solutions if the underlying cause is vocal misuse of the speaking voice. Repeated episodes of voice problems may indicate vocal misuse and a need for training of the speaking voice.

Who should do vocal rehabilitation for the speaking voice? Training the speaking voice requires a sophisticated ear, and retraining or rehabilitating a misused speaking voice demands an experienced, clinically trained voice pathologist who works with voice disorders, and also one who has knowledge of the singing voice and vocal styles and their effect on the speaking voice.

Even singers who do not have vocal misuse of the speaking voice may benefit from vocal training for it. Singers may need more efficient and more aesthetic speaking voices for stage work, movies, television, and public speaking. The poor sound and quality of the speaking voice are often quite a contrast to the singing voice that is well focused, efficient, and aesthetic. A bad speaking voice does a great disservice to a good singing voice, to the singer, and to the listeners. Using the correct speaking voice makes speaking as effortless and pleasurable as good singing.

BIBLIOGRAPHY

Cooper, Morton. *Modern Techniques of Vocal Rehabilitation.* Springfield, Illinois: Charles C. Thomas, 1973.

——. "Vocal Suicide of the Speaking Voice in Singers," *Music Educators Journal* 57 (September 1970), 53–54.

——. "Vocal Suicide in Singers," *Bulletin of the National Association of Teachers of Singing* 26 (February/March 1970), 7–10, 31.

——, and Cooper, Marcia (eds.). *Approaches to Vocal Rehabilitation.* Springfield, Illinois: Charles C. Thomas, 1977.

Kawashima, Dale. "Singers Must Take Care of Speaking Voice, Doctor Says," *Cashbox* 38 (February 3, 1979).

Franco Corelli

Franco Corelli, a native of Ancona, Italy, sang first at Spoleto in his native country in 1952. His debut role was Don José in CARMEN. *His large tenor voice from the beginning was ideal for the heroic Italian repertoire, and he has excited audiences all over the world in such roles as Radames, Andrea Chénier, Manrico, Calaf, and Cavaradossi. After his Metropolitan Opera debut in 1961 (as Manrico) he became one of the Met's most popular singers.* 🎭

IN 1957 I made my debut at La Scala in the title role of Handel's *Hercules,* surrounded by a star-studded cast that included Elisabeth Schwarzkopf, Fedora Barbieri, Ettore Bastianini, and Franco Corelli. The main reason for my being chosen for the role undoubtedly was my size (six foot six and two hundred forty pounds), and it soon appeared to be the main reason for concern to Franco Corelli. At that time he was the tallest, handsomest figure on the Italian stage, and I topped him by two and a half inches. I was unaware of the complex my height was giving our tenor from Ancona until the bootmaker came to my dressing room to fit my boots. I suddenly realized that Lucia, my wife, was measuring the heels of my boots with her fingers and was asking the bootmaker to add at least three inches to my height. I began to protest.

"Calm yourself, darling," she said, smiling very sweetly, "I know what I'm doing." She had been tipped off that Franco, stewing over my size, had insisted on extra-high heels for his boots. At the first costume rehearsal Franco stalked on stage a towering six foot seven, and found me waiting for him at six foot ten. He never quite got over it: years later, when we sang together at the Met, he always greeted me with, "*Non tacchi alti,** okay?" And every time we

* "No high heels."

took a curtain call together, he would firmly hold me down with one hand while he took his bow on tiptoes.

During those years I found Franco to be a very simpatico, friendly colleague. He had a quick, smiling way about him despite his obviously high-strung personality. Many stories circulated about his temperament, and, I am sure, with a good share of exaggeration. But to deny he has a highly emotional makeup would be a downright falsehood, and indeed, it probably contributes much to the excitement he creates on stage, an animal excitement, as some describe it. All singers get nervous before important performances, and Franco is no exception, but he always seems to transform his nerves into dynamic energy on the stage, resulting in an electrifying performance.

From the mid-1970s on, Franco and I have become very close personal friends, and have had many opportunities to discuss vocal technique. An honest appraisal of his sensational career discloses that below the surface of that high-voltage nature lies a keen, determined mind, consumed with a passionate desire to know more and more about the voice.

Franco had sung with me during my vocal slump, which had begun in the late 1960s, and my recovery after 1972 fascinated him. He often questioned me, trying to fathom how I had engineered such a recovery. This developed into a series of discussions, sometimes highlighted with a look at Franco's vocal cords, or a turn at the piano sharing the challenge of some difficult vocal exercises.

One time in 1978 I showed him a type of fast-moving scale that he simply could not begin to do. It was then that I got an in-depth view of the driving spirit in Corelli that had impelled him to stardom. I didn't realize how much it upset and challenged him to find he couldn't master this type of scale, until I saw him several days later and discovered he had spent most of his waking hours attacking the problem with a bulldog tenacity, almost with a fury. Not only did he conquer it in the next two weeks, but he put it in his throat all the way up to a high C sharp. This fierce desire for self-mastery must be taken into account when one tries to understand how he achieved such great vocal heights.

I got Franco's interview for this book one spring day while we were driving to south Jersey in my Caddie, the cassette machine on the seat between us.

HINES: Did you sing as a child?*

CORELLI: No, I never sang until I was eighteen.

HINES: That's interesting. You are the only singer in my book, besides me, who did not sing as a child. I have heard rumors to the effect that you never formally studied voice. Is that true?

CORELLI: No. When I discovered I had a voice, I entered a vocal contest. The composer Pizzetti was present, and he said, "It's a shame you don't study. It would be a sin to let such talent go to waste." You see, I had plenty of volume, but the voice was incomplete . . . I had no high notes, I was preoccupied singing even a B flat. It was a yell. So, when I returned home to Ancona, I began to do some vocalizing with a friend of mine, Scaravelli.

HINES: Was he a singing teacher?

CORELLI: No, but he himself was studying with Melocchi, the teacher of Del Monaco. He was a young man with a passion for trying to understand vocal technique. Working with him was like a scientific study, which I feel was important.

HINES: Did Scaravelli have other students?

CORELLI: No, he was a student himself. Melocchi was considered a truly great technician in Italy, so when Scaravelli returned home from his lessons, he brought me all of the information he had learned from him. I studied more or less with that method.

HINES: Did you ever study with Melocchi yourself?

CORELLI: I only went twice, and two times are not worth talking about.

HINES: How would you describe Melocchi's method?

CORELLI: It was a method based upon vocal emission note by note. [Franco then demonstrated by singing the vowel *awe* on one note at a time.] It was very simple, based upon a low larynx with maximum opening of the throat.

HINES: Would you explain what an open throat means to you?

CORELLI: To sing with the larynx low. There's no other way, it's like when you yawn. I believe that if you show a young singer how

---

* This interview was conducted in Italian and subsequently translated into English.

to lower his larynx, he can do it, but if you try it with a person who has already been singing for twenty years, he won't be able to. You need good muscles to sing with a low larynx. A person who is already forty-five or fifty, you will not get him to open his throat, you need young muscles. But the larynx must remain in that position without forcing.

HINES: In other words, when you open your throat, you must not hold it rigidly in position . . .

CORELLI: Exactly. Don't force. The voice must float, like the ball on the water jet.

HINES: Then Melocchi's method concentrates your attention more upon the larynx?

CORELLI: Yes, it is a laryngeal school of singing. You go *against the breath* with your singing. Practically speaking, since you use pressure of the breath there, these muscles [of the larynx] must work more. You must *appoggiare* [lean] upon the vocal cords themselves.

HINES: Explain what you mean by leaning upon the vocal cords.

CORELLI: You do *awe, awe, awe,* trying out the vocal cords [becoming aware of where they are located]. You lean on the voice there.

HINES: Do you actually become conscious of closing your cords?

CORELLI: No. You are only conscious that, as you sing higher, the larynx doesn't rise.

HINES: This reminds me a bit of Pavarotti, who spoke of biting the sound.

CORELLI: Yes, *ahì* [he sang], attacking *on* the vocal cords.

HINES: He maintains that the voice originates in the larynx, not in the mask.

CORELLI: That is logical, clear!

HINES: He used clear attacks . . . *awe, awe, awe* . . . from the diaphragm and larynx . . .

CORELLI: Yes, that is when you lean on the cords. That was the school of Melocchi. But it is important how you employ this method. When you make the attack here [the larynx], you have to see if your throat can take it. Because if you do *awe, awe, awe* [he attacked each note almost glottally] a hundred times, and then look in the mirror, you will see the cords are red. And many have sung this way.

HINES: Perhaps the way they use their breath determines whether or not they survive. From the interviews I have done, there seem to be various ways to use it.

CORELLI: All those you have interviewed are people who have arrived, people who have a throat adapted for singing. I believe that every one of them, whether they breathed this way or that, would have sung just the same. But in conclusion, the throat is relaxed, not forced. Open throat means a lowered tongue [and larynx] as in a yawn, but the throat does *not* participate in the sound.

HINES: But when you bite the sound, don't you feel the throat working?

CORELLI: It's logical that you feel that little effort you feel also when you speak. But the use of the voice leaves many questions. It is truly a mystery. Who knows whether if Titta Ruffo had not placed his voice in the nose [nasally], he would have ever become the great Titta Ruffo? And yet it was clear later that his method was not exactly right. Still, you can't be sure if it was his method or some unrelated physical problem that caused him to stop singing; he finished very young.

HINES: We touched on breathing a moment ago. What are your thoughts on this subject?

CORELLI: I'm in accord only with natural breathing: to *not* sing with the chest, but use the diaphragm. It's not necessary to make a great study, because if the diaphragm responds, you go. I know that much depends on what quantity of breath comes out, in what manner it comes out, with what velocity it comes out . . .

HINES: Some people advocate pushing the breath against the cords, others advocate just the opposite, and they speak of drinking the breath (or air), that it's good for the voice.

CORELLI: It's true in the sense of "drinking the sound" in order not to consume the breath. If you use a lot of breath, it is certainly not a good method. You must find a way to place the voice with very little breath. But bear in mind that there are many whose nature it is to use a lot of breath, and many whose nature it is to use little

Franco Corelli

breath. One thing is clear, *all* people who are *short* on breath are those who use too much breath.

HINES: Too great a quantity. They waste it.

CORELLI: Yes.

HINES: But you feel a person's physical nature enters into it as well?

CORELLI: It's like the gasoline your car consumes. [That reminded me to check the gas gauge.] There are cars that use more gasoline and there are cars that use less.

HINES: A good analogy. If I had driven my Vega today, it would have consumed half the gas. And a singer's vocal mechanism is a machine that consumes air.

How about the use of the tongue? Many singers insist the tongue must be forward, touching the back of the lower teeth. Yet there is the case of——[I mentioned a famous singer, not included in this book], a great artist, who sings all of his high notes with the tip of his tongue way up, just about touching his palate.

CORELLI: If he sings well with the tongue high, why should he lower it? He has made a sackful of money. Naturally, if you have a young student, you must try to train his voice according to a theory as perfect as possible. You try to have him maintain an open throat, as with the yawn. Then, if you see his tongue is up, you try to train it to go down. You see, you always need a maestro of great experience and with a good ear. Many sounds may be produced incorrectly, and still sound good. A maestro may say, "It's beautiful," and instead it might be a sound that can ruin you. But you can't always lay the blame on the maestro, because eighty percent of the time it is the student's fault, one who does not follow his teacher's advice, or does not take his studies seriously . . . or have the intelligence.

HINES: But, back to the tongue . . .

CORELLI: I don't know . . . I have heard it said that the tongue should be shaped like a spoon. I know that the tongue must be relaxed, because it is a muscle that is attached to the muscles of the throat. If the tongue stiffens, then the muscles of the throat stiffen. Singing should be based upon relaxation, except for the diaphragm. The tongue for me is a thing that I would not care to think about.

Franco Corelli

When the sound is in the right place, the tongue is down, the whole tongue, flat, below the teeth, as when you sleep.

HINES: Do you think of raising the soft palate?

CORELLI: I believe that the yawn raises it.

HINES: How about placement and projection of the voice? Some people object to the idea of placing the voice forward, or projecting it out in front of you.

CORELLI: That's not right. We are constructed in such a way that there's a curve . . . and that is the path of the breath.

I tried an experiment: I sang *ah*, and then put a wad of cotton in front of my mouth. I could no longer hear a sound. Also, with the cotton one or two centimeters from the mouth, the voice remained inside, the vibrations did not carry. But, with a piece of cotton in front of the nose or the eyes, the voice sounded normal. So the exit for the voice is the mouth. Then what is the purpose of aiming the voice up in the mask?

However, if you make a sound produced in the mouth alone, a strange voice comes out. It's an open, spread, uncontrolled sound. But if you think of sending the voice up in the head [the mask], the voice comes out round and focused, the color is sweeter, more simpatico. So it means that this part here [the mask] helps to protect the voice.

The vibrations that propagate in the cheeks, jaws, eye sockets, the frontal parts of the head, perhaps serve in directing the breath, giving beauty to the voice, giving a more effortless trajectory to the breath.

HINES: Where, more specifically, is this place in the mask, toward which one directs the voice?

CORELLI: It depends on one's anatomy, because one person has high cheekbones . . . One person puts it here, another puts it there, and no two have the same place. Some people say, "The more you open your mouth, the more you will hear the voice." That is not necessarily so! Someone singing with a small mouth can just as easily project a big sound. However, the important thing is, if you *feel* the voice striking in the mask, it means that the voice and throat are free. Because when the throat is free, and you let the breath

Franco Corelli

pass tranquilly, and the cords are healthy, only then the voice strikes in the mask.

I don't believe absolutes exist, but I do believe that ninety-nine percent of all voices can be placed with the result of a more or less beautiful singing sound. All would be able to sing, whether on pitch or not. But this would depend on having the good fortune to find a teacher with an absolutely exact ear.

HINES: How can a student know a good teacher?

CORELLI: This is not easy, because a teacher might have twenty students, not one of whom has the necessary qualities to make it. They might have the voice and not the intelligence, or the persistence in studying. So much depends on whether or not the student takes up singing with love and seriousness.

HINES: You mentioned earlier that in your first days of singing you had trouble with your high notes. This is a common problem among male singers.

CORELLI: Men must resolve this problem of the *passaggio* [passage, transition].

HINES: Which occurs on D natural [above middle C] more or less for the bass, E natural for the baritone, and F sharp for most tenors.

CORELLI: There are many beautiful voices that have not found the way to the high notes . . . how to *girare* [turn] the high notes. One thing is very clear: if you make a middle-voice sound and then go up to the range of the *passaggio*, singing with the same kind of sound, it's not going to work. You must make a change as you go up, otherwise . . . [He sang *ah* on a scale going up through the *passaggio* to the high voice without changing the color of the vowel. It ended up a spread yell.]

HINES: So one has to go from *awe* in the middle voice to *oo* in the high voice, with *oh* lying somewhere in between.

CORELLI: You have stated it clearly. Now this famous *passaggio*, between a note placed normally in the central voice on *awe* and the high note on *oo*, goes more in the mask, it goes higher [in placement]. Practically speaking, that is the path. Almost everybody knows that the *passaggio* is rounded out. If you sing an open *ah* you can arrive to an F sharp. But if you try to keep it *ah*, it won't turn until at least G sharp, because you are now spreading the sound.

For example, Caruso, in doing scales, began with *ah*, then in the *passaggio* used *oh*, and in the high notes *uh* [a sound between *up* in English and *awe*].

HINES: Actually, if one sings pure *oo* properly on a high note and opens his jaw as if to go to *awe*, the sound comes out *uh*. There is no question that the color of the vowel must change as you go up.

Franco, as you go up into the *passaggio*, do you make a bit more space in the throat?

CORELLI: Well, a general opening, including the mouth, is necessary.

HINES: Then this rounding out of the *passaggio* you spoke of, this is opening the throat more?

CORELLI: Obviously. But all of this should be carried out with the help of a good teacher. You can work alone also, perfecting the voice . . . but too much perfection can ruin you, because, unfortunately, the voice is a mystery. You can form the voice, mold it, to a certain point, but not beyond. You can take Caruso's records and imitate his voice. But you cannot go against your own nature too long. In the fury of imitation, you ruin your own nature.

HINES: Franco, when I first sang with you at La Scala, you had a noticeably fast vibrato.

CORELLI: That's true.

HINES: How is it called in Italian?

CORELLI: *Caprino* [little goat].

HINES: You mentioned to me several years ago that you didn't like this vibrato, so you got rid of it. In fact, ever since your Met debut, I've never detected a trace of it. That's remarkable. How did you accomplish this?

CORELLI: I believe this *caprino* is caused by breath that has not found its proper point [of placement]. I was not using my breath well, it was somewhat dispersed. When the breath was taught to go to the right place, the voice became steady. It was a vibrato that came from a certain physical force. It's not that you think of the

Franco Corelli

breath itself. When I sang in the beginning, I never thought where to place a note; I opened my mouth and I sang. That is not singing with technique, that is natural singing. Singing with technique is when you think where to place the voice. All the notes must go toward the same point . . . [He sang *ee, eh, awe, oh, oo,* then he repeated this incorrectly with each vowel done with different openings and closings, different types of placement, some bright and some dark.] All vowels must be directed to the same point. As my voice found an easier path, it grew steady. However, what changed was only the use of the breath, since the color of my voice remained unchanged.

HINES: This vibrato . . . did the body shake as well?

CORELLI: Also the body. But many famous singers had this, including Pertile, Supervia, Björling. Also Ruffo, a little. But much of this depends upon forcing.

HINES: How did you acquire your beautiful *passaggio* to the high notes?

CORELLI: I found it by imitation. I listened to many records, no one singer in particular. By finding the *passaggio* . . . no longer singing open, but rounded out . . . I found a greater range on top, up to the B natural, and with more ease. But in 1960 I found the way to sing up to D flat.

In the earlier years I had sung a very heavy repertoire. And I made the voice very heavy when I sang [he demonstrated with a phrase from *Norma* with a dark sound]. Then, when I began to sing *Trovatore* in 1958, and *Turandot*—very high operas—I tried to put the voice in a lighter position, a bit brighter. Before, the voice was more baritonal. This lightness gave me the extra notes, putting a little more sweetness, gentleness, in the voice. I sang more "on the breath."

HINES: Then, when we sang at La Scala, and you had this *caprino* sound . . . ?

CORELLI: I sang that deep, low way, with much breath in the mouth.

HINES: Now, let's discuss the role the imagination plays in singing.

Franco Corelli

CORELLI: Basically, it is the brain that commands. With the thought one forms the voice. But on the stage there are so many things to think about: you have to move, interpret, follow the conductor and follow the words. In spite of all this you still have to control the sound.

HINES: Then one should strive not to be a slave to technique when performing.

CORELLI: But technique does not come only from thinking about making a sweet, beautiful note. You must also think sweet *with* the technique. These things are tied together. Certainly you do not think of technique when you sing in the middle range. But instead, when you sing "Vincerò! Vincerò!" from *Turandot,* you *think*—and *how* you *think*—about *"vincerò."* You put yourself in position to take a good breath, all of your mind concentrates on dominating your throat . . . the color of the note . . . each thing related to everything else . . . and you think, "Now I'll let you hear a note." It isn't true that one can always be completely free from technique! Only when there's something easy to sing, you needn't think.

When the voice is placed right, singing is like walking. You don't usually think when you walk, but if you are climbing the stairs, you'd better pay attention to the steps, or you'll fall.

At this point in the interview, we arrived at our destination and our thoughts turned to other things.

Everyone knows about the glorious, emotion-packed career of Franco Corelli. In 1976, at the height of his vocal prowess, he dropped out of public sight. The terrible emotional price of delivering those sparkling, high-tension performances had temporarily exhausted Franco, and he found it more pleasant to relax and let the rest of us knock ourselves out doing our thing. Everyone would be overjoyed to see him return to the opera stage again.

In June of 1980 Franco did a great favor for Lucia (my wife is the chairman of the New Jersey State Opera's annual ball) by singing two numbers at her grandiose affair. The result was a pandemonium of joy from the audience as they heard the Franco Corelli of old, his beauty and power of voice undiminished.

Franco Corelli

The night after the ball I rejoined the Met on tour in Boston. Word had spread fast, and the management met me with the impassioned plea: *How can we get him?*

Cross your fingers.*

---

* Since the writing of this interview, Franco has begun doing select, triumphant performances in places such as the New Jersey State Arts Center in Holmdel. Relax your crossed fingers. It's working.

Fiorenza Cossotto

*Fiorenza Cossotto made her debut at La Scala, Milan, in a small
role in* Manon Lescaut *in 1958. She continued to sing small roles
at La Scala for several years. Then in 1962 she replaced an ailing
singer in the title role in* La Favorita *and since has become one of
the world's leading mezzo-sopranos. Amneris was the role of her
Metropolitan Opera debut in 1968. New York audiences have enjoyed her rich, warm voice in many roles, including Santuzza and
the Princess in* Adriana Lecouvreur.

"Signorina," the voice rasped nervously on the telephone, "La
Scala calling. Come to the theater immediately. Madame Simionato
just called saying that she cannot sing."*

Fiorenza Cossotto's heart sank. She had successfully jumped in at
the last moment twice during her first season in smaller parts at the
famous Teatro alla Scala, even learning one role in only three days.
But this was the title role in *La Favorita!* And our twenty-three-
year-old mezzo-soprano had just come home from six hours of rehearsals.

"It's too late," she cried. "It's seven-thirty, I've already eaten a
big bowl of minestra . . . no, no!"

"You must come, the theater is already full. We have given you
the opportunity to study and sing here. Now you must save this situation for us."

"But *Favorita* . . . without rehearsals . . ." Fiorenza knew that if
her heroic attempt to bail out the theater ended badly, it could
mean the end of her career before she had even gotten started.

With deep misgivings she accepted and hastened out into the
wintry night with her husband, Ivo Vinco. On her way to the the-

* This interview was conducted in Italian, and this is a free translation.

ater she bolstered her courage by thinking of her parents. They were poor, and had to work hard just to eat, and many was the time they did not eat so Fiorenza could afford her voice and music lessons. Their faith in her future was amply demonstrated and she could not let them down; she had to win the battle, and this is how she described it:

"Our destiny is written for us. I arrived in the theater at eight-thirty, and the performance was to begin in fifteen minutes. First we tried the costumes. They fit perfectly. Next, the wig, of perfect size. The hat was as if it had been made for me. Even the shoes were comfortable; imagine if they had been too tight, or too long! I was made up in ten minutes.

"But the groans when the public was told Simionato was not singing . . . I thought of my parents, I thought of Ivo, my husband, and I thought of our baby boy . . . All this gave me strength, and I went on the stage saying, 'I must now think only of singing and performing well. I have studied, and I know what I have to do; I must do well that which I love.'

"After that terribly difficult aria of the third act, I received the longest ovation of my entire career. When I came off stage at the end, amidst the congratulations of the tailors, the wigmakers, and the staff, I asked them all, 'Where is Ivo?' Nobody could find him; he was behind a curtain in the corridor crying his eyes out, weeping because of his great responsibility. Since we had first met in Milano, where he was already launched in his career, he advised me vocally, and I had great faith in him. We both knew that this impromptu performance at La Scala could easily ruin both of our careers, but, instead, all went well."

Fiorenza had given a most emotional account of her crucial debut as she relived those triumphant hours for my benefit. It was a heady reminder of stormy emotions and fiery furnaces through which all must pass who are destined for great operatic careers, but the way is littered with countless thousands of those who tried and lost. All the more beautiful, then, to hear of those who dared and won, and Fiorenza Cossotto has certainly been a winner.

I first sang with her in Buenos Aires, at the famous Teatro Colón, and she was a sensation as Eboli in *Don Carlos*. I then had the

Fiorenza Cossotto

privilege of singing in her debut at the Metropolitan when she did her first Amneris to the cheers of the New York public. And now, some years after, I was in Fiorenza's hotel room ready to delve into the secrets of her success; I had already found one: courage!

"Fiorenza, did you sing as a child?" I asked.

"I have sung as long as I can remember," she reflected. "I attended a school run by nuns in my little ancient village of Crescentino, near Torino. The school put on performances and I always had a leading part.

"My voice was different from the others. I had a dark sound. It was obvious I was a mezzo. Later I won a contest with my singing and got a scholarship to a conservatory. I received my diploma after five years of studying voice, piano, and music in general."

"Who was your teacher at the conservatory?"

"Paolo Della Torre. I then began studying stage deportment at La Scala, and they immediately took me for small parts. I was nineteen years old, and I still needed to study."

"What was your voice like at that age?" I asked.

"It was unusually dark, like that of a contralto, of great volume. It was mature only in the middle. I didn't have low notes; I did have the high notes, but they were shrill [*fischi*]; I still had to develop them.

"For five years my teacher had been afraid of ruining my voice, and had not allowed me to sing very high. Ivo said, 'My dear, you must not make such an enormous middle voice sound, because you must go up to the high voice with an even column of sound. You must content yourself with the middle voice of a mezzo-soprano [instead of a contralto].' And thus it became much easier for me.

"My teacher had always insisted that when a singer had a good middle voice, it was the foundation upon which to build the high voice and the low voice. If you begin to lose the middle voice, you lose the foundation.

"That is why I have always paid very strict attention to not exaggerating on the low notes, but to keeping the voice even, not shoving down on the chest tones like a man. Once in a while when a certain word requires a more dramatic intensity, or power, I darken the sound, but only for the moment.

Fiorenza Cossotto

"Naturally, on the low notes I use a little bit of chest, but I seek to equalize it with the middle voice."

"Did you principally use scales when you began to study?" I asked.

"Yes. My teacher started me on scales . . . fifths and ninths . . . on all vowels. Then we used sustained notes, taken softly, then louder, and back to pianissimo. Except for some early Italian arias, I studied for two years on scales alone."

"You still study on scales?" I asked.

"Always! I do my usual scales on *ah* and *eh* vowels but only to warm up the voice, since it is placed right. But when I study now, I take my example from the great concert pianists, who study hard passages from their repertoire, by the hour. The vocal cords are even harder to handle than the fingers. So I say, 'If the pianist has to study for hours in order to move two fingers, how much more zealously should I tackle difficult passages.' I feel a singer could study all of her life just to make one phrase come out well."

"How long does it take you to warm your voice up for a performance?"

"A minimum of an hour, beginning gently."

"Let's discuss technique in more detail," I suggested. "How did you straighten out the problem of your high notes?"

"I sought the position of my throat that would make them come out right. Ivo would say, 'That note was good.' Then I would try to feel the position . . . where I put the sound, and attempt to continue in the same path.

"There are various places in the throat where you can *appoggiare* [lean] on the voice, and I found *my* proper place. It would be different for someone else. I believe it would be a great mistake to try to describe my feeling of the *place* exactly, because it would put other people on the wrong track."

"Let's approach it this way," I said. "What does *open throat* mean to you?"

"Relaxed. It's a vertical feeling, up and down, almost like a yawn."

"Do you feel the base of the tongue should be down a little?"

"I have always believed that too much thinking about where you put the tongue, et cetera, causes rigidity. Instead, you should keep it as simple as possible."

"Perhaps you approach an open throat by simply thinking of the proper vowel sounds," I said.

"I have found the vowels that are too open [spread] don't work. The *ah* should tend toward *awe, o* toward *oo*. Never sing *aah* [she sang a white *ah* with the mouth opened horizontally]. At least, I speak for myself, *oh* toward *oo, ee* toward *eh*, because *ee* is already closed [*stretta*]."

"Then you feel that proper vowels mean proper singing?" I asked.

"Correct. For years my teacher made me sing *ah, eh, ee, oh, oo* on the same note without changing the position, and this becomes more difficult as you go up, and you cannot, after a certain point, keep the throat in exactly the same position."

"Do you use the lips in forming the vowels?"

"I try to use my lips in a natural way," she said. "You shouldn't make the *oo* different from the *oh*. Or, in going from *oh* to *ee*, you cannot do . . ." [She went from round lips on *oh* to a widened mouth on *ee*.] "Instead, you must do *oh . . . ee*." She kept her lips relatively round and unchanged.

"Try going from *awe* to *oo*," I suggested. As she did, the lips did not protrude for the *oo*.

"You only closed your jaw going to *oo*," I observed.

"But that's where you need a maestro," she said, "to control the color of the vowel. When I go from *ah* to *oo*, I cannot make a white *aah*. I must make an *awe* that resembles an *oo*, and I must make an *oo* that resembles an *awe*. I try to change the vowels as little as possible."

"Did you ever have a problem with the passage from chest voice to the middle voice?"

"No," she said. "I use chest voice, but I use it lightly. Now I can support it, and switch it . . ."

"What do you mean, 'switch it'?" I asked.

"The throat enlarges . . ."

"Where?" I asked.

"The part of the throat that immediately attaches to the palate.

Fiorenza Cossotto

It is the part behind the palate, down in the larynx, that enlarges."

"You mean that the pipe, here in the larynx, enlarges," I suggested.

"Right, but without force. Above all, think to not make the note rigid. There must always be a relaxation. I try to *appoggiare* [she was applying this term to the larynx, not the diaphragmatic area*] as if I were yawning in such a way that the note was accompanied by the breath, like taking a yawn with sound. This obligates you to breathe exactly at the moment that you are making the sound."

"How high do you take your chest voice?"

"I can go as high as G above middle C if I wish. If I don't wish, I don't. It is very important for the student to be able to unite the two registers [chest and middle]. They can equalize the voice by doing exercises that start above and go down as far as possible, both scales and arpeggios, keeping the voice light. Then you can do it contrarily, going from the low to the middle range with the voice well supported. You then develop two types of voice, one from above and one from below.

"When you sing passages with sweet, gentle words, that require a light production, you are prepared to sing them lightly. So you can lighten or *appoggiare* on the voice according to the words, whether they are gentle or dramatic. Now, when I sing a very focused and supported *eh* vowel down low, the throat is in a better position to go up to the middle voice.

"There is a chest sound that some singers use which is not focused; it is completely abandoned, but that is not the true beautiful sound. It is vulgar. I absolutely refuse to use such a sound. I keep the chest voice contained, always within certain limits, controlled by the breath, also in terms of volume. I never give all that I can, but I always try to focus the sound and I use it so all the way down."

"What is your normal passage from chest to middle?" I asked.

"E flat, E natural," she said, "and as you go into the middle voice, you must find a position in the throat that is absolutely different, the throat must have a vertical feeling, not horizontal."

* Observe that in this book some singers speak of *appoggio* (support) in connection with a sensation in the larynx as well as in the diaphragm.

Fiorenza Cossotto

"As you go up to the high notes, do you think of a higher position in the mask?"

"Yes, exactly. For mezzo-sopranos that have a large middle voice it is not possible to avoid a change of position. The whole musculature changes. Everything raises. Think of a pyramid. The point is at the top. The voice is like that: you cannot think of a high note being as large as the base, because you would never arrive up there. You must make it more pointed as you go up. Up above it is always concentrated. Think of the high notes as small [pointed], not large."

"Let's discuss placement of the voice," I said.

"There are things we all have in common, and there are certain rules that are invariable," she said, "but I believe each singer must find her own color, or sound, according to her constitution. She must find the right place for the note in her throat."

"In the throat? Or in the mask?" I asked.

"In the mask if it's a high note, but for central and low notes you must find them in the throat. It is not possible in the mask alone. When you go from the low notes up to the high notes, the voice goes more up into the mask. When you near the second passage, B, C, C sharp [above middle C], the voice already begins to get higher instinctively. There is nothing you can do about it. Even if you wished to keep it down, it would go up."

"When you go from *forte* to *piano,* what is the difference in technique?"

"You must give less breath and focus it more. There is no way you can keep a large space in the throat."

"Then the throat is more open for *forte* singing?" I proffered.

"And more focused for *piano* singing."

"Fiorenza, in conclusion, let us speak of *appoggio* with regard to the diaphragm."

"One thing is certain," she responded, "that we women should never use the low abdomen in breathing. You men use pressure down there, but we cannot, because it is very dangerous physiologically for the woman. They instead expand more here"—she expanded her lower rib cage—"and they don't push down, in order to protect a delicate part of their body. Expand here in the diaphragmatic area [the lower ribs and the stomach]. From the diaphragm on up there must be a slight raising, including the shoulders. If you make a beautiful sweeping gesture with your arms, you take a good breath, and your shoulders raise a bit.

"A famous stage director and ex-ballerina told me I breathed like a ballet dancer. Perhaps it is so, because I took two years of ballet, and maybe I have retained that. However, when I breathe, I pull up the diaphragm [her ribs expanded out and a bit up in the front], and the shoulders instinctively must raise up a little bit, otherwise where would the air go? Then there are two sets of muscles that act like suspenders." At this point I got the distinct impression that the "suspender" type muscles acted as a counterforce to the expansion in the upper chest.

"Everything must be in harmony. The breath must arrive tranquilly without thinking about it. You cannot think out everything as if you were a machine. There must be a harmony of movement in the whole body, and you can only do that through instinct. If you think, 'Where do I put the breath? Where does it come from? Where is it going?' then you tense up and lose this beautiful harmony."

As our interview came to a close, I realized how many times the word *instinct* had come up. I also thought of that crucial debut when Fiorenza had to close out all the clamoring doubts and thoughts and just think of beautiful *instinctive* singing. Trusting in one's technique to work *instinctively* takes a tremendous dose of courage!

Régine Crespin

Régine Crespin was born in France; her operatic debut was also in France: in Mulhouse as Elsa in LOHENGRIN *in 1951. Mme. Crespin has employed her exceptionally large dramatic soprano voice in a wide-ranging repertoire of French, German, and Italian operas. Among her outstanding roles have been Sieglinde, Dido, and the Marschallin. The Marschallin was the role of her Metropolitan Opera debut in 1962. More recently, she has been acclaimed as Carmen and as Madame de Croissy in the Met's production of* DIA-LOGUES OF THE CARMELITES. ♔

RÉGINE studied piano diligently as a teenager, but she also loved to sing, accompanying herself at the piano. And sing she did, day in and day out. Now her mother was a great music lover, but enough was enough.

"Régine," she cried, "you cannot learn something else . . . something a little more interesting?"

Impelled by her mother's complaints, Régine inquired of her piano teacher what she could sing that would be more interesting and challenging. Her teacher brought some music and Régine began singing it with her.

"My," said the teacher, "you have a lovely voice . . . you should do something with it . . . a little study, perhaps."

Her mother received the idea enthusiastically, hoping her daughter would not continue to bore her with her primitive repertoire.

With that, Régine began her first voice lessons with an elderly lady who "never really taught me anything; she just had me shouting."

Régine was sixteen when she began studying and before long left her hometown of Nîmes to continue her studies in Paris, despite her father's protestations; she was his only child, and also it was contrary to their family's tradition. Contrary or not, she was soon studying with Madame Cesberon-Vizeur at the National Conservatoire.

After four years of study, Régine made her debut in *Lohengrin* in the town of Mulhouse and soon after added *Tosca* to her repertoire. As our diva puts it:

"I had the voice for doing big parts. I started in heavy things very young."

I was interviewing Régine Crespin in her East Side apartment in New York. She was a bit down in spirit because of the recent death of her little poodle. I can sympathize because I too am a "poodle possessor" (or is it the other way around—I'm not sure who possesses whom). But her face soon brightened as she began to talk about the voice and the theater, two of the great loves in her life.

"Of course, singers should not push themselves too strongly, and, most important, they must *enjoy* singing. If you don't enjoy . . ." She shrugged her shoulders in frustration at the thought of someone singing without the love of it.

"You say you began your career, Régine, singing the heavier roles?" I asked.

"It's fine if you have the voice for it," she responded. "I always had a big voice. When I was twenty-three I made my debut at the Opéra Comique in *Tosca* and *Lohengrin*."

"That's something," I said. "A teacher will bring me a pupil and say, 'She's only twenty-eight, she's young.'"

"At twenty-eight she must be on the road already," she said.

"That's true," I agreed. "Most successful singers I know have been singing professionally since their early twenties. But there are exceptions."

"Of course. But you have to be at the top between thirty-five and forty-five. My second teacher in Paris, a tenor named Jouatte, always told me those were the best ten years of your life. And he was right, because I arrived in Bayreuth when I was twenty-nine, and went to Glyndebourne and New York when I was thirty-two. And it was the right time."

"Were your original studies based on scales?" I asked.

"Of course! Various ones on different vowels. Jouatte was using—

extremely—the 'n,' which I am not so in accord with now. For instance, we would use *nee, nah, no,* doing [she sang]:

(staccato)

"The first time my teacher asked me to do that I said, 'Are you crazy, Maestro, I'll never do that.' He put his glasses down, and said, 'In two weeks you are going to do it!' And two weeks later I was doing it."

"Did you principally work on fast-moving scales?"

"To start with, yes . . . with a closed sound like humming . . ." She demonstrated with a quick five-note scale coming down from G to C, then A to D, then B to E, etc. "Not so much sustained things, more moving things. My teacher said, 'When you are young, it's more difficult to sustain the sound, so you have to move the voice quick so the voice doesn't have time to get . . . get . . .'" She grimaced, tightening her neck muscles.

"Get rigid," I suggested.

"Yes. He was saying that you have to move a big voice, keep it light. Then we worked on arias using sustained sounds. That was when he was putting much attention on sustained singing, for instance, to give an intention to a sound, not to just have a sound last for one bar. He was always saying, 'Stop! Give a little less, then give a little more. What do you feel? What is the *personaggio?*'"

"When I began to go into the Wagnerian repertoire and the recital repertoire, I did something a little stupid. I literally forgot my voice in order to interpret the personage. I was too interested in the staging, acting, and I got in trouble, so I stopped singing and studied for one complete year, and you see what happened when I came back to the Met with *Carmen* four years ago."

"I worked for one year with Rudolf Bautz," she continued. "He understood immediately it was a psychological problem and not vocal. For instance, I was breathing like an animal." She demonstrated by taking a great breath.

"He said, 'Madame, cross your legs and cross your arms. Now, don't breathe . . . *sing!*'

"I said, 'I have to breathe.' He said, 'No! Just give me two or three notes, that's all.' And we started like this. And little by little the flexibility of the voice came back."

"Régine," I reflected, "I, too, have had to resort to this many times when I have gotten into trouble, and I recommend it highly. But let's go back a moment and finish our discussion of your early training with Jouatte. How much of your lesson was used for scales?"

"Twenty to twenty-five minutes of vocalizing on arpeggios and scales. We would start in the middle and go to, say, mi, fa . . ." She went to the piano and indicated a range from middle C to the second F above it.

"Then we would go up until I had used my full range. He was never insisting, for instance, to sing on my very high notes . . . except on scales . . ."

"But not on sustained tones," I added.

"Because," she continued, "if you build your low and center—Well, you don't build a house by starting with the roof . . . But not a very big low. Now I am a teacher myself, and I start teaching from the middle register down. Basically I give students scales with words put to them; in Italian, if you want, or German, or French, or starting on scales with *Brrr* or *Breee*. But it depends on what the voice needs."

"In your first six years of study, what did you have to acquire?" I asked.

"The bottom was never a problem for me, considering me as a soprano, since I am not really a mezzo. Once I had a little problem, that passage from chest to head voice. I solved that passage five years ago. I find out that when you try to go on chest, you have really to put your larynx down and open it." When she said, "open it," she put both her hands at the sides of her throat, with her fingers curled in, and pulled her hands apart.

Régine Crespin

"It must be down and as round as possible," she added, to my quizzical look.

"The open, round feeling is in the larynx itself?" I asked.

"Yes, exactly, without forgetting that the soft palate is high; never down. If you put your soft palate down, you lose the connection with the head tone." To demonstrate this connection, she reached way up with one hand, pulling down with the other in the region of her stomach, as if she were stretching an imaginary rubber band.

"May I use the analogy of a rubber band?" I asked.

"Yes, if you want, but I use a broom, or a cane. If you are singing medium high, medium low, you should imagine you have a cane coming down from the top of your head into your chest, and yet everything is open like a column, nothing is closed or tight. There is nothing in between. Oh, the vocal cords are there, but the muscles are supple. When I say *open*, it means nothing in the way. No jaw . . ." She pulled her jaw down tightly to show the wrong way.

"Does that column extend all the way down into the abdomen?"

"No," she said, "only to the chest, because there is not so much resonance below that. You know that in France, years ago, everybody was against singing in the chest. We were not permitted to do it. And that's why I had such a difficult time finding the way to balance and not have a break. For my type of voice I needed sometimes to have some chest, from A . . . where it was going almost naturally."

"I understand," I said. "Since chest was taboo, nobody taught how to smooth out that troublesome passage; you were only supposed to use head voice, thus avoiding the problem."

"But," she went on, "if I wanted to sing on chest on D flat, D, E flat, E, F [above middle C], I had to work hard. But now I know how to balance that, because I put my larynx down and just let it go free. It will go, because the chest is a natural sound. When we talk, we talk on it. Chest voice is the speaking voice."

I said, "I have heard many mezzos really sound as if they were yodeling as they went from chest to head and back."

"That is terrible."

"How can they overcome this problem?"

Régine Crespin

"With strong attention in preparing to go into the head tone, leaving the larynx open, but being careful to keep the soft palate high."

"Does keeping the soft palate high enable one to put more resonance in the nasal passages [the mask]?" I asked.

"Not too near the nose."

"Well," I continued, "some people feel a bit of nasality helps smooth out the passage."

"That, for me, works for the higher passage. I have to be careful beginning on middle C, and on F [second F above middle C]. That is the second one. I sing that a little too loud and too broad. Then I use a little nasality, not closed, but open, with the soft palate high."

"You never use the nasality in the lower passage?"

"Sometimes. It depends on the words."

"Do you associate open throat with yawning?"

"Careful," she warned. "When you start to yawn, everything goes up. When you finish yawning, everything is down. Well . . . it's the beginning, when you yawn politely. The end is not good . . . It's like smelling a rose . . . Ah!"

At first that made no sense to me until I tried sniffing as if smelling and I noticed that with each sniff my larynx dropped. Seeing my actions, she admonished me:

"Not too much, just the space you need, and that's enough. Not to do something which asks you to make an effect, the face as natural as possible."

"Do you use your lips to form the vowels?" I asked.

"I think the articulation is not to be made by the lips, really, but made inside the mouth, just behind the teeth. For instance, I can say '*awe, ee, eh, oh, oo*.'" She sang these vowels without using her lips. "Did you understand the vowels?"

"Yes," I said.

"Did I move my lips?"

"No."

"Completely without the lips. It is just behind in the mouth, not in the throat, of course. Now, what is carrying the voice? You cannot sing on the consonants, so it is the vowels."

"So, open the throat," I began to recapitulate.

Régine Crespin

"The beginning of the yawn, and I say to my students, 'Be suddenly, quickly astonished.'" She took a quick breath, her face lighting up . . . "*Ha, ha!* Start breathing by the nose, and be astonished, even in the high voice. Even the expression comes. It's the eyes . . . a smile . . . a surprise, which is good.

"We should also sing with the cheeks a little high. No tension," she warned, as she saw me trying it, "just a little high like the beginning of a slight smile. You smell a rose, and the smile remains. And it gives you an expression of kindness, or sweetness, or sadness. You can have any expression on the face that you want."

"Do you feel that the chest voice is more relaxed, less placed in the mask?" I asked.

"Yes. But it has to be connected always with the mask. Chest voice is more relaxed. Sometimes I start in the higher register and the breathing is not so easy, and I immediately go back to the chest tone. Immediately the breathing is easier, and I have more breath. And it relaxes me for going up."

"You can't really sing chest without relaxing, can you?"

"Absolutely not! Unless you push."

"When you speak of pushing, what does that mean to you?"

"Pushing, for me, is the question of breathing. If you take too much breath, you blow a lot of air against the vocal cords. What can they [the vocal cords] do?" She demonstrated by hitting her hands hard together. "My teacher said, 'To sing well, the vocal cords have to vibrate *côte à côte* [edge to edge] but not to be tight. *That* is pushing. As soon as you take a big breath it's . . . Ha!" [She gave a harsh, damaging attack.]

I suggested, "Let's talk about *support,* since we're on the subject of breath."

"Support is just having the breath you need, with the lower ribs open, and the diaphragm down. And then as you sing it goes up. Of course, when you breathe, you . . ." She pushed in her lower abdomen and immediately the upper region of her stomach popped out.

"Is it a pressure and counterpressure, one in balance against the other?"

"Exactly! One teacher said, 'The lower abdomen out!' I'm not very much for that pushing out."

"It's a good way to get a hernia," I said.

"I think if you breathe like a balloon . . . not a balloon, but a kind of something very smooth, very round inside, getting a little narrow going up, not forced, not pushed, but just to shut off the breath . . ." She dipped her hands down, making a sort of semi-sphere in the diaphragmatic area, ". . . but don't forget the ribs. When I take a big breath, I am full of breath . . ." She expanded all around her body, searching for words.

"All around, not so much in the chest," I offered.

"Never in the chest—almost never. Sometimes you have to use it for emergency. If so, think you have a kind of elastic pouch under your arms." With this she hooked her thumbs under her shoulders—or pectoral muscles—her fingertips touching in front of her chest.

"Like a rubber band across your chest?" I asked.

"Yes. I breathe down and suddenly you feel that you push against the rubber band to open it. And that is done by the upper back . . ." She pulled her shoulder blades back, expanding her chest a bit in front. "The back takes the work."

"So," I observed, "when you want a little extra expansion of the chest you do it by pulling the shoulders back a bit."

"And those muscles in the high back . . ."

"They take the tension," I volunteered.

"But not to be used always . . . only in case of emergency. For instance, if you sing sitting, and you are not so comfortable, then you can use a little bit of that."

"I notice, Régine, that when your shoulders go back like that, the chest does not enter into the attack."

"Never," she responded. "In fact, that should never move . . . like the shoulders. The real breathing is from here." With that she took a breath from the solar plexus right down to the lower abdomen, and expanded her chest all around the sides.

"The waist," she said, "and the ribs out. And if you could, leave your ribs constantly open." Her upper chest was without motion as the rest of her breathing apparatus expanded and contracted rhythmically.

"I read García. He said, for women, they should breathe only with the shoulders and the chest," she said. "Why? Because at that time the women wore corsets."

"So they couldn't use diaphragmatic breathing," I exclaimed.

"Right. So that's why they had such little head tones and not a big voice."

"Régine, as you go up in range, do you feel any change in the configuration of your throat?"

"In the chest voice I feel my larynx very low down. After the *passaggio*, in the middle, before the high notes, it takes its natural position. But I discover the larynx should go down again for the very high notes. And something else I discovered, do not open the mouth too much as you go up to the very high notes."

"Do you open or close the mouth more in the low range?" I asked.

"I can open it, or close it. If I want to make it pianissimo, I have to open the mouth a little more. If I want to keep it on the chest . . ." She demonstrated with a more closed mouth.

"That's a more focused sound," I said.

"It's focused," she agreed, "but the diminuendo is a bit more difficult, because I am not a real mezzo. The less I open my mouth, the more the sound is narrow, focused, well projected. That's my problem too, because I sing too wide. All of us sing too loud and too wide. If you have a big voice, you want to give even more. But if it's a big sound to you here, it doesn't carry."

"What does focus mean to you?"

"A little hole, making it a little tighter. Not tight!"

"Do you focus more as you go into the first passage from chest to head voice?" I asked.

"If you sing too wide, what can you do? On that *passaggio* you make it more narrow, almost *stringere* [squeeze, in Italian], but *not* squeezed. And higher," she added. "Don't go down with the soft palate."

"Shall we discuss placement?" I said.

"Putting the voice in the mask? In France we have an expression, 'He sings in the mask,' which is terribly good and terribly bad," she said. "To sing in the mask means to use all the resonance we have in the face, but in front! When you do . . ." she made an ugly nasal *aah* . . . "in the nose . . . the sound that goes in the nose stays there. You have to use that space which is *behind* the nose.

"You, for instance, are a foreigner. When you sing French it is fabulous, because when you use our terribly difficult nasals, you use them very well . . . using the back of the nose."

"By that you mean . . . ?"

"*Nasalité*, in French," she said, "not *in* the nose, but just behind. There is a way to see if the sound is *in* the nose. You say 'mon,'" and she made an improper nasal tone and pinched her nose closed. The sound stopped. Then she made a proper nasal tone and pinched her nose. The sound remained almost unchanged.

"Ah, I see," I exclaimed enthusiastically, "the sound stops when the soft palate is down, touching the back of the tongue. This shuts off the air and resonance to the mouth, producing a purely ugly nasal sound." With that she sang a correct nasalized vowel.

"Now, my soft palate is very high," she said.

"We singers can change the color of our voices at will. How does one find his own natural color?" I asked. "Isn't it found by seeking the pure vowels?"

"Of course. You have to have your own color, and the teacher who wants a student to sing like him, or someone special, is not a good teacher. I'm sorry, you have to consider the voice you have. If the quality is not so good, you try to arrange it, but you can never change the natural quality. The rules are mainly the same, but everybody is different."

"In other words," I said, "if we all sang the same way, the sounds would still all be different, because we are constructed differently in terms of shape and size, not different in muscular structure or physiology.

"Régine, in conclusion, what is most important for a singer?"

"I never forget the joy in singing; you have to be happy. I think that is the biggest, important thing, to make people think you've a happy open face, open eyes and ears, breathing happy. I am sure it is a physical response we have, because, after all, people who sing, generally speaking, they are happy people. They laugh a lot."

So this interview ended happily, and the next time I sang on the Met stage with Régine, I couldn't help but note how her warm heart had infected those on the other side of the footlights. What a joyous roar shook that mighty hall as she once again walked off with the show.

What a magnificent artist. Where there's joy of singing there's always joy of hearing.

Gilda Cruz-Romo

Gilda Cruz-Romo was born and trained in Mexico. She also made her debut in Mexico, in 1962, as Ortlinde in Die Walküre. *In 1970, Miss Cruz-Romo won a Metropolitan Opera contract in the Metropolitan Opera Auditions. She has performed many roles at the Met since, particularly the soprano heroines of Puccini and Verdi, including Suor Angelica, Madama Butterfly, and Amelia in* Un Ballo in Maschera. *Her portrayal of Desdemona in* Otello *was televised in the "Live from the Met" series.* 🎵

"The only thing left for me now is to go sell peanuts in front of Bellas Artes."* Gilda Cruz-Romo, with her Latin eyes twinkling, looked like a daughter of the Conquistadors as she recounted a desperate period of her student days in Mexico City. She had been at her wits' end over financial problems, walking three miles to her lessons to save the bus fare, with a threat of eviction hanging over her head. No wonder she had had a terrible lesson that ended in anguished tears.

"Now, why should you sell peanuts in front of Bellas Artes?" asked her teacher, Angel Esquival, in a kindly, paternal tone.

"I'm done," she wailed in desperation. "I'm singing just as I did at my very first lesson. I can't get out of this problem."

Gilda had a wide range with the low voice of a contralto and a rich middle, but earlier study with a bad teacher had produced shrill high notes with no velvet to the sound. Now, under the burden of personal problems, she had slipped back to where she had started and was ready to give up.

Esquival, with a beautiful smile, said, "You have not even started and you are already desperate? A career is full of sacrifice and deprivation. You really have to develop patience."

* Bellas Artes is the Cultural Arts Center of Mexico City.

Gilda Cruz-Romo

"I do have patience," she sobbed.

"Then tell me, what are you crying for?"

"Because what I am doing is so bad!"

Esquival smiled. "*You* say it's bad. You're just singing . . . I have to listen to it and have you heard me complain? If you think *you* have patience, I can tell you I have much more patience."

Then, as if nothing had happened, Esquival returned to finishing the lesson. The air had cleared and suddenly all became much easier.

After only six months of study Gilda was already performing the role of one of the Walküres on the opera stage and after a year was happily ringing out one after another of those round, beautiful high notes she had so desperately sought. Still having severe financial needs, she brought in extra revenue by singing also in a zarzuela company headed by the parents of Placido Domingo. Gilda had a very early start on the professional stage, and this daughter of the Conquistadors was destined to go far.

Our interview was a far cry from the tropical setting of Mexico City as we sat in a Holiday Inn in central Philadelphia on a cold, blustery day between rehearsals for Verdi's *Attila*.

"What is your routine on the day of a performance?" I began.

"Well," she responded, "I treat it like any other day, only I wouldn't perhaps do any strenuous shopping. Nothing extreme. After a good night's sleep I have breakfast and then wait until noon or 1 P.M. before I try my voice. We all have a little phlegm in the morning from sleep, which disappears by midday. If I am singing something difficult like *Attila* or *Trovatore* I vocalize for fifteen minutes. For other operas like *Butterfly* I can warm up in the theater or on stage."

"What do you do when you vocalize?" I asked.

"I start in the middle voice, on one note, singing *ee, eh, ah, oh, oo*. I do this over a range of about one octave, not too high. Then I do a five-note scale on *ah*, followed by a nine-note scale. I start easy and don't lean on the high notes. I feel they come by themselves. And that's it until I'm in the theater, where I do a couple more scales and go."

"Do you continue to study voice using scales, arpeggios, et cetera?" I asked.

"No," she said. "My teacher, Esquival, died while I was still young. Soon after I came to New York. I coach operatic roles with Alberta Masiello, but I don't study voice by using formal scales. I usually use phrases from operas I am learning, especially the hardest ones, and sing them over and over until I have mastered them. Scales with no meaning are too boring."

"When you work on scales and discover you are not in good voice, what do you do?" I asked.

"Under these conditions a singer should keep his, or her, big mouth shut! But I never go for a long period of time without singing. It is important to keep the voice in condition by using it. Also, when a singer is not in perfect condition there is a tendency to cough and clear the throat. A singer must never do that. It is like sandpaper to the vocal cords."

"Now," I said, "let's talk about technique."

She said pensively, "Well, first you must look for beauty of sound. Sharp sounds should be used sparingly for special expression. And glottal attacks should never be used, not even for special effects."

"Let us discuss breath support," I said.

"Now, breath support is a mystery," she began. "Air you cannot see."

"I know it's hard to explain," I said patiently, "but we must try to put it into words."

"First you should inhale through the mouth, but with the tongue raised up a bit so the air doesn't dry the larynx."

"Some people say you should inhale through the nose," I said.

"No!" was her emphatic answer. "It should always be through the mouth." She paused, eyes twinkling. "At least to my way of thinking. What is good for me may not be good for someone else. But with a very fast breath between two quick phrases you simply cannot breathe through your nose. When you have plenty of time, then you can breathe through your nose.

"Now," putting her hands under her ribs, she continued, "the diaphragm must expand all around down here—but *no chest move-*

Gilda Cruz-Romo

ment. Look at a baby. It does not breathe with its chest. If all people breathed like that they would be much healthier."

I broke in. "I have often heard it said that if you breathe correctly, you sing correctly."

"Oh no," she said, "there is much more to it than that—well, that's again *my* way of thinking. You must know how to place the voice. It must not be thought of as in the throat. It should be high up here," she said, pointing to a spot on her forehead, just above her eyes. "When you place the voice there, you don't force it."

"What do you mean by forcing?" I asked.

"When I don't have any more to give—that's forcing. You must always feel you have something left in reserve. You should really feel as though you were inhaling the sound into the vibrating cavities of the head."

"Now to placement of the voice," I said.

"One should begin with the chest voice as a base and then build the rest upon it," she began.

"What do you mean by chest voice?" I asked.

"Oh, chest voice is a meaty sound, it has a more open feeling. The talking voice is chest voice. When you teach a beginner you say, 'Talk to me.' Then: 'Now sing that way.' But with the chest we have too wide vowels. Then you must round the sound out, mellow it. It must be covered and made more beautiful. But you must not force on the chest. If you do, you will not be able to carry that force to the high notes. The voice becomes too heavy."

I stopped her again. "I have heard some singers say that chest is too dangerous to use."

"That is because they have never learned to mix the chest voice with the head," she said emphatically. "Maybe it's not for everybody, but . . ."

"I know," I laughed, "it's your way of thinking."

"Well, I'm a *spinto*, and when I sing with a big orchestra it is necessary to use chest voice mixed in to cut through the sound of all those instruments. Of course you mustn't use chest beyond F sharp above middle C. Chest must be used gently, I can't say it enough—carefully."

"You mentioned mixing chest voice with the higher voice. What do you mean by that?"

"I get a mix between the chest voice and the head voice by . . . thinking in the nose," she said. "I hesitate to say this because it might be taken wrong, but . . . actually, by thinking nasal. I didn't want to come right out and say 'nasal' because a student following this advice might be tempted to sing everything nasal, whereas I mean it to apply only to the range where the break can occur. But every singer needs a good *teacher* to avoid getting on the wrong track. My first teacher ruined my high notes."

"And it took a year for Angel Esquival to undo the damage that was done," I added.

"Right. I had been handicapped with a fear of my screechy high notes. I was always able to get them, even up to a high E or F, but I had been taught to produce them incorrectly.

"I conquered that problem with Esquival, and I feel my best feature now is my ability to sing round, free high notes, which I can easily reduce from forte to pianissimo. I had a good pianissimo from the beginning, but I improved it even more by hard work."

"What do you feel is the basic difference between pianissimo and forte?" I asked.

"It is in the quantity of air, less for pianissimo, more for forte. Also, in singing pianissimo, there is a sensation of narrowing the column of air in the throat a bit. It is very important to have a good pianissimo, but it never should be used as a gimmick. It must be used as a part of the artistic coloring of phrases. It should always have meaning. When you begin using pianissimo as a trick to impress the audience, you are not a good artist anymore."

"Now, one final question," I said. "This round, free high voice you have found, is it different in feeling from the middle voice?"

"Absolutely," was her quick reply. "For high notes the opening of the mouth is larger. At the same time there is a deeper spacing in the throat. Yet you must leave the sound free to go way up high in the cavities." To demonstrate the deep spacing in the throat, Gilda cupped her hands in the shape of a bowl just below her larynx.

Gilda Cruz-Romo

"I wish our readers could see that," I laughed. "There really are some things that are hard for a singer to put into words."

"I was right," she said, "there is much mystery in singing. But to sum it up as best I can—some people make the voice large on the bottom and it narrows down as they go up, like an egg with the pointed end up. Others do just the opposite, small on the bottom, large on top. But ideally the voice should be like a cylinder, even all the way up and down."

"Ideally . . ." I began.

"Well, that's my way of thinking."

Several nights later, as I sat on Attila's throne and reigned briefly on the stage of Philadelphia's Academy of Music, I listened with special interest as Gilda strode on the stage and valiantly bombarded the theater with free, round high notes and easily conquered the colossal challenge of Verdi's Odabella. Considering a career that was almost diverted into vending peanuts because of shrill, tight high notes, I realized that this was a challenge which could have been met only by the indomitable courage and determination of a true Conquistador.

Cristina Deutekom

Cristina Deutekom is in the forefront of dramatic coloratura singers. Born and raised in Holland, she made her debut in 1963 in Amsterdam as the Queen of the Night in Mozart's THE MAGIC FLUTE. *She also made her Metropolitan Opera debut as the Queen, in 1967. Her dramatic approach to this role, her ability to sing the difficult coloratura music with security and ease, and the size of her voice— unusually large for a singer of this role—have made her an outstanding interpreter of the Queen of the Night. On the opening night of the Met's 1974–75 season, she sang the leading soprano role of Elena in Verdi's* I VESPRI SICILIANI. ♐

WHEN I heard that I was to do *Attila* with Cristina Deutekom in Edmonton, Alberta, I was quite curious as to what she really looked like. I had previously sung with her in *The Magic Flute,* and as the Queen of the Night, she wore a most ghastly blue makeup. I had never seen her in real life. But I was also curious as to the technique that produced such high-precision singing.

When I met Cristina in Edmonton, I found myself immediately liking her cherubic Dutch face. Her warm personality conveyed nothing of the cold, hard Queen of the Night. One chilly spring afternoon, we sat down to discuss her vocal technique.

"I always sang as a child, but I was not allowed to sing in the chorus because my voice was too loud," she began. She then related details of her youth: how she never thought to be a professional singer, and how, after joining an adult choir at the age of twenty, the choir director began to teach her voice. It was immediately obvious that she had an unusual gift. She studied in Amsterdam for the next eight years, then made her professional debut there in 1963 as the Queen of the Night. She still follows the basics taught her by her first teacher, although she now studies with another in Holland.

The conversation turned to technique and I asked her if she vocalized often.

"If I don't feel like singing I know I'm really ill! On vacation I vocalize every day. I vocalize in the bathroom . . . everywhere," she exclaimed with her jolly eyes twinkling. "It bothers me when I have guests who stay all day and I cannot vocalize. Not that I'm disturbing them, but that they're disturbing me!"

"What sort of vocalizing do you do?"

"I start with a one-octave scale, using words based on *oo*: du Blume du. I feel *oo* is the softest . . . gentlest vowel. I start pianissimo, then I put *ohs* together with the *oos*, not always using real words: non-ro-du-ro-muth-voll-rufen [It sounded like German but . . .]."

"Then there are the consonants, which sometimes are more important than the vowels. They force you to open your mouth. It has to do with the throat, of course."

"Now that you've mentioned the throat, what does an open throat mean to you?" I asked.

"*Not* the tongue forward," she stated. "I learned to lower the larynx, as when you yawn . . . The feeling should be *down* and *up*, like an egg on end . . . not spread wide."

"How about the use of the breath?" I asked.

"A soprano needs two different ways of using the breath. For singing a long high note you must distribute the amount of breath. You use two sets of muscles in tension—one against the other—to control so as to not push on the larynx. You must avoid having the breath too close to the larynx. If you lose the internal counterpressure, force goes to the vocal cords and trouble begins. It feels as if the air is higher than the muscles. To avoid this, I take the breath low in the abdomen and think of my body as a drum, with the sound originating from the diaphragm."

"What exactly are these two uses of breath that you mentioned?" I asked.

"Well, for high notes you strongly hold the diaphragm in balance to avoid pressure on the larynx. You use the muscles of the upper back, too. But it's different in the middle voice . . . the diaphragm is lower."

"What do you mean, the diaphragm is lower for the middle voice?" I asked, genuinely puzzled.

With that, Cristina demonstrated by taking a deep abdominal breath and then shifted the position of the diaphragm up, raising the whole rib cage up and out as the abdomen pressed in.

"It is wrong," she said, "not to bring up the diaphragm for the higher range."

I spent the next few minutes trying what she had just told me, in order to be sure I understood her correctly. You take a deep abdominal breath. If the attack is on a low note, you keep the diaphragm in that position. If the attack is in the middle voice, you shift the diaphragm up a small amount by tucking in the abdomen a bit, raising the rib cage with this action. If the attack is on a high note, you shift the diaphragm and rib cage as high as they will go, without forcing.

As Cristina sang up and down scales, I could see the different amounts of lift in her rib cage according to the range she was singing in. It was all done with skillful perfection. When I commented on this, she said she was a Virgo, which means she wants to be perfect.

"Cristina, as a dramatic coloratura, do you use chest voice?"

"Yes, but never just chest voice alone, and I never use pure head voice alone. It is always a balanced mixture of the two. There are three registers in a woman's voice:* the first goes up to B or C above middle C, the second to E or F above this, and the third as far above this as the voice will go."

"How do you conquer these transitions so it all sounds like one voice?" I asked. "Do you manage it by placing the voice in any special way?"

"I never thought about voice placement," was her reply.

"Then you don't place, or feel in the area of the nose, or . . . ?"

"I only feel it in the nose when I have a cold," she said, laughing. "When I'm singing at my best, I feel as though someone is lightly touching the hinge of my jaw, by my ears . . . but inside my head.

* Here, obviously, Cristina is speaking of the coloratura voice.

It's a sensation of tensing muscles directly in front of the middle of my ears. My notes are sitting there . . . not in front of my nose. Really high, high notes seem to be outside of my body . . . behind and around my head. And on my very high notes I still bring in some chest voice."

"How do you bring in chest to very high notes?"

"Keeping the breath away from the larynx is bringing in chest."

"How do you overcome the problems of transition between registers?"

"You conquer these passages by the use of the breath. In the middle-voice passage you must keep the breath down. You sing from the stomach in this range . . . not only the front of the body, but the back muscles too. But this is only when singing low . . . and not in the high voice."

We were between *Attila* rehearsals and, unfortunately, I had time for only one more question before we had to return to being Odabella and the Hun.

"When you vocalize for your performances beginning at the end of this week, what will your routine be?"

"I start vocalizing on slow scales with words using *oo* and *oh*, as we discussed before. I don't go too high at first . . . to B flat only. Then arpeggios . . . slowly, like:

using the words *du Blume** with two or three notes per syllable. This is good for developing the legato. Then I use other words also but I use only the *ee* vowel when I'm warmed up. Then I do all sorts of improvisations on arpeggios.

"Finally I do fast descending passages starting on the C above middle C, using the word *weise* over and over with three notes to a syllable. Then I use *weise bist du*† also with three notes to a syllable":

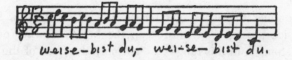

weise-bist du,- wei-se- bist du.

Three days later we were on the stage together and the audience and I were treated to the pleasure of hearing Odabella's extremely difficult dramatic coloratura music performed with such precision as only a perfectionist could achieve. What chance does a Scorpio like me have with these Virgos around?

* In German that would be "you flower."
† In German that would be "you are wise."

Placido Domingo

Placido Domingo is one of the outstanding tenors of his generation. He was born in Spain and grew up in Mexico, where his parents managed a zarzuela theater. His operatic debut was in 1959 in Mexico in a small role in RIGOLETTO. *In New York he sang first at the New York City Opera for several seasons, then made his Metropolitan Opera debut in 1968 as Maurizio in Cilèa's* ADRIANA LECOUVREUR. *He quickly became one of the Met's most popular artists and soon was acclaimed internationally for his beautiful voice and superior musicianship. Among his many successes have been appearances as Otello on the opening night of the Met's 1979–80 season and as Hoffmann in a new production of* TALES OF HOFFMANN *at the 1980 Salzburg Festival.* 🎵

ON a warm fall afternoon in the quiet recesses of a Metropolitan Opera dressing room, Placido Domingo, with his soft-spoken voice, distinctive in its Spanish flavor, unfolded his life story. Born of a musical family in Madrid and raised in Mexico City, he bears the cultural heritage of the Old World with the simple, democratic mien of the New. Perhaps this marriage of the Old and New helps to account for the atypical development of this unusual and prolific artist, one of the true superstars of today.

As a child, Placido was always in the theater, whether doing two lines, singing, or just watching. During his teen years he was constantly immersed in any form of theatrical or musical expression to be had. He worked with his father, developing his voice with scales, acting in zarzuelas and conducting, as well as doing some musical comedy.

He went to a conservatory and studied music, piano, harmony, and composition, but—strangely enough—*never* did he formally study voice. Obviously, he is one of those rare singers who achieve great heights without teachers per se, but other singers and musicians have played an important part in his development. We retraced the path that led him to vocal stardom.

"As your parents began teaching you to sing, did you use scales?" I asked.

"Absolutely."

"What kind of scales did you use?"

"Usually I used the fifth . . ." and he sang:

"I suppose you still use that exercise. How high do you go on that?" I asked.

"Well, it depends. I go a lot higher than I need for the performance . . . which should be an insurance. Is very bad the day you cannot . . . You know you are . . ."

"In trouble," I finished.

"When you can go a tone higher . . ." he went on, "a lot higher, it's wonderful."

"What other scales did you use?"

"Arpeggios with the thirds . . ." Again he sang:

And again:

Placido Domingo

"After your informal training with your father, what were the major influences on your vocal development?" I asked.

"One was Carlo Morelli, who was at the Met. He was a marvelous interpreter. He was a great believer in the strength of the mind on anything in life . . . if you really want to make things work.

"When I was at the conservatory studying, I started going to his classes. He wouldn't teach you how to sing, but how to interpret. I was singing as a baritone . . . really a lazy tenor. I sang the Prologue to *Pagliacci* for him. He said, 'You have a voice, but I think you are a tenor.' So I went to him for interpretation lessons and I learned from that man basically what is the whole meaning of my singing. A big percentage of my singing is based only on interpretation of what I am saying."

"And after that, who influenced you the most?" I asked.

"It was a colleague . . . a Mexican baritone called Iglesias, who has an incredible knowledge of singing. We used to be together in Tel Aviv, he and my wife. I used to go to a performance . . . and I was singing Faust . . . and every time that B natural was coming . . . 'Je t'aime, je t'aime, je t'aime,' I would crack! And I would feel very bad about it.

"So he told me one day, 'Placido, the voice is there, but you don't support.' It was the first time in my life that I hear the word *support*. And he, with the help of my wife, who was also there . . . the three of us used to listen to each other . . . He talked to me about the diaphragm, *supporting*. And he was, together with my wife, the great help that I've had. He never saw me for studying . . . Just going to the theater on an empty stage and singing . . . projecting a phrase. I aquired my first knowledge of singing vocalizing with my parents. But seriously speaking, of somebody you go to . . ." He groped for the words.

"Yes," I added, "somebody you go to regularly to study formally . . ."

"I never had that," he said. "But, intuition . . . and how you are willing to take things . . . they are the best things. Sometimes people vocalize three or four times a week, making the same mistakes over and over. So one finds a teacher who really is marvelous . . . he would be really lucky, you know . . . But I have been lucky."

Placido Domingo

"When and where was your opera debut?" I asked.

"I did Borsa in *Rigoletto* with MacNeil in 1959 in Mexico. I was eighteen years old. Then it was *Traviata* and *Tosca* in 1961."

"And after that . . . ?"

"I went to Tel Aviv, which was a fantastic school, because I sang two hundred eighty performances in two and a half years . . . eleven operas. I sang most of them in the original language. *Onegin and Pearl Fishers* I used to sing in Hebrew. Those years were really the most fantastic training. I was earning, with my wife, three hundred twenty dollars a month . . . Those were really hard days . . . days that I wouldn't change for anything in this world. It was like a knife that has two edges, because you would go ready or be destroyed . . . In two and a half years if you sing two hundred eighty performances that's . . ." He shrugged.

He related how Julius Rudel engaged him for the New York City Opera, opening with Alberto Ginastera's *Don Rodrigo* in 1966. He came to the Met in 1968 and sang in both houses until 1971. The rest is well-recorded history.

"Were there any other influences on your vocal technique?" I asked.

"I was most influenced by recordings of Caruso . . . that quality of sound . . . that incredible power of his voice . . . I used to hear a lot of his recordings . . . I could do a very bad imitation of him; I wasn't trying to imitate Caruso, I was just trying to find out what he was doing. And one day, when I recorded, I still had great problems with high notes . . . I tried to imitate him . . . and suddenly I realized I could sing anything. So that day I went alone to the piano and I sang about twenty-five arias, because I realized it [Caruso's method] was based on the old technique . . . [in] which they don't waste any kind of breath singing. And that was the singing of Titta Ruffo.

"If you hear most of the singers in Europe, like Gobbi, they sing in that old technique . . . it's only working the air . . . It was my next step, hearing the Caruso recordings. And since then I have found a consistency in my column of sound, equal from bottom to top."

Placido Domingo

"You have a beautiful smooth *passaggio* to the high notes," I observed.

"Really?" His response was so disarmingly surprised and pleased that I delighted in his open, genuine character. It was obvious that his wholehearted attention is constantly directed at self-improvement rather than contemplation of his accomplishments.

"It's such a smooth, even transition, rather than being . . ." I groped for the right words.

"Yes, I don't show the switch," he said thoughtfully. "It's done in a way that one cannot tell when you do it. The public should know that you have the technique, but you shouldn't show it. In fact, it's disturbing in some singers that you can see their technique. When they approach high notes they tend to hold their"—he struck a typical singer's pose with the hands folded in front of him, knuckles white with tension—"depending on which note is coming . . . or a mouth position . . . or you hear the closing [covering] as soon as there is an F. You will hear

Ah ————— oo

You will hear it [the *ah* to *oo* switch] so you are aware [of it]. It [the transition] is there, it *has* to be. There are limits . . . in tenors especially. You have fine tenors and they didn't close at all. They did a couple of performances and they break the voice. And then you have heard some, they were beautiful singers, but unexciting because they used to cover much too early [too low]. The excitement of the voice didn't come out."

"Describe to me what you think when you take a breath," I said.

"If a note is properly supported," he explained, "when you are singing, somebody might even be able to hit you"—he indicated the stomach area—"and that note is still there. I used to breathe like this . . ." He demonstrated by lifting his chest and shoulders high. "You cannot support, and many people sing that way. It should be deeper"—he gestured with his hands to show expansion, indicating filling his whole abdomen from the ribs on down—"everything expanding out. In the middle register, you don't use this to full potency. You leave it a little relaxed. When you're going to the high notes, *then* . . ."

"Then you use it a little stronger," I said.

"Yes, yes. When I started to support, in order for me to remember, I used to have a very tight elastic belt . . . which I still use. And also, to sing against the piano . . . I push the piano away." With this, Placido went to the piano and pushed it away with his diaphragm. "So my feeling is that when I am singing, I should be able to push anything that is against me."

"And, as you said, somebody could hit you in the stomach and it wouldn't change the tone . . ."*

"It wouldn't change the tone. That's the reason it's good to have something elastic . . . You are working *here* . . ." He indicated the stomach area. "I don't use the elastic belt very much today, because I know what I am doing.

"If a singer is singing for me, I find out immediately about the supporting [his support]. When they're doing a note you push your hand against them, they feel the pressure and the voice starts to support. Then the sound starts to really come."

"In other words," I broke in, "that is what the belt does."

"Yes!"

"How wide is the belt?"

"It depends," he said. "It could be elastic shorts . . . and there are those that go higher . . . or it could be a separate belt. I have both."

"Where does one buy these things?" I asked.

"Orthopedic supplies."

"What does *placement* mean to you?" I said, taking another tack.

"Position," he said. "I think there is one very important thing—especially when we sing in theaters as big as the Metropolitan—not that you have to sing loudly, because that's impossible. You sing

---

* As I was transcribing this interview, I went into the kitchen and asked my wife Lucia to punch me in the stomach a couple of times while I was holding a note. Since I had misbehaved earlier that morning, she complied with extra enthusiasm. Placido's idea worked; the tone held. I called my doctor for repairs afterward. Lucia's little, but she's strong!

with *your* voice in a small house and you sing with *your* voice in a big house. It is nonsense when they tell you it is a little house and you can save. You don't change the technique. Maybe in a small house they might be able to hear you better. My thinking of singing is *over there.*" He gestured out in front of himself. "Way out in front of me. I always try to place the voice like it was a front tennis ball . . ." He groped for the words, swinging at waist level with his right hand.

"Oh," I said, "a forehand tennis stroke."

"With the racket," he added, "or jai alai, you know, when the ball is going there I have to have the feeling that the ball is going to that wall, which should be the public, and coming back. That's my feeling of placing."

"Then you're not thinking of placing the voice in the mask?"

"No, no," he said emphatically. "I'm thinking of *going out.*

"But I do have a basic problem which I discovered only lately. Sometimes I am recording . . . feeling really fantastic . . . and all of a sudden the voice starts to sound, from one phrase to another, different. Suddenly I realize I have a vocal defect. In many notes my tongue goes up. I do that very often, not constantly. You can hear the change of the sound in the microphone. Now, when I do my recordings, I want to put a mirror near my music stand, and I want to control that tone until the tongue will go down by itself automatically."

"While we're on the subject of the tongue," I said. "Many singers feel that an open throat means the back of the tongue, or the larynx, is down, as in a yawn. Do you feel this to be the case?"

"Yes," he said.

"Another vocal function, which we have already touched on, is covering, or closing. Can you put in words what you mean by cover?" I asked.

"I just don't know the explanation," he said thoughtfully.

"You just do it," I said unhappily.

"Yes."

"When you start to close," I pursued doggedly, "is there any sensation of thinking deeper in the throat?"

"Physiologically I cannot tell you the glottis did that or . . . It's just the fact of singing and automatically making, in a way, a darker sound."

"What do you mean by a darker sound? Do you start thinking deeper in position when you go up there?"

"Yes," he said. "There is a need of covering. One way to start is feeling the change from *ah* to *oh* . . . the vowel itself will be darker."

"Do you mean a deeper sensation in the throat?" I asked.

"I think so, because giving a deeper kind of position, and you are having a horizontal sound . . . to think vertical, in a way."

That momentarily confused me. "You mean the sound becomes vertical instead of horizontal when you cover," I prompted.

"Yes."

"In other words, you can have a horizontal feeling in the middle voice, but when you go to the deeper, covered tone, the sensation in the throat becomes vertical . . . up *and* down."

"Yes!"

"That's an interesting thought." I now comprehended his meaning. "Many singers say that when they sing high notes they think deeper in the larynx and higher in placement, giving a sort of two-way stretch up and down, whereas, in the middle voice, you can think laterally."

"It has to be," he responded. "All of a sudden you start to get vertical. It's a bit up . . ."

"Up and down at the same time," I said.

"Yes, that's interesting," he mused, "because one never stops thinking."

"And then," I went on, "some people speak of having to narrow down in the *passaggio* . . . as they begin to cover . . . which implies also going from horizontal to vertical. They're almost talking the same language.

"Well, we have covered some basics on technique," I said. "Do you have anything to add regarding your vocal discipline, say, scales?"

"Something very special, which many people may not agree with," he said. "I do my scales and when I arrive at the top note of my register, I don't go down."

Placido Domingo

"You stop at the top?"

"Yes, I don't do descendant [descending on the scales]. I think this is unnecessarily tiring yourself. And the top notes you *touch only*. You don't have to concentrate on them the whole time."

"In other words you shouldn't spend too much time on high notes when vocalizing?"

"No," he said emphatically. "You are working with the whole register. That's enough . . . going up. You don't have to go back. That's a personal opinion."

"As you warm up the voice you do increasingly difficult things, right?"

"Yes."

"When you get to the most difficult things, do you go back to something easier before you stop?"

"No! When I go to the most difficult I leave it for a while. Then my next proceedings would be singing easy passages from that particular opera, whatever I am to perform or study. Then I start to do the hard passages and then I just leave it."

"What is the most difficult scale you do?" I asked.

"I do the fifth, the ninth, and then go all the way to the twelfth." He demonstrated with

"By then the diaphragm is surely working. For me the feeling is that you should never start to sing before the diaphragm is really proper.

"Sometimes, to people that *chop* very much their singing, I recommend this type of exercise . . ." He then repeated the exercise of arpeggios on thirds that he had demonstrated at the beginning of the interview, but much slower, with an exaggerated portamento, or slur, between the notes. "To use portamento in order to make one's diaphragm . . ."

"Wake up," I suggested.

He nodded. "And don't chop!"

"On a day you have no performance, but wish to vocalize, how much time would you spend at it?"

"Not much," he responded. "Just enough to know that if I had a performance then I would be ready. There are days when you just open the mouth and ten minutes is enough. Other days you realize it's difficult and you start. I may have something to eat, then I vocalize a little more. It all depends."

"Do you always vocalize in small segments?" I asked.

"Small segments . . . yes!"

"Then you wouldn't do a complete set of a half hour of scales at a time?"

"No! You get tired without any reason. Some artists sing ten times the role during the day before going on the stage. Incredible!"

"What's your routine on a performance day?"

"I like very much to talk, but I try to do minimal talking the day before. I sleep to about eleven-thirty, then I have a shower and breakfast. I cannot start the day if I do not have a shower . . . especially the day of singing. After that I do my first trying [vocally] . . . ten minutes. Then I like to walk, because that wakes me up. I go to the theater where I am going to sing and maybe I try my voice again . . . only five minutes, to have that feeling. Then I have a very light lunch about two: consommé, steak, and coffee. Then I walk more and have a little nap for an hour, or an hour and a half. Then I take another shower about five-thirty, I walk to the theater, and I do a couple of scales. I sing some of the phrases that I have in the performance . . . some of the difficult stuff I want to try out . . . before I go on the stage."

At this point I was sorry the interview was coming to a close, because it was a most pleasant time. Was it his Spanish charm or the New World's informality? No, it was a splendid marriage of the two!

Pablo Elvira

Pablo Elvira made his debut as Rigoletto in 1968 at the Indiana University School of Music in Bloomington. A native of Puerto Rico, he had been a trumpet player and the leader of a dance band before his operatic career. For several seasons he sang at the New York City Opera. His lyric baritone was first heard at the Metropolitan Opera as Tonio in I PAGLIACCI. *He is also well known as Figaro in* THE BARBER OF SEVILLE. 🎺

"I STUDIED piano with my uncle until I broke my left arm. Then I started another instrument, alto sax, which I played in my uncle's orchestra until I broke my left arm a second time. Then I went to a conservatory, studying bass fiddle, and broke my left arm a third time. I finally decided to pick up the trumpet, with which I used my right hand, because my left hand was beginning to lose some of its facility."

In a short time Pablo Elvira was recognized as one of the two best trumpet players in Puerto Rico, performing with his own orchestra in hotels for six hundred dollars a week. He came from a musical family; both his father and his uncle were musicians and had their own popular orchestras, so Pablo had his sights set on music all of his life. He never thought about singing, though, until he saw the movie *The Great Caruso* with Mario Lanza. He began studying voice, but he could not sing above an E flat, because he "didn't know how to cover the high notes." This would sound strange to anyone knowing him today, since the high range is one of the best features of his voice.

I first met Pablo in 1967. I was producing my opera *I Am the Way* with the Indianapolis Symphony, Iszler Solomon conducting. My John the Baptist had dropped out of the production a month before our premiere, and I was hard put to find another baritone who could sing the grueling part, let alone learn its difficult music in the short time left. It was recommended that we use Pablo Elvira, who was currently teaching at Indiana University.

I was enormously impressed by this young man's technique and beautiful voice, and after his success singing in the Indianapolis production, it was natural for me to invite him to participate in the production we were planning for Palm Sunday at the Metropolitan Opera House in 1968. Again he sang the difficult role so easily that I was most curious about his vocal technique.

Now more than ten years had passed. Pablo had rung up successes in big European opera houses and made four important operatic recordings. I sat in the back row of Symphony Hall, Newark, and listened to him doing the dress rehearsal of *Il Trovatore* with the New Jersey State Opera. At intermission I went backstage to greet him.

I was well into writing this book, which was intended to be a series of interviews with internationally acclaimed singers who had had many, many years of experience. But Pablo, who had just signed his first Met contract, was an exception in my mind. I still had an insatiable curiosity to know how he did it. I proposed that he be included in the book and he quickly accepted. We met a short time later in a Met dressing room, and this is how the interview went:

"I believe the human voice, being a muscle, has so many hours . . . miles . . . When your voice is developed you can stretch the durability of your voice for fifty years, or you can use it up in ten. The best way for a physical body to recuperate from work is to give it a rest, because the body heals itself. So I take a minimum of two months' vacation a year."

"Do you vocalize during that period?" I asked.

"No. Not at all! Total rest."

"How long does it take to get your voice back?"

"Four or five days."

"Your voice returns quickly. Not mine," I observed.

"Our physical bodies are different," he said.

"I think it has to do with the way you sing. You don't use any force when you sing."

Pablo Elvira

"I don't force, no! And the force I use," he said, "is mostly the diaphragm. Two months won't harm it. And I climb mountains."

"With me it's two months of scuba in the Dutch Antilles," I said. "What do you consider the most important aspect of technique, Pablo?"

"Support, *appoggia*, because I believe that you sing *on* the air, and not *with* the air. First of all, you breathe *down*. You never breathe *up*. But you're tightening that lower part," he said, indicating the low abdominal muscles, "which is the *floor*, and tighten your rear end. Now you have a foundation there. Then you have the air . . ." He had his hands in the region of his stomach and ribs, then he spread his arms and hands outward. "The lungs fill that way."

"They fill laterally," I observed.

"Exactly. Never up. You take a balloon and fill it up with air. If you press it sideways, you get the air out . . . okay? But if that balloon is placed upon a flat surface and you press down . . . you're going to get it faster out. But the idea of having the lower part as hard as a rock means that you can apply pressure from every direction, and it will go up, because that's the only way it *can* go. It's the only way you can do long phrases," he continued, "because you have a tremendous way of using the air. It's not that I have more air in my lungs than anybody else . . . it's the way you press it . . . squeeze it out."

"With this balloon in the stomach, the floor is solid," I concluded. "Then you press in from the sides . . ."

"And the front . . . every way," he said.

"But you're *not* pushing down with the chest?"

"No, no, no! It's this motion . . ." He had his hands touching in front, elbows out. He then squeezed in with his elbows, with the hands still touching in front. "There are many singers that sing like this . . . the chest is *up*, but the stomach is *in*. They can sing, but only with half of the air, because the lungs are being supported from beneath. You can use the air in your chest, but when it's over . . . it's over.

"If you go like this"—he took a breath and his diaphragm protruded out farther than his chest—"then you use all the air you have in your chest when you're singing . . . pressing, pressing . . ."

"You allow the chest to move?" I interrupted.

"Yes, definitely! Only, it is not muscular, because there are no muscles, only bones. Also the ribs, if you expand them, they're going to go back. But the only place you're using is the diaphragm."

(I subsequently understood that the only rib action was lateral, not *up*, using the shoulders.)

"You develop the breath," he went on, "by using scales. Then you go to the vocal cords and exercises."

"What is the relation of the breath to the larynx? Should one attempt to keep that pressure away from the cords?"

"Absolutely! There must not be any tension," he explained, "from your neck up, in your face, in your cheeks, lips, tongue, palate, throat, larynx . . . that must all be relaxed. Of course there are muscles that have to be pulled in order to produce the tone, but basically every other muscle around should be relaxed.

"The most simple thing, which is the most hard to teach, is how to *lift* the *palate* . . . feel that the soft palate is kind of going up so that you can have that space that you need when you sing. Now you apply the pressure from the diaphragm, and what's coming is a tremendous force of air that is going to make the cords vibrate . . . so the cords will be well trained . . . exercising, doing lots of scales."

"In order to strengthen the proper muscles?"

"Also that they are flexible," he said.

"Do you believe in using fast-moving scales?"

"Absolutely! The fast-moving scales are the best way to develop the top," he said. "You *cannot* develop the top by sustaining it. You have to get up there and come down. Stretch the vocal cords to the height and come down again. And keep doing it until finally you can go up and stay there. How can you learn to sing a high C if you don't sing it short? It's abnormal! You're stretching the vocal cords beyond the normal range.

"You can develop the top, which is what everybody has trouble with, simply by scales, up and down, up and down. Eventually you go up and stay a little. And they crack once, but after a few months

Pablo Elvira

of work, getting those muscles ready for it, they can go up and stay up."

"Then you shouldn't ever try learning high notes by sustaining them?" I mused.

"You can do that, but you kill the poor guy, because you hurt the vocal cords. He's not ready for it."

"What sort of scales do you use to teach?"

"I start them with short exercises like":

"Do you take this all the way, to the top voice?"

"No, with the short ones you can't go all the way. I do the third, the fifth, the ninth, then I do":

"And then I put them together":

"That makes the support very strong halfway to the end. In other words, you will be able to sing a phrase and still go to a high note when you have only—"

"Only a little breath left," I added.

"If you give them only short exercises, they always develop a tremendous attack . . . I have met many singers that can sing a high note, but only for two or three seconds. After that they die, turn purple. They have developed only an attack."

"They cannot sustain long phrases," I said.

"The way you can develop that is to do long vocalises in which the last part of the vocalise is the hardest and the highest. That builds the stamina without working, because it's on scales.

"After the scales and development you can begin producing different sounds. Now, there's a secret that I'm going to reveal. There was a Puerto Rican dramatic tenor in the time of Caruso named Don Antonio Paoli. He sang for the tsars. He went back to Puerto Rico to die, and he taught a few people there.

"He vocalized all the time with the vowel *oo*. This is something I used myself, and I have developed more [range] than I need. I can sing a high C. I can sing a B flat anytime. And I can sing low. It's because of this vowel *oo*. All these vocalises that I talked about, he would vocalize on the vowel *oo*, trying to keep the *oo* with the *squillo* [penetrating or carrying brilliance]. And that's why I can do whatever I want. I never studied with him, but I observed his students teaching some other people. He said the hardest vowel to sing was *oo*. When you master the difficult one, the others are easy. When you make the vowel *oo*, you lift your palate. If you do *ah*, you have to think like when you're yawning to lift the palate, and that's a little more abnormal."

"Then students should be started on an *oo* . . ."

"Being careful," he added, "because you can hurt them tremendously if they do it wrong."

"How can you do the *oo* wrong?" I asked.

"It doesn't have *squillo*."

"Should the lips be used in making the *oo* . . . or any of the five basic vowels?"

"No, if you don't want to. All of that can be at your command. The formation of the lips, in certain individuals, helps to focus the sound a little better. But the idea is to be able to do it when you want to, and not for it to be a crutch."

"Some singers have to use their lips as part of their basic technique," I observed.

"That's wrong! It's very important to have a completely blank expression. I don't want anybody to come and wrinkle the forehead. That isn't going to help you sing."

"A while ago you mentioned the yawning position."

"Yes, but it should always be up," he said. "Sometimes when you yawn you *pull* your tongue down."

"But when you yawn, your larynx does move down, doesn't it?"

"Yes, but the larynx should never be *pulled* down."

"Should one think of the beginning of a yawn, not the end?"

"Exactly!"

"The end of the yawn stretches laterally," I said.

"Absolutely! Wrong! And you should never feel a *down pull*. One thing is a little push to the front . . . the tongue . . . but relaxed. You must feel it is coming, a little out of the throat, and the palate lifting . . . only about one hundredth of an inch. You open your throat, it's not *uugh* [like singing in a barrel].

"After that you find the proper placement . . . *not* through your nose," he said with a nasal twang. "Some people sing through the nose and nowhere else. It's so inhuman, so artificial. It doesn't work, because, first of all, it makes the voice very light. It's *squillante* [brilliant], but it's not beautiful."

"How should one differentiate between *nasal* and *in the mask?*" I asked.

"When you put it in the *mask*, the nose is closed." He sang nasally and then shifted to what he meant by *in the mask*. "See, I close my nose and immediately it sounds round and solid. I think the secret is that your nose must be closed somehow, from the inside."

"That reminds me of scuba diving. A diver must learn to take off his face plate and have the knack of still breathing through the regulator without allowing any water to enter his nose. You close the nose off internally."

"As individuals," Pablo continued, "we all have different cavities of resonance. The placement for some people is a little farther back, and for some a little farther forward. You have to be able to play with that *after* the voice is developed, not before the basics are present. That is the point at which a teacher is very important."

"How about the problem of the *passaggio?*"

"This is only one of the problems that the *oo* vowel solves . . . it's already covered. But if you do"—he sang an ascending scale on an *ah* vowel, opening more and more as he went up—"then you have to teach him how to break that *passaggio.* But if you use the *oo,* it's already there [covered]."

"But then *ee* is also a covered vowel. Why not use it as the foundation?" I asked.

"Yes, but the problem with *ee* is that it can be very tense. And the *oo* forces you to relax . . . or else!

"Let the low notes always float light. The higher you go, increase the sound, lowering the jaw. Coming down, relax again, making it light, and close the jaw. It gives the voice a rest. You can't sing the high D with the same pressure as the low D. But no matter what you do, it must have that high *squillo.*"

As the interview ended and I left the stage door of the Met, I was glad I had included this new young face from the Met. It was a most informative interview. I trust the reader will profit not only by it, but also by many future years of happy listening to one of the Met's new young stars.

Lucia Evangelista

Lucia Evangelista, world-renowned soprano, was born in Genoa, Italy, where she received all of her early musical training. She made her opera debut at the famed Carlo Felice Theater in Genoa. Following a tour throughout Italy, Miss Evangelista made her debut at La Scala, Milan. In 1946 she immigrated to the United States, where she starred in several transcontinental tours. She sang with many important U.S. companies including San Francisco and the New York City Opera. In 1953 she married Met basso Jerome Hines, and after having four sons retired from the opera scene. Her movie of Verdi's LA TRAVIATA *has had worldwide showings.* 🎵

MANY people have fond memories of Lucia's beautiful performances of Violetta and Mimi, and I have been asked countless times if she too would have a chapter in this book. Since her marriage to me and the subsequent arrival of our four sons drew her away from the opera stage just as her career began to blossom, I have felt vague qualms of guilt for having deprived the opera public of such a stunning singing actress, so I decided that the least I could do was to include a few pages on her technique.

Knowing Lucia's modest temperament, I approached my interview with her most delicately.

"Darling," I said, "I feel it would be a great loss to the musical world if you did not share with us some precious insights into how you managed to sing so exquisitely. Now, what can you tell us?"

"Sweetie . . . I was born with it."

Well, I tried. You see what I have to live with.

Nicolai Gedda

Nicolai Gedda has had a long career as one of the premier tenors in the world. He made his debut in 1952 in Stockholm, the city of his birth, in Adam's POSTILLON DE LONGJUMEAU, but he had been singing in church long before his operatic beginning. Producer Walter Legge engaged him for what proved to be a long phonographic affiliation with EMI in England, and the series of recordings Gedda made beginning in the fifties introduced his pure, sweet voice to millions and hastened his rise to eminence. He is known as a superb stylist and for his outstanding diction. Every syllable he sings can be clearly heard and understood whether the language is Italian, French, German, Russian, or English. He made his Metropolitan Opera debut in the title role of FAUST in 1957 and has been associated with the company for more than twenty years. Some of his roles have been Hoffmann in TALES OF HOFFMANN, Lensky in EUGENE ONEGIN, and Belmonte in DIE ENTFÜHRUNG AUS DEM SERAIL. 🎺

IF any key word epitomizes the career of Nicolai Gedda, it is style. I was immediately aware of it that night in 1957 when the young tenor debuted at the Met in Gounod's *Faust*. I was the Méphistophélès in that evening's performance, and I was very impressed by Nicky's rare combination of beautiful voice and clear enunciation, as well as a profound sense of French style. This initial impression was strongly reinforced when I later heard his Don Ottavio in *Don Giovanni*. Again beautiful voice and impeccable enunciation, but this time in Italian, and a clean Mozartean style. Over the years I have sung with this talented man in everything from Verdi to Moussorgsky, and always it is the same satisfying experience. Nicky's sense of style for each composer is well known and respected by all of his colleagues. And all of this has always been matched by a beautiful, polished technique. How much of this was molded into his life and how much was just his nature?

Nicky and I sat down in a Met dressing room where we spent a very pleasant two and a half hours. Our tenor was born in Stockholm of a Russian father and a Swedish mother. Undoubtedly, his extraordinary linguistic ability had been stimulated by the experiences of his early life. His native language was Swedish, but at the age of three he was taken to live in Germany, only to return to the land of his birth at the age of nine. To complicate the linguistic situation further, he sang in a Russian choir while in Leipzig, where his father was the choir director and cantor in the Russian Orthodox church. It was there that his father began teaching him to sing as well as to play the harmonium.

Nicky attended college in Sweden, graduating with a degree in Latin and history in 1945. In addition to being trilingual from childhood, his college education added Latin, English, and French to his repertoire, giving him mastery (and I mean mastery) of six languages.

After his graduation he took a job in a bank, singing on the side, but only in church. He was looking for a singing teacher, and one of the clients at the bank took him to the Swedish tenor Carl Martin Oehman, who had discovered Jussi Björling when he was young.

"He taught me about support," Nicky began. "First of all, he said, 'Your posture must always be erect. It is very important, when you are on the stage, to hold the chest as high as possible.'"

"How do you take a breath to sing?" I asked.

"The only muscles which should work are these . . ." He indicated the area just under the ribs in the front. "That's my diaphragm. When you inhale you fill the lower parts of the lungs first, so automatically your ribs have a movement out. The support is the movement, with the help of your abdomen, under the sides of the rib cage."

"If you sing a high note," I asked, "what do you feel with regard to the diaphragm?"

"I think it's a double kind of movement . . . of working of muscles . . . even up a little. It's both."

"Like a pressure and counterpressure?"

"Yes. Of course you can't write it down, but it's like a bowel movement. [Who says I can't write it down?] If one could see through the body, I would say that the rib cage, through that muscle work, is expanding outward . . . and something in between is holding it up. The outer muscles below the ribs have a tendency to go out. You use your chest also as a resonator . . . as a support."

"Would the lower abdominal muscles be pushing up too?"

"I really don't have any concern about lower muscles. I don't feel any . . ."

"What else did you learn from Oehman besides support?" I asked.

"He explained to me the mask . . . the bone structures under the eyes. We have cavities behind the nose, under both eyes. The tone has to travel through the throat and be placed above the nose, and we play with the tone in all of those cavities. Of course, too many think that to sing in the mask means to sing nasal sounds. Very often older singers have very nasal tones, many also in the Russian school."

"Some people say the throat should feel as though it were nonexistent," I said.

"That I believe in, yes! My first teacher taught that the position of the throat, when singing, should be the same position you have when you are yawning: wide open without any muscles . . . no tension whatsoever. So I think you should forget about the throat. By inhaling properly, as when you yawn, your Adam's apple automatically goes into a low position."

"Would you agree," I probed, "that we are only speaking of the beginning of the yawn?"

"Yes! Yes! Now, I don't just take a breath and exercise. I do a whole procedure. I have the mouth closed and I inhale . . . not through the nostrils only . . . but deeper, so I have a sensation behind the nose."

"Do you mean feeling the sensation also in the sinuses?"

"Yes. I have the impression that I open all those cavities." With that Nicky demonstrated.

Nicolai Gedda

"I hear a slight sighing sound," I said. "You try to produce a sinus resonance as you inhale?"

"Exactly," was his enthusiastic reply. "And that gives me the sensation that, when I start to sing, I already have the mask open."

"What else did Oehman contribute to your technique?"

"He was very severe about the pronunciation of the consonants, especially in the beginning of the word, so every consonant would be heard clearly. In *bel canto*, energetic pronunciation of these consonants should not ruin the line. They should come at the very last moment after a vowel."

"Some people stay too much on the first consonant, like *mmmmee*, and they tense everything because of it," I said.

"True. He had that fault, my first teacher—yes. I had to moderate that. But, for instance, the Italian word *tremo . . . trrr . . . trremo . . .* you can take your time there. The *m* is more dangerous. He sometimes overdid it and the vowel was not proper.

"Another rule is, whatever you sing, in whatever position, or key, the consonant with which you start a word should be on the same height as your vowel. If you sing, for example, *mio* on a high note . . ." He demonstrated.

"Ha," I said, "*m* is a sounding consonant, and its sound must be on the same pitch as the vowel you are about to sing."

"Right!"

"You've obviously thought a lot about proper use of consonants. No wonder you are well known for your excellent diction in all languages."

"I can thank this man for that," he added.

"Going back to this rule," I said, "*s* is not a sounded consonant. Should it, just the same, be pitched correctly in the mind?"

"Yes. The consonants should help you produce the beautiful vowels."

"How many years did you study with Oehman before you debuted in opera?"

"Three years."

"Did you use a regular system of scales?"

"I don't think my first teacher had any routine. My second one,

Novicova, did. Her system was scales, first with rather small intervals, like:

and then longer ones:

Then maybe":

"These are usually fast-moving scales?" I asked.
"Yes. Then she would do arpeggios":

"What vowels did you use?"
"First *ah,* and then the other vowels. Then she would finish it off with:

And every exercise I do this . . ." He demonstrated again the slow breathing through the nose.

"She also taught me the *sorriso* [smile] position of the mouth . . . a *slight* smile."

"Now tell me," I said, "what do head voice and chest voice mean to you?"

"Head voice to me means the falsetto. That is a tone that is absolutely not supported. I have learned to sing a very high *mezza voce*, and I always support it. I can't sing falsetto anymore."*

"What is the difference between an unsupported falsetto for a tenor and a supported pianissimo?" I asked.

"Falsetto . . . it's very high-pitched, but a tone I cannot do anything with. Pianissimo . . . I support it and I can make a crescendo on it."

"Did you always have a high pianissimo?"

"No, no!"

"How did you acquire it?"

"It can only be acquired by working on the placement of the voice. The higher the voice is placed the more you can play with it."

"You mean *high* in the mask?"

"Yes. The more the voice is *égalisée* . . . equalized . . . there are absolutely no breaks in the voice from the low to the high . . . no registers."

"Then the first step is to eliminate register changes as you go up," I said.

"Absolutely! And that takes time. We tenors have those difficult notes in the *passaggio*—F sharp, G—that have to be overcome."

"What would you recommend for smoothing out that passage?"

"As a tenor, for the position in the throat around F sharp and G, one must think of yawning even more. The *ah* should be covered. I was taught that one should think more an *oh*. It can't be an open *ah*, as in the lower register."

"You say you use more of the yawning position in the passage. Does that mean you think of holding the larynx down even more?"

* This is reminiscent of Jussi Björling, who used to claim the same thing.

"No! I think of it in terms of the working of the muscles of the diaphragm."

"More tension in the diaphragm as you go up?"

"Yes, yes!"

"Do you think a little deeper as you go up?"

"A little deeper would be the right expression."

"Along with more spacing in the throat?"

"Definitely."

"By that we mean in the larynx area, right?"

"Yes. It's very hard to explain."

"Of course, no student will be able to learn to sing solely from reading this book," I said.

"Definitely," was his firm reply. "You cannot overcome problems that come in different passages and pitches by listening to yourself. You need another ear."

"Back to the *passaggio* for a moment," I said. "Some people say they can smooth it out by thinking a bit nasal in that critical range."

"I would say yes . . . it means exactly that. The tone has to be as much forward as possible . . . *not nasal* . . . but really *in the mask*. The thought is *forward*. You take a point somewhere there . . ." He indicated a point a foot or more in front of his face. "And you sing to that point."

"When you say forward you mean . . . ?"

"It's all up here," he said, indicating the mask.

"And you don't think in terms of using the throat?"

"I was taught to sing the vowels."

"In other words, if you sing the correct vowels, you sing properly," I prompted.

"If you hear the great singers of the past there are always pure vowels. If I teach, I will stress very much that young people learn the languages and pronunciation.

"The French say that the non-French singers who speak the language sing French better than the French, because the French are exaggerating the nasals too much. They're closing and they lose the line."

"French should be slightly Italianized," I offered.

"Exactly! Of course, we should say *sans* . . ." He demonstrated the French nasal vowel. "But the French are overdoing it. I was lucky to work with people who were very, very strict with legato, expression, line, and style. The fact that I was brought up with Mozart is very important . . . as for instance, you have a *gruppetto* . . ."

"What's a *gruppetto?*" I asked.

"Well:

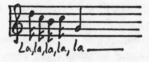

Something like that, or:

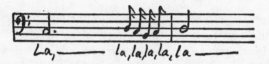

as in *La Calunnia,*" he said, giving me an example from the bass repertoire. "If you have something like that in Donizetti, or in Italian opera, you always have an aspirated *h* in between. That's a crime in Mozart. Also in Schubert songs. And also, the more you speak and pronounce the language, the more help you get. You find the essence of the style."

It was most appropriate that the interview ended with the word "style." Of course, there are some famous singers who have had great style which they used effectively to disguise their shameful lack of technique. But Nicky's style has nothing to hide: it is more than matched by the masterful use of his voice.

Bonaldo Giaiotti

Bonaldo Giaiotti was born in Udine, Italy, and made his debut in 1958 in Milan as Colline in Puccini's LA BOHÈME. *Shortly afterward, in 1960, he debuted at the Metropolitan Opera as the High Priest in Verdi's* NABUCCO. *For more than twenty years, Mr. Giaiotti has continued his association with the Met, where his rich, beautiful bass voice has been heard in many roles, from Méphistophélès in Gounod's* FAUST *to King Henry in Wagner's* LOHENGRIN.

BONALDO greeted me warmly at the elevator and ushered me into his spacious New York apartment overlooking Central Park West. Our interview began with assorted refreshments, occasionally interrupted by a business call. It was a scene of bustling, friendly activity. As my host left the room to speak on the phone with his opera coach, Maestro Marzollo, I couldn't help wonder at the unpredictable fate that had brought a sturdy country boy from Udine, Italy, to the great opera stages of the world. What influence did his humble rural origin bring to bear on his already long and successful career? One usually associates simplicity with provincial life, and are not the greatest truths usually the simplest?

Truth and honesty are the handmaidens of sustained success, and I recalled the simple honesty of Bonaldo in 1963, when I saw him sadly walking about backstage at the Old Met.

"What's the matter, Bonaldo?" I asked.

"Oh, Signor Jerry," he sighed heavily, "I am in grave difficulty with my voice and I am afraid it will mean the end of my career. I have been to the doctor and he says I am developing nodes on my vocal cords and must have an operation."

"Nodes," I said. "How long have you had this condition?"

"A couple of weeks," was his answer.

"Wait a minute," I countered, "it takes six to eight months for nodes to form. I want you to get another opinion. Will you go see Dr. Leo Reckford? I'll pay the bill myself."

Bonaldo agreed to visit Dr. Reckford and I received the report a few days later. Bonaldo had some redness and swelling from vocal fatigue. With three or four days' rest he would be back in good shape.

"No sign of nodes?" I asked the doctor.

"Nodes? Of course not!"

I then explained the previous diagnosis. Dr. Reckford was incensed. The other doctor had a reputation for operating excessively, and Bonaldo was the victim of an irresponsible diagnosis. Fortunately, due to his honesty with a colleague, he was spared a possible tragedy and quickly returned to performing at the Met again.

At this point in my reverie Bonaldo reentered the room and we began the interview. Eighteen successful years had passed since this incident and by now it was all but forgotten. Before discussing technique he wanted to give me his background.

Bonaldo sang in church as a boy until the age of twelve. There were no musicians in his family, but his father had a beautiful untrained voice. Bonaldo felt he had inherited his father's voice as well as his mother's talent for doing imitations.

When he was twenty years of age, the football team on which he played lost an important game. That evening, seated in an inn with his defeated and melancholy colleagues, he decided to dispel the gloom by doing an imitation of a Russian bass he had heard on the radio that morning.

Everyone was surprised by his extraordinary voice, including a friend who sang in the local opera chorus. He subsequently took Bonaldo to the lady choral director, who not only inducted him into the company but began to give him private voice lessons.

The day of his first lesson he returned home with the news that he was a tenor and he hoped soon to be singing everything from Rodolfo to Radames. The day of his second lesson he was told that he was a baritone instead. He and his family quickly adjusted to that with the thought of his becoming a great Iago or Rigoletto. The day of his third lesson he was told that he was a bass!

"I cried," he said. Being a bass, I understood perfectly.

Bonaldo Giaiotti

Within a year he was presented in a solo recital and then taken to Trieste for an audition with an important maestro. The verdict: "A beautiful voice. It's a shame he has such a tight throat, but it's obviously his nature and there is nothing to do about it."

Undaunted by the expert's opinion, Bonaldo set out on a quest for an "open throat."

When he returned home he set his mind on finding the solution. The thought entered his mind that chickens on the farm, when fed large amounts of cornmeal two weeks before being killed, fattened up, their necks growing much thicker. Surely with a neck that size the chicken must have an open throat. With that thought in mind he proceeded to take a healthy quantity of cornmeal and pour it down his throat. Fortunately, some water was nearby and he quickly got it down before he strangled to death on the powdery meal. Still determined, he returned to his lessons.

After two years of interrupted study he went to Milan for another year of vocal studies. He then began a full-time vocal career and soon found himself singing at the Metropolitan Opera. For five years he sang with no more formal study, and during this time, he confessed, he began to have vocal problems. Finally in 1963 he had a serious vocal collapse, bringing about the incident I described.

"I have always been extremely honest and outspoken when I've had problems with my voice," he said, "and I feel this is what saved me. When I was in trouble I readily admitted it to myself and my friends. I asked help from everyone and they all gave me bits of advice. I put it together and developed my technique."

I was duly impressed because such a situation creates emotional as well as intellectual confusion. The pressures of a career and an ailing voice combined with the multitudinous and often conflicting opinions of well-meaning colleagues can be disastrous. It takes a lot of cool, clear thinking to find one's way out of such a problem, and I have seen many great voices come to an untimely end under such circumstances.

During this crisis Bonaldo began coaching roles with Maestro Marzollo.

"The great drama in the singer's life," he continued, "is that he can judge others correctly, but not himself. I had the ability to imitate what other singers could do and this seemed to help in my earlier years. Then I realized that imitation of another singer is dangerous, particularly if one does not know *how* the other singer does it. Working with Marzollo helped me to find what I really was myself, and it convinced me of the need of another pair of expert ears to listen to me and say 'yes' and 'no.'"

"Bonaldo," I said, "a few moments ago you said you took bits of advice from your friends and then put it all together and developed your own technique. Just what is that technique?"

"I do not believe that singing scales has anything to do with the development of the voice," he said. "Scales serve only to develop musicality. You must find and develop the mechanics of the voice before you make sounds."

He then demonstrated the concept of an open throat by reproducing the beginning of a yawn, breathing deeply, which caused his Adam's apple to descend firmly all the way down, accompanied by a lowering of the *back* of the tongue without pulling down on the jaw. He clarified this by repeating that it is the *beginning* of the yawn, not the latter part, which spreads the back of the throat wide, closing off the larynx. He repeatedly demonstrated this downward motion of the entire larynx, independent of the jaw, which remained loose but unmoving.

The other important factor in vocal mechanics, he felt, is the use of the diaphragm. Suddenly he was lying flat on his back on the floor demonstrating the sort of muscle flexing used in proper breathing.

"You see, the first moment you begin to do a sit-up, you feel certain abdominal muscles tensing. These are the correct muscles to use in breathing."

Jumping to his feet, he then demonstrated how he warms up his vocal apparatus for a performance. It was a soundless exercise that consisted of taking a deep abdominal breath coincident with opening the throat by lowering the larynx together with the back of the tongue. He does this simple exercise each day for ten to thirty minutes.

Regarding the use of the breath coordinated with the vocal cords, Bonaldo felt that one either sings *sul fiato* (on the breath) or *col fiato* (with the breath). *Sul fiato* he described as the "tone sitting on the breath," as in the classical case of the ball bouncing and floating on top of a fountain of water. *Col fiato* was the "breath that runs behind the sound." The former floats and the latter is impelled. Fundamentally the voice should be based *sul fiato. Col fiato* can be used sparingly for some special effect or vocal color, but not as a basic technique.

"In summation," he said, "one must open the throat by lowering the back [or base] of the tongue, with the tip of the tongue resting, *not pushed*, against the lower teeth. The tongue must not enter into the formation of the sound, but must be kept out of the way. To form the sound by lifting the tip of the tongue to the roof of the mouth, or by lifting the back of the tongue, is dangerous. Properly lowering the larynx then neutralizes the tongue, allowing the fullest resonance of sound in both the head and chest."

With this summary our interview closed. I left with the distinct impression that Bonaldo Giaiotti had never forgotten the early criticism of his "tight throat" and had persisted with great tenacity until he had found its solution. I had encountered an artist dedicated to simplicity, truth, and honesty. You can't beat that.

Jerome Hines

Jerome Hines has been a leading basso at the Metropolitan Opera for many years. He debuted with the company in 1946 as the Sergeant in BORIS GODUNOV. At the publication of this book, he was entering his thirty-seventh season with the Met; the previous record holder was Antonio Scotti with thirty-four seasons. Born in Hollywood, Mr. Hines made his opera debut in November 1941 with the San Francisco Opera as Monterone in RIGOLETTO. His mellifluous bass voice is outstanding in many roles, among them Gurnemanz in PARSIFAL and Sarastro in THE MAGIC FLUTE. He has been a pioneer of American singing; he was the first native-born American to sing Boris Godunov at the Met; Philip II in DON CARLOS at the Met, the Teatro Colón in Buenos Aires, and in Palermo; and Wotan in DIE WALKÜRE and DAS RHEINGOLD at the Met and at the Bayreuth Festival. Mr. Hines has also composed an opera, I AM THE WAY, the life of Jesus, which he produced at the Metropolitan Opera House in 1968. 𝄢

IN the 1980–81 season I had the privilege of breaking the all-time record for longevity for a leading singer at the Metropolitan Opera, racking up thirty-five consecutive years of service. I am happy to report that at the writing of this chapter, three more years with the Met are already contracted. It is more than forty years since I first set my foot on the operatic stage with the San Francisco Opera in 1941. They have been satisfying years in retrospect, some of them exhilarating, and some devastating. All in all, I love my profession; opera has been good to me and I hope I have brought some measurable good to opera in return. I have also sung approximately thirteen hundred recitals and orchestra concerts since my debut at the Metropolitan, which perhaps types me as more of a recitalist than an opera singer.

It has been a long road and a hard one and I thank God for every moment of it. Three major factors, other than my basic vocal studies, have been the cause of my durability. The first is my deep and abiding Christian faith. The second is my more recent commitment to a real "health nut" discipline of nutrition, fasting, and exercise. The third has been the compiling and writing of this book.

I have, in essence, been given the privilege of having a singing lesson with each and every great singer who has been interviewed for this book, and that truly has been one of the great experiences of my life. Previous to undertaking this assignment, I had studied voice continuously for over forty-four years, and with the finest of teachers, to whom I owe an enormous debt. Yet I must in all honesty say that I have learned more about singing, at least in head knowledge, while writing this book, than I had previously learned since my first voice lesson with Gennaro Curci in the spring of 1938. (Subsequently I studied also with Rocco Pandiscio and Samuel Margolis.)

In all honesty, I truly believed my career was about to come to a close in 1971. I was down to two performances a season at the Met, and Mr. Bing had dropped me from the roster for the forthcoming season under Goran Gentele (who subsequently gave me a foot back in the door with three performances of *La Bohème*).

Through a powerful spiritual motivation I began to fight vigorously despite a seriously growing threat from a devastating bout with osteoarthritis. I then became a health nut, just to survive in my profession, which provided the fortuitous spin-off of rejuvenating my tired and ailing vocal cords.

Then late in 1977, I began the series of interviews in this book. That was the deciding factor, and a flood of encouragement began to pour in from the media and friends alike. First they said I sounded so young, and finally some began to say I had never sounded as good in my younger days. Be that as it may, it is obvious that something most unusual has happened in this singer's career, and what I have acquired in vocal know-how in subsequent years has had a crucial influence.

I had originally intended to espouse my personal ideas on vocal technique in this chapter, but I have changed my mind. I have decided to tantalize you, dear reader, by suggesting you extract that technique out of these interviews just as I did . . . the hard way. I am not going to make it easy for you because there is truly no easy way to sustained success. I am not being capriciously perverse in this, I think the discipline will be good for you. I want you to eventually become tough, as I have become tough. A serious opera career is not for the weak and the lazy.

What are you waiting for? Get to work. If I did it, so can you.

Note: I must add that in one period of major vocal problems, I visited Dr. Morton Cooper, who pointed out that much of my trouble had its roots in incorrect speaking habits. Giving heed to this has also been most valuable. For further information, consult the chapters on Dr. Morton Cooper and Rita Shane.

Marilyn Horne

Marilyn Horne is one of the outstanding singers of bel canto *operas in the world today. Her phenomenal technique, coupled with her rich, deep mezzo-soprano/soprano voice, has given much pleasure to many audiences throughout the world. Miss Horne was born in Pennsylvania but studied in California. Her debut was as Hata in* THE BARTERED BRIDE *in 1954 with the LA Guild Opera. In 1970 she made her Metropolitan Opera debut, as Adalgisa in* NORMA. *Among her outstanding roles have been three Rossini interpretations: Rosina, Isabella in* L'ITALIANA IN ALGERI, *and Arsace in* SEMIRAMIDE. *She is also a successful and popular Carmen.* ℘*

I AM sitting here in my living room sifting through my impressions of "Jackie," as Marilyn Horne is called by her friends, trying to come up with some outstanding attribute of her personality that would help explain this brilliant artist's career. My reflections take me back four years, and in my vivid recollection there she is sitting on the couch across from where I am now, conversing in her cherubic, animated way as her husband, Henry Lewis, paces the floor chain-smoking. Henry has a pained look on his face since I have just handed him a custom-made ashtray shaped like a coffin, with "Ashes to Ashes" embossed upon it. My other impressions of Jackie include performances we have done together, television appearances, including a most charming sequence on "The Odd Couple" and our two-and-a-half-hour interview in her apartment.

What strikes me most forcibly is that there is no single outstanding attribute that propelled this Pennsylvania cherub to stardom, but rather a happy amalgamation of all the important attributes necessary to a great career: persistence, energy, intelligence, a great voice, and many others. All of these were in evidence when I interviewed Jackie on her vocal technique.

We began discussing the use of the breath. I asked her how important she thought it was.

"I think it's ninety percent at least," was her response.

"How do you take a breath?"

"First of all, stand straight! Not exaggerated, but with an excellent military-type posture. By standing straight you automatically put yourself in a position to have maximum support. Stand with your feet a little bit apart. As I inhale my diaphragm goes out," she said as she indicated the area just below her rib cage.

"Do you think down?" I asked.

"No, I think out. The ribs expand automatically. I was very fortunate, Jerry, I had a teacher when I was seven years old—I started at five—that lady taught me how to breathe properly at that age. I'm not saying I always used it properly, but it was always in the back of my head, and I could think of it and call upon it.

"Like all young kids I went through periods in my teens when I thought I should sound like Stignani and Tebaldi combined, because they were my favorites. So I did all kinds of experimentation, lost my high notes, got them back . . . that kind of nonsense. Luckily all that happened to me before I was twenty.

"Anyway, when I breathe, my diaphragm goes out, the whole rib cage fills, and the back muscles are absolutely engaged to their fullest. It's almost as though there's air around there too. It's as if the whole thing just opens up, an automatic mechanism that happens by pushing out the diaphragm."

"By diaphragm," I interjected, "you mean the stomach area underneath the ribs?"

"Yes. It is fat," she jokingly patted her tummy, "but it's hard as a rock."

"No raising of the chest and shoulders?"

"No way! Now, the breath . . . Depending on the difficulty of the phrase, I will engage other muscles in my body. I sing a lot of dramatic coloratura. In order to negotiate that coloratura cleanly, with a big enough sound . . . otherwise I would not be set apart from the others if I were not able to do these things on a fairly big sound . . . I find that I must use my buttocks. It's almost as if the buttocks muscles tighten also, like a support below the support. To maintain this lower chest area at its maximum strength, at certain times I engage these muscles even more strongly. The muscles in the legs are like an added support underneath all of this, too. Sometimes after an important performance my legs are really stiff. When you go for an extremely high note, your back stiffens, goes very straight."

"As you sing a phrase, do you continue to think of pushing out in the diaphragm area?"

"Constantly! Pushing out, out, out. Now, that also has a great residual to it. That will take away stage fright in two seconds. Excuse me . . . that won't take the fright away, but that will take the shake away. When you start pushing on that diaphragm, that's going to start controlling your voice immediately.

"I also find certain days like yesterday," she said, "when I just can't support my voice. So, what did I do? I got to the piano and got my diaphragm . . ." She demonstrated, pushing against the piano. "I push right against it, and that will warm up all of the muscles that I need . . . down in this area"—she indicated her diaphragm—"so that finally I can support my voice."

"Now let us relate support to the functioning of the larynx," I said.

"I think, in breathing correctly, your larynx goes down automatically, you're already in a position for singing, so that you're not singing with a raised larynx. Then, of course, the higher you go, the lower the larynx has got to go."

"What imagery would you offer the student to help achieve this lowered larynx?" I asked.

"I would say that he could yawn, and the larynx would go down . . . the beginning of the yawn. And the tongue goes flat. The female voice . . . the higher she goes, the flatter it should go, and the bigger the groove, pushing against the lower teeth with the tip of the tongue."

"Jackie, some people, to get the tongue against the teeth, do this . . ." I demonstrated by raising the tongue up against the back of my teeth so it filled the entire aperture of the mouth.

"That's terrible," she grimaced. "That's a raised tongue. You've got to get a groove in it."

"How should it be grooved?" I asked. She demonstrated by folding her tongue so a groove formed, running from the tip back.

"That's sort of the maximum to work for, Jerry. Seventy-five percent of most famous singers, especially sopranos, their tongues wag and wobble all over the place, because they don't get that tongue down when they go up high. It is lack of support. They are keeping their tongues too high for the high register.

"This didn't come about a hundred fifty years ago; this came about when the orchestras got bigger. Voices were trained to sing beautifully, and to carry as far as they could carry, but they were not trained to have this big cavernous sound."

"Since we're talking about the larynx, some, not many, singers say that's where the voice has to start," I said.

"It has to," she said firmly. "The sound begins there."

"And how about placement?"

"I don't think about placement. I've a natural placement, but there are times when I've had to analyze a little bit what's going on."

"You say the voice starts in the larynx," I said. "Now, what does that mean to you in terms of actual singing? Some people think of the cords as if they were up in the dome of the palate . . ."

"That's absolutely ridiculous!"

"Then you have the sensation of making the sound in the larynx?"

"Of course! You're making the sound there. I feel that my whole concentration is coming out here in the front . . . in the mask . . . but I don't concentrate on that either.

"I have a wonderful pianist and he was making a great study of me the whole time he was playing for me. He said, 'You rarely really open your mouth very much when you sing. It's basically inside the mouth cavity where the sound is taking place.' And that is absolutely true. But at some point when you go for the high notes, with the female voice, the mouth has got to come way open or you can't really get them out. You've got to get the jaw down."

"What do you consider the most difficult part of the voice to master?"

"The middle voice," she responded.

"The transition area between head and chest voice?"

"Right!"

"What are head and chest voice?"

"Resonance cavities. In the chest voice your chest is the major resonator, God knows why. The whole area of danger is the middle voice."

"Did you always have this natural middle voice, or *passaggio,* or did you have to work it out?"

"I worked it out when I was between the ages of seventeen and twenty. I did exercises with my voice teacher at USC, William Vennard. He always said, 'I want to stay out of your way, because you have a natural placement, and I don't want to fool around with that.'"

"What did you do specifically to smooth out that passage? And what influence did it have on your high voice?"

"We decided to really work to make the high notes come to fruition," she said. "They were there, but they didn't blossom as they should. And one of the things we did . . . we really tightened up the middle and especially the *passaggio.* We squeezed on that *passaggio* to get it really . . . you could say 'tight.'"

"Which *passaggio* are you talking about?"

"My higher *passaggio.* It starts around D [the second D above middle C]. We did exercises to get the most beautiful tone without opening the mouth . . . and you have to tighten it . . . and you have to use tremendous support.

"He [Vennard] used an exercise where he would start in pure head register, without any problem of pulling any kind of chest, and he would take me down and then back up to the note." She demonstrated with:

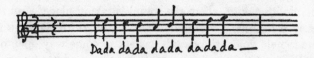

"I started out pure head softly. By the time I got to the lowest note of that scale I made a big crescendo. And when I came back up I made a decrescendo, so that I ended up softly again. And he would take me down as far as my voice would go. Some days it would be A below low C [the first C below middle C], so that when we came back in the danger area, which is past middle C—E and F are the trouble spots—by then I was in the habit of leaving off weight in the chest register. I would crescendo, decrescendo . . . you start with an almost childlike voice so you have no tendency then to bring up the weight, and I think that has kept that break in the voice . . . smooth."

"What is the overall sensation as you go from the chest voice, through the middle and up to the top?" I asked.

"It's like an hourglass, or it's like two pyramids, one upside down."

"Their tips touching one another," I ventured.

"Exactly! Therefore you have this point at the beginning of the middle voice, or the break . . . I base this on García's teachings. García called it, in his earliest books, the *falsetto*, then in his third book he changed the name falsetto to middle voice.

"I had a conception of what a male falsetto sounded like, so I could imitate it. Therefore I was able to learn how to sing those notes loudly without really pulling the chest voice.

"Then, to continue, the whole middle area, let's say from E above middle C up to C or C sharp above . . . that whole range has a very narrow production, and the best way to say that is that the mouth is fairly closed at all times."

"You close the jaw, too?"

"Yes. It's relaxed. The jaw is not tight."

"And this tightening you mentioned is inside the larynx, rather than being associated with the jaw," I said.

"Exactly! Nothing to do with the jaw. It's an internal thing and the megaphone for the sound is inside the mouth. The roof of the mouth and all that cavity in there is what's causing the sound to come out.

"Then, from C sharp on, begins the point of the pyramid upside down, so that you start getting bigger and bigger as you go up, and your voice should really blossom when you're at the top.

"I have the ability to color my voice in so many ways in the famous break area that I don't even consider it a problem area. I can sing it all head resonance, I can sing it all chest resonance, I can sing it fifty-fifty, I can sing it sixty-forty. But I call that coloration.

"And I would like to say a little bit of what I think constitutes the middle voice, and this is also based on García. He maintained that whether you were soprano, mezzo, or contralto, at some point you left off a full chest sound. We know from the records we've heard from Golden Age people that they didn't bother to smooth over the break. They just broke, went into the chest, and that was it.

"García maintained that a soprano's head voice came down one half step lower than a mezzo's, and that the contralto's chest voice went up the highest of anybody's. He wrote, for the contralto, the chest voice should stop at F, and in parenthesis F sharp. For mezzo he put E, parenthesis E natural, and he meant stop pure chest.

"Now my theory is . . . you take a ratio of fractions, so that you stop a pure chest on an E, say . . . the F is going to be seven eighths chest voice and one eighth head voice, and as you go up by half steps it increases and decreases, so that by the time you get to the B you're seven eighths head voice. And that's why it's very hard sometimes—for mezzos—to get the balance of the head and the chest around the A, B flat, and B natural. That's where so many great mezzos suddenly get this terrific hole in the voice for two or three notes . . . and they can spring into the head voice and they're fine."

"I've heard some mezzos sound as if they're yodeling," I observed, "and others just get foggy."

"Right! They're hooty-sounding, and now we have these huge orchestras to get over. Basically, the conductors don't have any mercy on us, and we have bigger houses to sing in, and they want the orchestra to sound like stereophonic sound while the human voice hasn't changed any. Therefore you have most females relying on this overblown . . ." She demonstrated with a hooty sound. "They're trying to get this big fat sound out instead of a carrying sound that's going to pierce through, which is the way the early gals were trained, and boys too. You had people like Plançon, who could sing incredible coloraturas. Obviously he sang on a very slender emission of air.

"I had a great compliment given to me. Martinelli heard me sing *Semiramide*. He came backstage and said, 'Madame Horne, you are dedicated to the economy of air.' And it's true. I am!"

"I think one of the ways I have learned a more slender emission of air," I said, "was imitating a police siren, sliding up and down the scale on a really clear mouthful of sound."

"You do? So do I. I use a siren a lot in vocalizing. When I first start I try to find a very pure head sound around C, D, E. I want to sound like a young girl, a girl soprano, and from that pure head sound I gradually start warming up. I use the siren when I'm fairly well warmed up."

"It requires more muscle," I interjected.

"It does. I find that the siren also helps me to warm up the resonators of the mask.

"All of these things I basically worked out with Henry. I'm not saying he can do that with everybody. I mean . . . after all, I'm *me*, with my talent, but I basically worked all of this out with him. I would say that Vennard and the work that Henry and I did together were the most important of my whole career. Jerry, when I was singing in my early days in Germany, I was a lyric soprano. I may have been doing wrong roles, but I always had a good technique. I'm rather glad that I sang soprano all of those years, because I feel that I might not have the extension on my upper voice that I have now. I laid off the chest voice until I was mature enough to use it, because the chest voice used too young, I think, is misused. Then you can really get into much more danger than if you use your high voice."

"Many sopranos say they never touch the chest voice if they can help it," I said.

"Which is crazy! They're afraid of it, because teachers don't know how to teach it. The chest voice should be taught, and sopranos should have it."

"Tell me more about how you vocalize," I said.

"I vocalize an *ah* almost exclusively. A lot of people we know vocalize on *ee*. I don't believe that you need this. If you want to use the *ee* vowel, then you've got to go:

because you can't sing *ee* up there. There's just no way. You modify it, I don't care what you're singing. If you're in the upper register you must modify it. I would say that the highest possible pitch at which a soprano can probably sing decent vowels and words is a G, and for mezzos an F or F sharp. Then you've got to start modifying."

"One more question on technique," I said. "Going up a scale, using an *ah* vowel, as you get into the high voice, do you feel more spacing in the throat or deepening of the position of the larynx?"

"Yes, yes." Jackie then sang a scale observing herself as she did it. "The larynx is going down . . . and the mouth's going open," she said.

"Let me touch again on placement. You said there were times when you had to analyze it a bit. What did you come up with?"

"I basically think it's like a pencil, and you have the eraser holding down the larynx, and the point behind your teeth."

"Am I getting an impression of a two-way stretch?" I asked. She nodded. Then I asked, "And the eraser's pushing down on the larynx?"

"Down. And the point is pushing the tone out. I always have the feeling, especially in opera, I am sending my voice out. I automatically do something in the hall that I don't do when I rehearse in the room. I have a feeling of a little more lift on the teeth, the mouth, right in that area . . . that I'm projecting the sound out there. I can't do it any other way. I can't do it by adding air . . ." Then she corrected herself. "Of course I can! But that's not what I feel is correct. And I can't do it by jamming the larynx farther down, trying to get a bigger sound, opening the throat more, and going very much *ingollata* [throaty]. For me the whole thing is just to keep singing it out . . . with the larynx down, of course," she said.

"Jackie"—I got up and stretched, preparatory to running to my next appointment—"you have just reconfirmed my opinion that successful singers who endure are endowed . . . upstairs."

"Singing *is* ninety-five percent brains," she said.

"Ninety-five percent brains," I thought as I left the apartment. "Ha, ninety-five percent brains, ninety-five percent talent, ninety-five percent perseverance, ninety-five percent guts . . ." This monologue continued all the way down in the elevator and out into the street.

All the important attributes!

Cornell MacNeil

Cornell MacNeil's debut at the Metropolitan Opera was as Rigoletto on March 21, 1959, and since then he has remained a leading baritone at the Met. TV audiences around the country saw his interpretation of Rigoletto in a "Live from the Met" telecast. Another Verdi role, Germont in LA TRAVIATA, served as his debut at the New York City Opera in 1953. Among the many roles in the Minneapolis-born Mr. MacNeil's repertoire are Iago in OTELLO and Scarpia in TOSCA. 𝄢

"I WANT to go on record that I don't think this book should be written! It's a mistake! It will do more harm than good!"

I had just punched the record button on my cassette machine for an interview with Cornell MacNeil. I flashed a smile and braced myself for the "happy hour" to come. Much of the time I am in a quandary whether to take Mac seriously or not, and this was no exception. I had had on many occasions the opportunity to observe his keen, clear intellect. But I had also observed that his intellect was amply matched by his sharp humor.

I relaxed my fighting stance as a warm twinkle came into his eyes.

"I was joking with Dennis at lunch," he said, referring to his son, who had just left the room, "and I said, 'I don't know what Jerry's doing this book for anyway. It's going to confuse people more than anything. Obviously he's going to interview twenty-five famous singers and the only one who knows sh—— about it is me!'" This opening volley ended in a grand burst of baritone laughter.

"May I quote you?" I asked.

"Sure!"

As our controversial interview unfolded, I steadily grew more

Cornell MacNeil

cheerful as it dawned on me that I had found myself a most colorful devil's advocate.

"Mac," I began, "your contrary point of view could prove highly interesting, and I am sure you have serious reasons for thinking as you do. I will by no means try to con you into seeing it my way. I prefer that you speak out clearly on your feelings, which obviously you would do anyhow if I wanted you to or not."

"I don't think you can learn to sing from a book. I think a lot of people will read it with glee because they'll say, 'What does that jerk know about singing? I never liked the way he sang anyway.'"

"Mac, you and I are accustomed to the sight of our own blood. We've lived with critics most of our lives. Let's face it, we were pretty tough critics ourselves in our younger years."

"Well, I still am. That doesn't mean I was right," he conceded with appropriate modesty.

"Very well," I said, tackling the core of the problem, "I am willing to grant that one cannot learn to sing just from a book alone, but you feel that the whole thing is—"

"Useless in terms of anybody learning to sing. It's too difficult a process . . . it's too peculiar . . . the teacher-pupil relationship—which may, for some reason, have the proper chemistry to work between the teacher and . . . one pupil.

"Everybody says, 'This wonderful singer learned to sing with Joe Blow. I will go off and study with Joe Blow.' It doesn't work. Some teachers end up with one pupil in an entire lifetime and never come up with anything else."

"In 1949 I changed teachers and went to Samuel Margolis," I said, "and after six months of study I showed real improvement. Immediately half a dozen other Met soloists beat a path to his door. But in a few months most of them had again flitted off to someone else."

"It's the singer's syndrome," Mac observed. "The Fairy Godmother will touch me with a wand and I will turn into a *toad—* which is usually what happens."

"A singer should stay with a teacher long enough to let his ideas sink in," I said.

"Well, the semantics of the thing are so elusive," he continued, "that somebody going to a new teacher could spend three months before learning the language, so that what the teacher says means to you what the teacher means it to mean. I've often said it would be an extremely important project to write a singer's dictionary."

"But," I broke in, "what two singers would ever agree on what any single term meant?"

"You wouldn't have to," he countered. "You have to have someplace to start from. Let us take a word commonly used by singers—*support*. What does it mean? To some people it means absolute rigidity, which will destroy them!"

"Support is usually equated with the Italian word *appoggio*," I volunteered.

"*Appoggio* . . . which means *setting upon* . . . something completely different from *support*," he said. "We think of support as propping something underneath, which immediately suggests rigidity and tension."

"Apropos of this conflict in meaning," I interjected, "the word *legato* to a German-trained musician means going from one pitch to another as quickly as possible with no connection or slur between them. To an Italian-trained musician *legato* means a tiny portamento between notes."

"If you were to sit down and give even those two different descriptions of it, you'd give people someplace to start from," Mac said. "It would only be a parting place. You could say to your teacher, 'Maestro, my Grove's Dictionary of Singing Semantics says here that *legato* means this or that. What does it mean to you?' If there's some confusion you'd have a frame of reference in which to work."

"I feel that one of the more . . . critical functions of a teacher is to say yes or no," I added. "That is something a book cannot do."

"Well, it's one thing to say yes or no," Mac observed. "You could write for the New York *Times* as a critic and be able to say yes or no. The problem is to be able to say, 'This is *why* yes, or no.'"

Now was the time, I felt, to dig into specifics.

"Mac, when you were seventeen years old, did you already have those beautiful high notes you are so famous for?"

"Absolutely," was his firm reply. "But I didn't know squawk about singing."

"Now, suppose you get another singer who, at seventeen, doesn't know squawk about high notes and can't seem to find the way to produce them . . . What do you do with him?"

Mac fixed me with a grim stare. "Then maybe he shouldn't be a singer." I didn't know if he was serious or not. If he was serious he had just eliminated at least half of the singers I have interviewed for this book, as well as myself.

"But suppose he could acquire them?"

"I think he's going to have a long, difficult problem."

"I had that problem," I countered. "I had nothing above a D natural when I began."

"There's no question about it that you can learn it," he conceded with a mercurial turn of mind. (I *think* he conceded, but it is not like him . . . maybe he was pulling my leg the whole time . . . I'll never know.)

"Now," I pursued, "you didn't have to be taught to sing those high notes?"

"Why do you need a teacher to sing? It's a natural function. It's just imposing pitch on speaking. The problem with singing is that most people complicate it enormously. It was natural enough to me until I was well into my career. I had to learn things like languages and style. That's what I concentrated on because I didn't really have any vocal problems. But as you start to have a career you'll get a maestro who will say to you, 'Here I'd like you to be a little darker, or brighter . . . you need a big, open, mysterious sound' . . . and you start applying all these nebulous kinds of things, and if you think the conductor knows what he wants, and you'd like to accommodate him, you begin to do something that's not natural, probably not even good vocalism.

"Most people call it *coloring*, which I don't believe in at all. There's no way that you can *color* anything . . . a voice particularly!"

"What do you mean, you can't color a voice?" I contended.

"All you can have is *intention*," was the firm interjection.

"And just what is the difference between *coloring* and *inten-*

tion?" I asked, honestly puzzled. I began to wish there were a Dictionary of Vocal Semantics.

"I don't believe in color!" Mac was adamant. "I can't talk with you about colors! This part of the dictionary shouldn't exist. Sing properly and with *intention.*"

"Well, then, intention will come out in terms of what?" I asked.

"It certainly does not come out by distorting your vocalism in order to accomplish it."

That was a point well made. In over forty years of vocal experience I have seen many famous interpreters, famous for their ability to "color their voices," lose those voices permanently because of constant vocal distortion.

"In other words, one should not depart from the vocal line for special effects," I said.

"For whatever reason," was his quick reply. "A lot of people have not admired my Scarpia because most of those who have been famous for singing it within the last ten years do as much yelling—I mean *real* yelling—as much *parlando* . . . They do *not* sing it. So the public is accustomed to people who do more yelling, who do more coloring . . . which I do not agree with . . . who do not sing the pitches that are written, and there are only about two places in the opera where he [Puccini] does not write pitches for the baritone.

"You accommodate a stage director who says, 'This has to have *bite!* Nonsense! How do you bite a sound?

"They change the music, they change the rhythm. To save your voice do it the way he wrote it. Sing the rhythm and the pitch with the proper . . . I started to say *force,* but I hate the word because . . ."

"What," I asked, "does the word 'forcing' mean to you?"

"It simply means you've gotten yourself completely unbalanced to the point where in order to make a sound you have to force."

"Force *what?*" I persisted, unsatisfied by this circular definition.

"Most usually you set up counterforces. Somebody who over-tightens his vocal cords has to force more air through them in order to make a given sound. Now there are all kinds of singers . . . you can watch their entire body shake . . . you can see the cords in their necks standing out. This is the setting up of counterforces in order to have *control,* which of course is another word that is nonsense!"

"Like breath control?" I ventured.

"Breath control."

"You feel the term 'breath control' should not be used?"

"I don't think it should be."

"But," I said, "most singers talk in terms of open throat, support, placement . . . don't all of these words imply control? If not, well, what should one think in terms of?"

"Open throat, support . . . all of these things . . . it is a balance; it is gymnastic; it is, in a singing sense, as demonstrable as Arnold Palmer's swing, Ted Williams swinging a bat, Joe DiMaggio going after a fly in the outfield. It is fluid, it is balanced. It's not rigid, it's not supported, it's not pushed, not forced . . . There is no strain in it at all, except making the exceptional sound that an opera singer has to make.

"This balance is almost a gymnastic preparation. It does not imply that you are terribly muscular, but that you have a kind of vocal gracefulness and are able to deliver a sound which is pleasing."

"Let's back up a little and return to high notes," I said. "When you vocalize do you stay with the middle voice, not using the high notes until you feel you're ready for them . . . or is the high always ready to go?"

"No," he replied, "you have to warm it up. Sometimes in the middle register I won't be happy with what I am doing. The thing is . . . if you *have* high notes, it's very difficult to muff them up, there's only one way to sing them. You can't monkey around on a high note.

"When I vocalize sometimes I will go up to a high note and be very careful how I come down on the descending scale. And if I start off a little out of whack in the middle I can correct it by singing the high note . . . bringing it down . . . careful how I come down."

"Aren't you in essence saying one should take the best part of the voice and extend it from there?" I prompted. "If a certain part of the voice feels good at the moment . . ."

"This is the method of getting the voice in shape," he said.

"Do you think everybody should work from the high voice down," I asked, "or is it just that that works for you?"

"It works well for me."

"Then," I said, "if a person has a good middle sound, and doesn't have excellent high notes, maybe working from the middle up would be more natural for him?"

"More than likely," he said.

"Now, let's get down to your definitions of some basic concepts commonly used by singers."

"Well, some of it will most surely run counter to all the other things you've heard," he said.

"Great!" I added. "I would be bored to tears if everybody said the same thing . . . except that there must be some basic thread of truth to which great singers approximate."

"What great singers do these days is distort. The more they distort, the more popular they become. You make a lot of records and you distort more and more. Take the poor record company that's making its forty-fourth album of *La Bohème.* They'd better get somebody who sounds different. The same thing creeps into conducting. Rather than doing what the composer obviously asks for, the conductor distorts it and becomes controversial. He becomes a great interpreter!"

"Early in the interview we touched on support," I said. "Let's pursue that further."

"I don't think in terms of support," was his reply.

"All right, *appoggio,* or whatever you do to vibrate that column of air."

"When you talk about a column of . . . whatever you want to call it . . . obviously you have to be flexible. It cannot be built upon concrete, otherwise it doesn't move. If you have a boat and you set it on a block of concrete, it's held up . . . but it's not *galleggiando* [floating] . . . it won't move across the waves. And if it's struck by any particularly violent force, it will break. Sitting in the water is completely different from—"

"—from sitting on concrete," I offered.

"Yeah. I think the diaphragm is enormously overrated as a method of support. I think it comes more from the floating ribs in the back. I think by far most of us take in much more breath than we really need."

"That's interesting," I observed. "When I studied with Rocco Pandiscio from 1946 to 1948, one thing he always insisted on was *not* taking a breath before singing a phrase. Your breathing apparatus began in the neutral position instead of . . ." I demonstrated by inhaling an enormous breath.

"When you do what you did there," Mac observed, "you set up a blockage and a tension. When you take a breath, with a deliverance of breath in order to sing, it is a microsecond sort of thing, and it should be continuous. If you take too much air, you're already in trouble. You're already creating tensions. Breathing is not separated from singing. It's all the same gymnastic action. It would be like standing at the end of the diving board before you take your bounce. You start there but, between jumping up in the air and down on the board, you can't stop it. It's continuous action once you've initiated it."

"So if you take in too much air before you start the phrase, you'll have to interrupt the process," I concluded.

"Almost certainly. All your system is so engulfed with air that you cannot possibly have decent balance. You will find that you can take much less air than most people think.

"Now, that column of air that we were talking about . . . at one end of it is your body supporting it, in *my* mind, preferably as low as you can. You extend that column of air as high and as low as you can. Your entire physique is working, the whole column will vibrate . . . You can't do it if you've made it rigid in any sense."

"Does this provide an open throat? Or rather, what does an open throat mean to you?"

"It doesn't mean anything to me," Mac snapped back. "I think it's nonsense!"

"Some singers speak about the beginning of a yawn," I proffered.

"It's great for yawning!"

"Drop or pull the larynx down," I tried again.

"As soon as you pull something somewhere, you've already created a tension. Then you're going to have to adjust something else if you're going to make an acceptable sound."

"How about those clichés like: think low when you sing high, and think high when you sing low?"

"I haven't the vaguest idea what it means. I think it's nonsense because if people believe as I do that that column is there, then it has to operate at both ends. You cannot operate with only half of it. Therefore, if you're talking about a column of air which is free to vibrate, your vocal cords and your larynx have absolutely nothing to do with it, and you should never think of them at all. They don't do anything except vibrate for you. You leave them alone."

"Is there any basic difference," I asked, "in the shaping of your throat as you go up and down in pitch?"

"It happens automatically," was the reply.

"That doesn't answer my question."

"Of course there is a difference!"

"What is that difference?" I prodded.

"It's automatic and I don't like to think about it!"

"But just for the sake of the book, *think* about it." I was determined to be as pleasantly obstinate about it as Mac was. "You're blessed that it's automatic. We are not all so blessed."

"This is that electronic miracle that takes place which nobody really knows much about."

"But can't you just say, 'I am singing automatically . . . Now let me sit back and observe what is happening'?" While I was envisioning myself as a dentist extracting teeth, Mac was probably envisioning taking a hammer to my cranium.

"Well, there are all kinds of things that happen to it."

"Can you describe them?" I pleaded.

"I'm not sure that I want to because I think that it will be enormously mistaken."

"*Try!* It's fun to make mistakes once in a while!" My felicity felt out of place since I saw Mac was dead serious.

"No. I will conduct this interview with you as though I were speaking to a young singer. They often say to me, 'How do you get those high notes?' And I am just not about to try and explain it to them, because what kind of damage can I do trying to explain to somebody in fifteen minutes' conversation—or even an hour's conversation—how I do these things?"

Mac really was serious about this, so I decided not to pursue it.

"Well, then," I said, "let's wind it up by considering one more common term used by singers . . . placement."

"Placement is nonsense . . . utter, complete crap. You begin setting up in somebody's mind, 'Place it here.' You think, 'Okay, I will place this tone in my left ear!' That stuff simply doesn't work . . . that column of air, if you try and bend it so it goes around . . . People say, 'Sing it forward! Spit it out!' All nonsense! You sing it backward and you keep the sound . . . the word . . . on top of that column in the back of your throat."

"By backward you mean what?" I asked.

"As opposed to forward."

"But *what* is backward?" I pursued doggedly.

"Obviously, if you're going to have a column of air, as in an organ pipe . . . organ pipes are built in a straight configuration whether they're square, or round, or whatever. They don't bend around corners. Neither can the human voice. It can go above the mouth's opening, obviously. There are nasal cavities, all of which should vibrate to give a particular kind of sound. But it reflects back and goes forward."

"But you don't aim it," I observed.

"I certainly don't aim it forward. One of the other words that's death to the singer is *project*. What are you . . . a *rifle?* No! You can't project it anywhere! You can allow it . . . make it free to go where it knows to go itself.

"The *non-effort* . . . the enormous concentration of the non-effort of the non-setting up of tensions and blocks and all of these things . . . that's what's difficult about it."

"Can we return a moment to the word *back*, because that's one that might be wrongly understood by the student, to his detriment," I said.

"Well," he said, "everybody thinks, 'I've got to get my voice out there,' so you start to project. You distort the vowel. How many people do you know who sing out of the side of their mouth, or raise their upper teeth so you think their upper plate's going to fall out?

"The other thing students must be aware of is DIC-TION TEACH-ERS," he said with exaggerated emphasis, "who always want you to get the sound *out on the lips*. And, quite plainly, nobody pronounces on the lips. You pronounce way in the back of your throat, at the hinge of your jaw, particularly if you're singing Italian."

"One main thing I can conclude from this interview is that singing must be free of controls and tensions and as unconscious and natural as possible," I said.

"If you start to get out of the balance," Mac said, "if you start to adjust one thing, as sure as night follows day, you must adjust what comes after it. Imagine the kind of terror that comes over a singer if he's trying to adjust every single note that he sings. Is it any wonder that some opera singers are considered bad actors if they have a technique that's based upon having to adjust? It's like trying to walk tightrope on something that's zigzag and wiggling at the same time. The only answer to interpreting at all is to have the security of a single vocal production which is adjusted only in the sense that it is adjusted to meet the dramatic requirements, but never outside of the framework of what is your vocal stature, equipment, and possibility."

"One thing in closing," I said. "I have noticed in your singing something I employ basically: a crooning or breathy kind of attack."

"Most modern singers," he observed, "do not believe in the use of the *h*."

"My teacher, Margolis, calls it a *half h*," I said.

"You can call it anything you want," he retorted. "You can even do it by thinking of it. But obviously it's not *ah*"—he made an attack on the cords . . . almost glottal—"not that kind of attack."

"It should start with that little breath of air . . . a relaxed attack," I observed. "Do you pursue the same concept of attacking with the *h* all the way up to the top too?"

"No. It's usually at the start of a phrase. If somebody goes out in the street and says to a kid, 'Opera singer,' he immediately gets into a strange position with his hands folded in front of him, and he takes a deep breath . . . Automatically singing becomes something that's rigid, loud, and overblown. Well . . . opera singers are over-blown people. Most all of us are very big and strong. Opera is an excessive art form populated by excessive people. We make it more excessive than necessary. Singing is really a very simple thing . . . except it's difficult to acquire."

"Well, Mac, we have to be bigger than life to score in our profes-sion," I said. With that we ended our interview. As I stepped out onto Fifty-seventh Street and deeply inhaled New York's refreshing brown smog, I mused upon how much bigger than life Mac was. Where among the countless myriads of people in this great city could one find Mac's equal as the devil's advocate for the arts?

P.S. I just realized I didn't say much about Mac as a singer, I was so absorbed in his extraordinary, mercurial personality. Forgive me, Mac, I've been your faithful fan since I first heard you in the early 1950s. Bigger than life? And how, as a superb artist and a superb man!

James McCracken

James McCracken, a native of Gary, Indiana, made his Metropolitan Opera debut in 1953 as Parpignol, the toy seller in LA BOHÈME. *For several years he sang small roles at the Met, then went to Europe to work and study. He began to sing leading dramatic tenor roles and became a famous Otello, which was the role of his return to the Met as a leading singer. Other roles that have figured prominently in his career are Manrico in* IL TROVATORE, *Don José in* CARMEN, *and Tannhäuser.* 🎵

JIMMY is built like a bull, and he has a dramatic tenor voice to match. Everybody knows the story of how he had the courage to leave the Met (as a *comprimario*) and bulldoze his way through European theaters with his lusty Otello, finally returning to the Metropolitan Opera as a star.

I have sung with him in many operas and his vocal stamina is prodigious. We had, at one point, been on stage a whole week preparing *Le Prophète*, which for the tenor is devilishly difficult. Our rehearsal routine was interrupted by an *Aïda* performance. Jimmy did his usual sturdy Radames, I was the Ramphis, and the next morning at ten we were both back on stage as Anabaptists. To my immense surprise Jimmy began the rehearsal in clear, full voice with no trace of vocal fatigue. His cords were in excellent shape as he sang all the clear falsettones the conductor had demanded of him, followed by ringing fortes when called for. He had to be doing something right. In contrast, we had had several tenors attempt the Radames recently who either couldn't finish the performance or shouldn't even have started.

Was Jimmy's powerful physique the answer? I doubted it. I had seen many singers during my career with strong, stocky bodies whose physical strength was their worst enemy. I brought this up

James McCracken

as I sat in the chaotic surroundings of his New York apartment. He and Sandra were packing and leaving for Florida subsequent to his recent collision with the Met Opera management.

"Don't you feel a strong physique could get in the way of some singers, Jimmy? What should they do to avoid forcing the voice?"

"Probably what it is is coordination," he said, "from the standpoint that you are not pressing in any one place, or forcing in any one area. It's like the really fine bowler . . . it's all in one motion. I had a teacher a long time ago . . . I was kind of tense . . . and he had me pretend to bowl while I was doing my vocalises. I would also pretend to be golfing . . . just something to keep me moving, the golf swing or the tennis swing. I learned to be in motion when I was singing, rather than being very static and rigid."

"You spoke of a 'long time ago.' When did you start?"

"I sang Gilbert and Sullivan things in high school. My first teacher was in Gary, Indiana; she was a high school teacher. She gave me what she had, which was good. Her thing was panting like a dog . . . and it's still useful . . . the diaphragm in motion . . . if you can do it without drying out your throat."

He then disclosed some of his vocal background: singing in the Navy, then later at the Roxy Theater in New York as well as in Broadway shows. Then he went directly to the Met at the age of twenty-six, where he put in four years of doing small parts. During his first year there he met Sandra Warfield, who had also just joined the company, and soon after they married. Finally they took the big step of leaving the Met and sought and found their fortunes in Europe.

Getting back to square one on technique, I said, "Where does a young singer begin?"

"Do the natural thing," he responded. "A lot of voice teachers think that all voices have to come up through Donizetti, Mozart, and light things. 'You're young, so sing something light.' As a rule of thumb, that might work, but it's not going to work for everybody. I was singing things like *Trovatore, Pagliacci* and *Otello* at a very young age, because they seemed easy for me. If a person will sing naturally, and what comes out is done without any particular pressing or effort, then I say people should sing what's easiest for them."

"You say *pressing*. Pressing what?" I asked.

"If you constrict your sound in the throat, you can press in a lot of places."

"How does one constrict a sound?"

"A sound that will not feel free," he said. "There's a right way and a wrong way to force. If you support the sound and you force with your body, down low, and have a column of air . . . a kind of feeling through the whole body, through the chest cage clear down, that kind of effort, as long as the throat does not close up on you, won't hurt you."

"You're using words that have to be explained, like *support*. How do you take a breath?" I asked.

"I don't breathe much differently than when I am talking. It's much easier to let the breath happen. Don't lift your shoulders and take it too high up. To take it down low doesn't mean raising the chest, because that, somehow, gives a feeling of constriction up closer to where the vocal cords are. This support, or *appoggiare*, or whatever you're going to call this—I call it *functions*—I can get my voice ready to sing without ever uttering a note."

"What are these *functions* that you perform without making sounds?"

Jimmy began making little puffing sounds with his lips and breath . . . a sort of *puh, puh, puh*. His diaphragm was working as these vowelless sounds were emitted.

"I have a simile of a bow and arrow. It [the arrow] goes down and compresses. You're going to shoot for the high note, but you're pulling it down, down. You don't reach for the high note by pushing the air. You reach for the high note by bringing it [the arrow] down. A bow and an arrow. It's not a bad simile."

"Let me get this straight," I intervened. "You mean the feathered tail is down in the abdomen with the point aiming up to be shot?"

"Yes, yes! I find that if I have a holiday, and I don't sing very much, but manage to do these functions, I keep the body muscles strong . . . I don't have to vocalize as much."

"Before we discuss functions, let's finish with support," I said.

"Where do you feel this compression of the breath, down below or on the vocal cords?"

"Way down. It's from the breastbone down. If you feel compression up here"—he indicated the larynx—"you've got a problem. No compression in the voice box. It stops here," he said, indicating the solar plexus. "There is a cylinder of air that is under compression. When it's needed it makes the sound, but without any particular effort.

"If you're going to get tired on the stage, it's going to be the diaphragm, and down under the diaphragm. You don't get tired in the throat. We singers must conceive the sound we want to make, and make it using all our resources, not just the vocal cords, or the area around the vocal cords. We should use our entire physical being, our entire psyche, our entire spiritual being. All should be coordinated when we sing. You show me a really fine athlete, and I'll show you somebody who's not doing one thing at a time. I feel, when a singer's singing really well, it's his entire anatomy that's doing the job."

"When you speak of compression, I get the picture of a force and counterforce . . . one set of muscles starts to compress the breath against the cords, and another set says, 'Oh, no you don't!'"

"That's not bad," he said. "I would say that that counterstrength . . . it's metering it [the breath] out. That's why I say it's a column of air under compression. Now, I still get red when I sing . . . Did you ever see a baby cry?"

"They get red," I laughed.

"Oh, boy! And do they hurt themselves? They cry just as hard ten minutes from now as they're crying now."

"One more question on support and we'll go on," I said. "Is there any difference in support between singing *forte* and *piano?*"

"I think you need more support to sing soft," he said. "But you've got to be careful of this. If I were a teacher, I would teach pianissimo singing after the student knew how to sing quite well. Once they start singing soft wrong, you've got a problem."

"Now let's go to chest voice and head voice; what do they mean to you?"

"Chest voice is probably below the *passaggio*, and the head voice is above the *passaggio*."

"Do you think of more compression as you go higher?" I asked.

"Yes. The higher you go, the more down you should go."

"You're speaking about the diaphragm," I prompted.

"You're going to shoot for the high note, but you're pulling it down, down: the bow and arrow."

"Some singers speak of narrowing down as they approach the passage," I said.

"I know what they're talking about. If you're thinking in terms of a wide sound, especially at the *passaggio*, at E and F, you'll be getting into some kind of trouble. If you just keep it thin . . . keep this column of air under a small kind of control, rather than let it get wide . . . with your thinking, instead of *aaa* [he made a spread, white sound], as you go through the *passaggio* [he then went to *ah* and then *awe*, indicating the more proper vowel as one approaches the *passaggio*]."

"A more focused feeling," I suggested.

"Yes, exactly."

"How about open throat?" I asked.

"Watch," he said. He then began making almost inaudible clicking sounds with his vocal cords, using little puffs of air. Here was another of his functions. "Now you do that." I did. "Now, close your mouth. Does your throat feel open? It does something that makes my throat feel comfortable."

"What you're doing," I said, "seems to be a closing of the cords over and over again without making a real sound."

"But the throat seems open," he persisted. "It feels as if maybe you could swallow an egg without touching the sides. My throat feels very open now, back there."

"Some people speak of the beginning of a yawn," I began.

"Yes, that's right," he said. "Watch"—he made the clicking sound again—"the beginning of the yawn."

"But that little clicking sound . . ."

"I don't have to make that," he said, smiling. "That's just for you."

"Do you have any other functions that give a feeling of throat

James McCracken

spacing?" I asked. His next offering was a long-drawn-out muffled sound like *ooomuh, muh, muh,* with a cavernous spacing in the back of the throat.

"It gives a cavernous feeling in the back of the pharynx," I said.

"Yeah, that gives you the body," he replied.

"And almost as if you were inhaling the *ooom* sound," I added.

"Yeah, yeah, inhaling it. Also, for me, I think constantly in a narrow up and down . . . never spread out."

"What are some of the other functions you use?"

First he yawned and then did *"Bzzzih, bzzzih, bzzzih.* There's no way you're going to get tension if it's going to be like that. It's a loosening."

"Do we agree that an open throat has to do with the larynx being slightly down?" I suggested.

"Yep."

"Any other functions?" I asked.

He immediately sounded off with sounds starting with the rolled *r*: *"Brrrrr! Brrrreel Brrrray! Brrrrih! Brrroh! Brrrrool* How does one have a tongue that's stiff if you're going, 'Brrrr'? How do you get a stiff face if you're going, 'Wee, wee, way, way'? But never open the jaw. Whatever comes out. Don't keep it too closed . . . don't open. Look what happens: I open my mouth, drop my jaw . . . too wide . . . and right away there's tension."

"Now," I said, "how about placement?"

"Be careful about this singing in the mask," he said firmly, "because there are parts of that that just don't work. If somebody decides he's going to sing in the mask before he knows how to sing, he's channeling his sound into places in the front of the face without allowing it to happen in the back of the neck, and in the skull, and in the chest cavity. A lot of people think they're doing a great deal of good singing by singing in the mask, and they begin to sound a tiny bit nasal, and it's thin. And yet there are an awful lot of voice teachers around who teach this method. There's not enough undertone, not enough body resonance."

"All head, no deeper resonance," I said.

"You have to have both," he concluded. "We're back to balance.

It's a coordination, it's like walking a tightrope. You don't want to do any one thing too much."

"Some of our colleagues say that putting the voice a little bit nasal in the *passaggio* helps smooth it out," I observed.

"I've done this," he said. "Going into the *passaggio* with a little bit of thought toward the nasal makes it a little easier. I don't think it's necessary if you're strong. What will supplant that is just a little more support. But if your body's tired, it's the ninth inning and you're wondering if you're going to make it or not . . . yes, I'll get into the *passaggio* a little nasal. I've gotten myself out of what has to be the beginnings of some trouble on a given day . . . with falsetto," he said.

"I use the falsetto as a conditioner, too, when I'm in trouble," I exclaimed. "What do you do, specifically?"

He did some humming with the falsetto on slow and fast five-tone scales, and then began going, "*Hoo, hoo, hoo, hoo,*" using these four-note falsetto sounds, successively going up by half steps after each fourth note. "But still that has to have a certain amount of support under there."

"I just noticed now, before you used your falsetto, you took a breath and sat down on it, and compressed it. You're actually supporting it as if it were a legitimate tone," I said.

"Well, Jimmy . . . in conclusion, what can we add that will round off all this technical talk and help a singer face that moment of truth when the lights go down and the curtain comes up?"

"When I get in the theater, and I'm making up," he reflected, "I'll hum . . . let out a few notes . . . But just before I go on it's more of a mental thing. I try to be quiet and call on the powers that are, and have myself be a reflection of spirit . . . or God . . . rather than have my own ego get in the way too much."

"I suppose singers need a certain amount of ego to make a career, though," I thought out loud.

"But you have to control it or it will ruin you. And I think in singing that if a person can somehow realize forces that are out and beyond us are working through us on the stage, it seems to help a lot. You don't have all of the responsibility. But then you have to understand that when you're a big success, it's also not your fault. You can't say, 'Well, see what I did!'"

I guess that amply answered my opening thought: Jimmy's strong performances and unusual stamina . . . was Jimmy's powerful physique the whole answer? Obviously not!

Zinka Milanov

Zinka Milanov has been hailed as one of the greatest of all dramatic sopranos. She was born in Zagreb, Yugoslavia, and made her debut in 1927 in Ljubljana. In 1937 she sang in Verdi's REQUIEM *at Salzburg, and was invited by the Metropolitan Opera to make her debut as Leonora in* IL TROVATORE *later that year. She sang at the Met until her retirement in 1966, performing Gioconda, Norma, and many dramatic Verdi roles including Aïda and the* FORZA *Leonora. Madame Milanov was particularly noted for the beauty of her voice and for her ethereal high pianissimos.* 𝄞

"WHO else are you interviewing for this book?"

This question was fielded to me by Shirley Verrett at the beginning of our interview on her vocal technique. I mentioned several names including Zinka Milanov.

"That's the one I'd like to read," Shirley said enthusiastically. "I want to know what Zinka has to say."

I had already had the same reaction from other singers as well, and having sung many times with Zinka myself, I understood their enthusiasm. Hers was not only a long, arduous career of singing the heaviest dramatic Italian repertoire, but also one of a consistently beautiful technique that didn't vary perceptibly over the years. She did not seem to suffer the major vocal slumps that occur in so many careers; hers was just a long series of excellent performances, justifiably appreciated by her colleagues and audiences alike. No wonder the younger singers wanted to probe her secrets; they had seen too many famous divas of that period expire vocally all too soon.

Zinka's childhood followed the pattern of the typical operatic achiever: she was totally immersed in singing from an early age. This is how she tells it:

"I was born in Zagreb, Yugoslavia, and I sang as long as I remember. When I was eight years old I had a beautiful contralto. When I changed from a girl, my voice suddenly got up to a high C.

"My childhood was spent only in music, and my brother, Božidar Kunz, was a *Wunderkind* as a pianist. He played piano when he was eight. When other children were playing, I went on the balcony and sang for hours. Whatever my brother played for me I sang. I didn't have to study, you know, it just came.

"My father and brother took me to a teacher in Zagreb. I sang Butterfly and he said, 'Where did you study?' My father said, 'She's fourteen years old, she's just starting.'

"'That's impossible! The voice is so well placed that I can't believe she didn't study with anybody.'

"I studied with this man just a few times, and I had this feeling, 'There is something I don't like.'

"At that time Milka Ternina was engaged by the Academy, so she held auditions, and I was the only one to be accepted. I went every day to her home and I was taking lessons with her for five years. She was a very nervous lady, you know, a very serious person and very demanding. I left many times in tears, but I am not sorry. She was a very good teacher and after that five years she was checking on me all the time. Then I made my debut in *Trovatore* when I was twenty. I sang all kinds of repertoire—Marschallin, Tosca, Gioconda, when I was a youngster. You know how the European houses are, you have to sing everything they ask you to. Turandot I sang, I don't know how many times, a little bit later. I was very fortunate they didn't ruin me, but I never gave more than I had, and that's what we should know. No teacher can advise you in that respect, but, you know, you have to study and work all of your life.

"Then my brother stepped into that business of seeing and watching me. He was my exclusive coach. We were a team, and he played piano for me."

Zinka then told me that after ten years of singing in Yugoslavia and being *discovered* by Bruno Walter, she was given a contract for the Metropolitan Opera: seventy-five dollars a week with a clause demanding that she lose twenty-five pounds. (On that salary it should have been easy.) She never felt she was well treated by the Edward Johnson regime, but her career really blossomed during the Rudolf Bing era. Then we began discussing technique.

"Zinka," I said, "you stated that you sang the Marschallin when you were a youngster, yet I don't recall you doing any German opera all the years I sang with you at the Met."

"I never wanted to accept German opera," she reflected, "while I was singing Italian opera. I sang in Yugoslavia Elsa and *Tannhäuser*, but in Yugoslav, not in German. In Dresden [before she came to the Met] I was engaged to sing *Trovatore* and *Aïda*. They asked me to do Strauss, and my brother stepped in and said, 'Not you. No Strauss for Zinka,' and I did not sign the contract. I like to stick always to *my* repertoire."

"Tell me a bit about your technique," I said.

"I always tried to put my *piano*, my *mezza voce*, my *legato* in all my parts. I don't believe it can be done well without it. In *Gioconda*, in the last act, there are beautiful things you can do, but naturally, the duet is louder. There is lots of pushing, and that famous B flat in the first act . . . you have to have it, *piano!* You know, you can lose it. The *piano* you cannot learn.* A real good *piano* . . . a head sound, this you have to *have*. You have to be born with it. And if you force, and you sing wrong, that goes first."

"How do you get it back?"

"You can't. Well . . ." she reflected, "it depends how much damage is done. Some singers, you know, they make so much damage, it may not come back. Some people don't watch themselves, they don't care. You're a soprano or you're a mezzo-soprano. You're a dramatic voice or you're a lyric. But to be a full lyric and go and sing dramatic parts is wrong. That's what the first mistake is."

Zinka's point here was well made with me. She was obviously a naturally born dramatic soprano and easily sang dramatic roles from an early age. I, similarly, was singing roles like Méphistophélès in *Faust* at the age of twenty without harming myself, because I had that kind of voice by nature. Despite many predictions to the contrary I have managed to sing beyond my twenty-

* I am beginning to believe this disappointing view. My wife, Lucia Evangelista, was likewise noted for her divine *piano*, and she agrees with Zinka.

fifth birthday. As Zinka pointed out, the danger lies in singing roles outside your natural vocal category. Zinka elaborated further on this idea.

"If they are mezzos, and they fortunately have good high notes, they think they are sopranos, but the timbre of the voice is a mezzo. You can go up high, but the *tessitura* . . . you are in trouble."

"Now let us get more specific on technique," I said. "Let's start with how to use the breath."

"People," she began, "first of all, when they are singing, are using breath too much or too little, and they don't know how to use it. They don't divide [ration] the breath. When they cannot come out with a phrase in one breath, then they use the tongue to help a little bit."

Zinka demonstrated this by singing a spread tone with the mouth opened wide from side to side, the teeth bared and the tongue lifted up and back in the throat.

"The moment you are using your tongue like that, you are abusing your vocal cords. You are not using the breath, you are using the tongue, which is pushed in the back, and then the hole closes in the back."

"So you maintain that one must in no way spread the mouth and throat horizontally, and should not bare the teeth," I observed.

"Not at all," was her emphatic reply. "You were singing with me a long time on the stage—*Aïda, Forza, Boccanegra*—I don't know if you noticed, but I *never* did . . . [she showed her teeth] never! I did . . ." She sang a pure, round Italian *awe* vowel with her mouth small and rounded.

"There's only *one* way of singing. They say, 'This one, she's a modern beauty, and that one, she's a classical beauty.' There's no modern beauty! There's only *one* beauty, and there's only *one* way of singing.

"I had a girl . . . she had such a wobble, you know . . . that's the most difficult thing to eliminate. It took me two years, Jerry, working with the breath . . . only breath. She could not sing . . ." Again Zinka demonstrated with that *awe* vowel; she then added a rolled *r* to the sound and continued on the *r* for a bit.

"The point of the tongue has to move. The tongue is very big, so when it goes back . . ." She shrugged and grimaced. "Her vocal cords were probably swollen. With correct singing the vocal cords will go back to normal. I would never allow her to sing anything on *ee* or *eh*, because when you sing *awe* the tongue goes on the side up [up on the sides], and in the middle it opens . . ." She demonstrated what she meant with her tongue.

"When you say 'in the middle it opens,'" I noted, "you mean it has a groove in it?"

"Yes," she said. "In the middle the breath goes through, with the tongue forward and flat."

"Now, we've been talking extensively about the position of the mouth and tongue," I said. "Some singers maintain they concentrate entirely on producing the voice in the larynx and don't believe in placement."

"It sounds like that, you know," she observed humorously.

"You don't agree with that, then?"

"No, the voice has to come out above your tongue with the breath."

"You feel the throat should be out of it entirely," I asked.

"No, no, no! Of course you feel this is always working [she indicated her larynx]. From here it goes out. But if you sing wrong, you get tired here, because it's the pressure on your whole instrument . . . here . . . inside . . . the muscles."

"For you, then, an *open throat* is formed basically by the position of the tongue?"

"And your lips too," she interjected. "This is all connected like a machine. When you sing . . . [she sang a white *aah*, spreading her mouth wide and showing her teeth] don't you feel how the tongue goes back? You close the hole, that is the *voce ingollata* [the throaty voice]. Open-throat singing, that is what is important! And, of course, it's very important to use the legato. The legato is just as important as the breath."

"Zinka, we have mentioned breath very often. Let's discuss your breathing a little more carefully. How do you take a breath before singing?"

"I don't make very much fuss about it . . . like some teachers put the singers lying down, and this and that."

"Do you breathe deeply?"

"It depends on how much time you have," she countered. "If you do not have much time, you have to know how to *snatch* some air."

"Suppose you have plenty of time," I insisted, "do you think of breathing deeply, or raising the shoulders?"

"No raising the shoulders," was her firm reply. "Nothing should move when you sing. You have to stay on your feet firm . . . no slumping. Everything has to work inside, not publicly."

"In other words, the public should not be aware of your breathing," I prompted.

"Absolutely!"

"What did your teacher tell you about breathing?"

"I didn't have trouble with breathing," she answered.

"How do you use your diaphragm?"

"When you take a breath, it's all here [she indicated her rib cage and the entire abdominal region from the stomach down]. The whole thing fills up."

"That includes expanding the chest?"

"Absolutely! You have the feeling, when you start to sing, like a snake would go from here over to here . . ." She moved her hand from the solar plexus region, just below the ribs, to the larynx and then to the mouth.

"You said an open throat is achieved by flattening the tongue, grooving it and keeping it forward. I assume this means the larynx is a bit down."

"And the uvula goes up." Zinka halted reflectively. "But if you put this kind of thing in a book, I think it is not good, you know, because the teachers are going to use that. People will use it in the wrong direction. This is not right! People will say, Milanov is using that, so I can use that too. And they do not do a good publicity for me, because they do not know how to do it. This is very delicate."

Zinka has made a most valid point here. I have heard university professors quote the most detailed techniques from the most profound textbooks of great masters all the way from García to Vennard. When I hear their pupils sing, it is obvious that their misinterpretation of these ideas has produced nothing but disaster.

"I realize, Zinka, the importance of what you have just said.

That's why I wish to be as detailed and accurate as possible, so there will be less room for misinterpretation. Let's move on to the subject of placement," I urged. "Did you ever think about placing the sound up in the nose or the cheeks?"

She responded by humming, then, "What is this? Vibration in the nose! [I noted she was humming on an *n*, which keeps the tongue forward.] Then, when you open your mouth, you shouldn't change anything, and the breath has to go with the opening of the mouth." (On reflection, I realized that this was as simple and practical a description of placement as is possible.)

"Some people talk about placing the voice out in front of the face," I said.

"This kind of talking doesn't help," she said flatly.

"All right. Now let's talk about chest voice and head voice," I said.

"I am personally against chest," she said.

"Did you ever use it at all?"

"Yes, I did, but only when I had to. Never a chest note on F [she indicated the first F above middle C on the piano]. When you do this [sing chest] too much on E and F, then the next two or three tones are hollow [she demonstrated with a breathy, empty sound]. I am against chest . . . especially for a soprano, you know. But for a mezzo-soprano too, it's very bad, because of this hollow part . . . they start to push there."

"How can a woman singer overcome this problem of the hollow sound just above the E and F?" I asked.

"With lots of breath, and connection . . . legato.

"I never used the chest. That's why I lasted so long, and I was so fresh. If I used chest, it was *covered chest*."

"What do you mean by covered chest?"

"Covered means you do not open, like also the top [high voice], the slender sound on the top."

"Then you used a slender sound on the chest?"

"Absolutely!" She sang a blatant, spread chest tone, and then corrected it by singing a low, pure, floating *awe*.

"How about the higher passage in the soprano voice, on the second F above middle C?" I asked.

"When that is heavy, that is murder! That is the most delicate one. Most of the sopranos have trouble on F [second F above middle C]. They are pushing it too much. It should be that covered sound."

"When you say covered, do you mean a more slender tone?"

"Narrower, yes, narrower. But some people don't understand what that means," she warned.

"Of course," I said. "Some people would take that to mean constricting the throat."

"Yes! Sometimes, to make narrow, they pinch the sound. When Nilsson sings, she sings very slender. That's why she can do *piano*. She has this big sound, but she is very seldom using the full amount. It's a focused sound without *sforzare*."

"In other words," I concluded, "it is all done with the breath, and never by expanding the back of the throat. You have to keep the breath pressure away from the cords."

"Sure, sure! It depends on with how much calm you sing. The vocal cords are very delicate. Keep it slender and never give your maximum. Never!

"Without *mezza voce* you cannot live as a singer. You cannot live on *mezza voce*, but you *must* have it; I wouldn't say *piano*, but *mezza voce*. I made my career on my *piano*, but you have to have a *forte*. When you hammer it out—sometimes you have to, you know, like for instance, 'Suicidio'—it needs a little soft attack. The tone is never as big as when you make a soft attack and then crescendo," she said.

"When you give immediately all you have, the sound gets hard after that. Never give more than you have! That's the biggest illness for the voice."

"Zinka, I remember, when I sang with you, that you attacked your famous high *piano* tones almost from a *mezzo-forte* and then took the sound immediately back to *piano*."

"The breath," she said, "must go the moment you open your mouth. When you sing a *piano*, or when you sing a *forte*, you have to use just as much breath . . . even more for a *piano*, so nothing happens. When you hum—and you cannot hum without breath—the moment you open your mouth, don't change anything."

Zinka Milanov

With that Zinka hummed softly on a high note, using the *n* consonant, and then opened her mouth, changing nothing. A lovely *piano* tone came forth. (This is worth trying, dear readers, both for placement and *piano* tones.)

"Zinka, in closing, I notice you've constantly demonstrated how you sing using a *small mouth*."

"Not big," she answered, "but not closed, either. Don't close the teeth!"

"Do you make a bigger space in the throat as you go from *piano* to *forte?*"

"No! It's only breath. The moment you . . . [she spread her mouth and throat] goodbye!"

"As you go up higher, do you think of more space in the throat?"

"You open your mouth more, this way . . ." She dropped her jaw down loosely.

"Never open horizontally?"

"No! And never . . ." She sang a sharp, sharp *ee* vowel. "Always . . ." She sang a rounder, darker *ee* vowel.

"With the correct *ee*," I observed, "you used practically an *oo* formation on the lips."

"Like the German *ü* [the umlauted *u*]," she said.

"Well, dear," I said, "I think we have covered the major points. But I must say, it is one thing to have talked about your voice, and quite another thing to have heard it in the theater and on the stage. We miss you and are all sorry you left off singing when you did. We would have enjoyed many more years."

"Since my brother died," she reflected sadly, "I didn't want to sing anymore, because I wasn't happy."

Shirley Verrett wants to know what Zinka has to say. I feel all singers should want to know what this great artist has to say.

Sherrill Milnes

Sherrill Milnes has been a leading baritone at the Metropolitan Opera since his debut there in 1965 as Valentin in FAUST. *Earlier Mr. Milnes, who was born in Illinois, had sung in Europe and at the New York City Opera. Among his triumphs at the Met have been Riccardo in Bellini's* I PURITANI, *Miller in Verdi's* LUISA MILLER, *and Iago in* OTELLO. *His portrayal of Iago was featured on a "Live from the Met" telecast.* 🎵

"THE idea that you either have a voice, or you don't . . . that you can't learn how to make a great sound . . . to a large degree is erroneous."

To hear such a phenomenal baritone as Sherrill Milnes make this statement immediately aroused my curiosity since so many of the singers I had interviewed stated that they learned very little from their earlier teachers because they seemed to have a natural technique and only came to know what they were doing later on as difficulties arose through career problems or poor health. I suspect that those who never succeed in analyzing their technique are the ones with short careers, because vocal problems come to all professional opera singers eventually.

Although Sherrill was "born on a farm and spent the first twenty-five years of his life milking cows," he was exposed to music and singing from a very early age. His mother was a church choir director and piano teacher and Sherrill not only sang as a boy soprano, but studied piano and violin extensively. He finally achieved a master's degree in music education, intending to teach for a living.

"In high school and college," he said, "I was not the hot talent. My brother had a more coordinated good tone."

He went on to say that in his first *Messiah* he sounded like "a thin nasal tenor" and he was a baritone.

Sherrill Milnes

"I was a great contest loser! I placed in the money . . . five hundred dollars, a thousand . . . from a whole series of contests, but I'd enter twelve or fifteen in a year, and if I picked up fifty or a hundred dollars that was great. But I was rarely the top dog. I entered the Met auditions in Chicago and was called back as one of the twenty-five semifinalists and then was eliminated. In the second year I went second in the Chicago region, so I never came to New York."

Then Sherrill said that his rate of vocal progress picked up at the age of twenty-one, and eventually he signed a contract with Boris Goldovsky and did over three hundred performances, including roles in *Rigoletto, Tosca, Don Giovanni,* and *La Bohème.* This he described as a "fantastic experience." He then debuted with the New York City Opera in 1964. His Met debut was in 1965 in the Old House in *Faust.* From there on his story is history. Obviously he built his voice by having a bright, inquiring mind that was able to put it all together, managing to become one of the greatest baritones of his time.

"All right," I began, "let's hear how you do it. What are your thoughts on breathing?"

"When we breathe in, the diaphragm, which is a curved muscle here [he indicated the bottom of the rib cage], as it starts to flatten, pulls the lungs down. That creates a partial vacuum and in goes air. As the diaphragm goes down it tends to displace organs and other things in a manner which makes expansion all the way around . . . *not* just in the front or the sides, but also in the back. This is one of the places some singers miss. They get enough front and side and they forget about back extension. That can be shown by somebody who lets the air out and bends over comfortably as far as he can . . . empty of air. Put your hands here on the soft part of the back and breathe in, bent over, and that will, by that posture, expand. That's the same kind of expansion that you should try to get standing up . . . also, of course, on the sides.

"Then comes the major difference in the schools of thought: the 'push in, squeeze in' school, or the 'stay out, pushing out' school, which I belong to. You can support by squeezing in. People do it and they are probably famous singers. I think the more efficient way is to expand the diaphragm and so forth all the way around the muscles. The maximum support from that expansion can be had by continuing the feeling of expansion through any musical phrase . . . continuing particularly this back expansion, because there are the big muscles. When these big muscles work harder, these small, specific throat muscles here will fatigue less, or not at all."

"Then the purpose of support is to keep the air pressure away from the vocal cords?" I asked.

"It also tends to keep the throat open," was his reply. "By the continued expansion—trying to keep this outward pushing, like going to the bathroom—in an exaggerated way, just setting to lift something . . . that can also be exaggerated too much . . . you can get a glottal slap on there. Too much push, that can be exaggerated, but the general feeling is the same: you're lifting a weight. You don't squeeze in here [the stomach region] as you're lifting a barbell weight. That's an outward push all around . . . a flexible feeling. It's not like a steel band.

"What happens then is you have two contrary forces . . . a physiological fact . . . the diaphragm is moving up into the chest cavity, back to its dome shape, preparing for the next breath, and the rest of the muscles, abdomen and back muscles, are continuing the outward pushing and you get this contrary energy force."

"Some people feel the pressure directed down," I observed.

"Instead of feeling it *down*," he said, "I think *out*. Posture is very important, too. Chest and shoulders comfortably high. The upper part of the chest should not pump. The point is that the main movement is low, the lower part of the ribs and the back. The shoulders should not raise up around the neck, nor should the upper chest heave . . . because that means shallow breathing.

"At the same time, chin position is important. There is no such thing as the one and only chin position, because we're all built somewhat differently. Generally speaking, a tucked chin . . . not, of course, jammed or forced down . . . but not the necktie tenor [he demonstrated, pulling his head back, chin high]. Now if I'm speaking and let my chin come up, you'll hear the sound thin out because it's stretching the throat . . . you're getting a smaller opening. It's as though you had a string, a pigtail, as if you're lifting the back of the head, and see where the chin goes. Or, standing up straight, chest and shoulders comfortably high, put your hands together [he clasped them behind his head] . . . not on the neck, but the high part of the head. Stand comfortably and take your hands away. There you've got a pretty good normal singing posture for the head. If the chin goes up you can support all over the place, but the throat opening is not going to be there."

"Now let's talk about open throat," I said.

"Open throat . . . low larynx," he said. "Those are in a sense the same thing. If your throat is open your larynx is low. Comfortably low. One can artificially depress—and young basses and bass-baritones do [he made a dark in-the-barrel sound]—because they want to sound mature. You can artificially darken the sound for a while, and sound older than you should. What happens if you keep doing that is, by the time you should be in your prime you sound like an old man! Pressing the larynx down, in a sense from above, is not right. It's another thing to open and let it drop, let it ride. Again . . . flexibility, *not* rigidity."

"Can you propose some form of imagery that will help the student achieve a lowered larynx?" I asked.

"*Trinken die Luft* . . . drinking the air. It's yawn . . . it's over the high transom . . . it's a whole set of imageries . . . noiseless breathing through your mouth and throat."

"What about the use of the soft palate in an open throat?" I asked.

"You mean the lifting of the soft palate? That's physiological fact! If someone thinks he's against it, he doesn't understand it. The soft palate is lifted in our kind of singing. In a beautiful sound . . . all of these phrases we are talking about . . . surprise breath . . . smell a rose . . . the yawn sensation . . . the soft palate goes up . . . Not with all young students does that happen. That's where a mirror can be very valuable. Check your posture . . . chest . . . see that you're not heaving, chin down . . . even mouth position . . . not singing too wide and spread . . . not fo— Deep . . ."

"You started to say 'focused,'" I noted.

"Yes. Now, one can support like crazy; however, if the cords are not approximating, that is, coming together, to their maximum efficiency . . ." With that he sang a very dull, breathy *ah* vowel on a five-note scale. "I sang what . . . five notes? I was out of breath because an enormous amount of air is going through the cords, not being used, not creating any resonance. The cords are wide apart.

"Most young students have an airy sound. And so focus has to do with *ping*. An unfocused sound doesn't go anywhere. One talks about making it more nasal . . . sometimes that can be valid, though even that can be carried too far, getting a nasal sound by losing your mouth and back space resonance. The nose for young students is a very valuable thing . . . they usually don't have enough. Chances are they need more point, more focus."

"You say 'more in the nose'?" I asked.

"Without losing space, and 'drink in the air' sensation. Or, if not nasal vowel sounds, lots of *m*'s and *n*'s preceding the vowels. They prevent using glottal strokes to start sounds.

"Obviously in any one lesson with a student, one will work on most of the elements of the sound. That is, let's say in an over-simplified way, there are five things in singing . . . there's focus; support; round, beautiful sound; resonances; and musicianship. You don't, of course, forget everything else . . . and work weeks and months to get support alone. There are people who think that that's the way you do it. Or, you need more focus in your tone, so we forget everything else and work on focus until it is perfect. Of course, that's silly, because all of these things *must go together*."

"Agreed," I said. "Now, what about placement?"

"Some people ridicule the phrase and say, 'You don't place your tone . . . you don't take it and *put* it.' All right, if that's their narrow meaning of the word placement. But nothing is foolish if it gets results. There *is* placement in the sense that one can encourage, and through encouraging add more resonances from various parts of the body. The whole body, in a certain sympathetic way, is a vibrator—but specifically from the throat up. Right above the larynx is the lower throat; with pharynx we have mouth, nose, sinus. A person's specific timbre, ugly or beautiful, is the result of the balance of resonances of these areas' resonating chambers. To make a sound more beautiful we have to alter the balance of resonances."

"Then placement," I said, "is . . ."

". . . the manipulation of these resonating chambers," he said. "That's what we are talking about when we use the word placement. Somebody else puts another connotation on it."

"Whether or not we are manipulating the resonance chambers themselves, we do feel different sensations in the face," I said.

"And in different registers of the voice and different vowel sounds . . . that's also what gives vowel sound its character . . . the change in resonances. Placement can be changed."

"Some people say they place the voice between the eyes; others, way out in the auditorium," I said.

"Any one of those phrases could be valid depending on the problems of that student. You can't say that everyone has the same set of problems," he argued.

"Okay," I agreed, "now let's take a word like 'cover.'"

"All of these words again, like 'placement,' are often ridiculed and/or misused. My first teacher, Andy White, used the word 'cover.' Some people hate it," he said.

"Some use the term 'hook,'" I said. "There is the school of hookers and another school that teaches you to smooth out the *passaggio* until it is undetectable."

"What you just said is the ideal way. As you're going up—B flat and C, D—we should have each note getting a little bit more top sound in it, a little more lift, more high resonance sensation, without losing that space. Then there comes a point where the sound will turn, or the sound will cover, or the sound will add enough head voice.

"You're never in trouble if there's an interval jump . . . E to G for a baritone. Lots of them can do E to G, even those who don't quite know what they're doing on top . . . it goes over because of an interval jump. But if it's . . . [he then sang *ah* on a scale between these notes] they don't know how to lift gradually, getting the higher resonance that we were talking about before, and then it turns at some point."

"Do you feel that smoothing out the passage is important for the actual placement of the high notes?" I asked. "Some hookers have good high notes, too."

"Oh yes! In certain operatic things you want to do some sort of a little *heiii*." He bounced from an upper middle note to a high note with a definite hook. "It's more exciting than just . . ." He repeated the interval with a smooth legato. "Just clean . . . look how easy it is! People don't want to think it's easy."

"You mentioned head voice," I said. "What, in your opinion, is the difference between head voice and chest voice?"

"Chest resonance . . . you feel buzz sensations, more in the chest and in the lower part of the throat (this *is* oversimplified).

"As singers go higher in the range, and if they do not feel the buzzes and the sensation of the resonances get higher in the face and head, then they are not employing head voice, they are keeping it chest. As a result, they will never be able to get any top voice, there will be no top extension. If you feel that high, back mouth, uvula, and behind the uvula, more nose and sinus resonance through the cheekbone, then you are starting to use more head resonance.

"One other thing about top voice: one aid to teaching it is the *oo* influence in *all* vowels, because there is vowel modification. In fact, there is an apparent dichotomy . . . conflicting phrases . . . One *must* have an *even scale*. Of course! But to have an even scale you sing unequal vowel sounds. We were just talking about chest and higher things. Another way of putting what is happening is that the vowel sound is slightly altering as you go higher. There is a little bit more *oo* influence."

"You are speaking about the *ah* vowel?" I asked.

"Yes. If you are singing an *oh* vowel, *oh* actually will turn slightly to *oo*. The *oo* influence in *ee* and *ey* . . . it doesn't sound like *oo*, but there is the *oo* influence on those two very bright, closed vowels. Some people will go into top voice automatically on an *oo* vowel, and no other vowel. So one then has to transfer, physiologically, sensationwise, what he does going from *oo* to *ah*."

"Is more spacing in the throat a help as you go up to the high notes?"

"The jaw needs to drop, particularly as you go up. It's not just a matter of doing this . . . [he flapped his jaw open and closed] but if you put your fingers below your ear, there's a space . . ." He held my fingers to the hinge of his jaw, and I could feel that the lower part of the hinge actually dropped. I realized I had been unconsciously doing the same thing for years without knowing it.

"The hinge drops . . ." I said.

"And then opens. There are students who have a very tight, locked hinge. Those muscles in there [about the hinge] are tight and they're not dropping."

"As you do a scale from low to high voice, do you have a sensation of more opening?"

"More spacing," he said. "More lift of the soft palate as you're going higher, and, if possible, more opening in the throat . . . the yawn sensation . . . however, without letting the sound fall back. You've got to keep that frontal, high feeling—nose, sinus . . ."

"A two-way stretch," I added.

"Yes. In a way, we're talking about contrary forces . . . in support . . . and that's where the kinetic energy comes from . . . that gives you the support. In another way, it's the same thing up here. You've got one force, whatever that force is, keeping space in the sound . . . for back, deep resonance . . . and at the same time another force keeping focus . . . keeping some bright, brilliant resonance going. But two things, each pulling equally, in a way, gives a sound . . . Well, there's another word I will throw in here: an *anchored* feeling. Sounds must be anchored . . . an anchored sound for you personally inside. Audiences respond. You've heard people say, 'Oh, when he, or she, sings I have such a relaxed feeling. I never worry about it. I love it.' Well, that's anchoring technique translating its feeling of security to the audience. If you don't give the audience that kind of feeling, you probably won't have a career."

"Well, Sherrill," I said, "you certainly have it well thought out. Fabulous!"

"Okay, I was not the hot talent in high school and college," he said. "Other people had better natural sounds. I was the better learner, though. I was a good analyzer. I'm the guy who could say, 'Let's see . . . put a little more *nose* in there. That was better.' Well, not only could I localize it, but I could repeat it. It wouldn't take me six weeks more of floundering around punching my fist in the water to get more focus. I could do it that day."

Sherrill may have been the great contest loser. But he proved it's not how many battles you lose, but *who wins the war*. He's a real winner in my book.

Anna Moffo

Anna Moffo, born in Pennsylvania, studied in Italy on a Fulbright scholarship. There she became an "overnight" star after a performance as Madama Butterfly on Italian television. Her lovely lyric soprano voice coupled with her slender good looks made her an ideal Cio-cio-san. She made her Metropolitan Opera debut in 1959 as Violetta in La Traviata, *and since has sung many roles with the company, including Liù in* Turandot *and all three heroines in* Tales of Hoffmann. *Miss Moffo has also appeared in many films in Italy.* ♪

"Hi, I'm the Virgin Mary."

A surprised young cadet looked the beautiful teenager over approvingly and slowly purred, "Weeelll, come right in!"

As he reached for her arm, Anna Moffo's father stepped out of the shadows surrounding the Valley Forge Military Academy's dormitory and firmly took his daughter into protective custody. They had been looking for the auditorium where the rehearsal for the Christmas play was scheduled, but had gotten lost. General Baker had persuaded Anna's most protective father to allow his twelve-year-old daughter to play the role of the Virgin, and Dad was now having second thoughts.

Two years later he began accompanying his cherished daughter as she delivered singing telegrams, and that kept him busy as she delivered over one hundred of them in the three years that followed. Her father wouldn't let her go anywhere without him.

Anna's cloistered life began in and near Philadelphia, and her loud singing voice almost caused her downfall in kindergarten, because her teacher said it was annoying the other children when they sang together. The teacher would make her sit in the corner, until, as she said, "I began not to sing anymore so she'd put me back in the class. It gave me a terrible complex. No matter how softly I thought I was singing, it was too much for the other kids, and they were very angry with me. So that's how I began singing solos in the first grade. Imagine, twenty percent of my life spent in a corner!"

Father Moffo's pride and joy was an achiever, graduating from high school at sixteen as captain of the hockey team and as the center for the basketball intervarsity. She then decided to enroll in Immaculate Heart Convent to become a nun, but the priest of the parish, knowing of her unusual singing accomplishments, persuaded her to reconsider. He felt God would not have given her such a great voice if He didn't intend for her to use it. The wisdom of his advice was quickly verified by a four-year scholarship to the Curtis Institute, where, in addition to voice, she studied piano and viola. Up to that time, singing had been fun. Then suddenly it became work. Under pressure she began getting nervous headaches and had to take aspirin before every lesson. She enrolled in classes that most singers would never have taken, such as orchestra, wind instruments, etc. She attended all recitals including tuba, French horn, and trumpet. Her first opera was *La Bohème* with di Stefano and Lucia Evangelista (the mother of my children), and she adored the Philadelphia Orchestra, but her parents wouldn't allow her to stay out late, forcing her to attend only matinees.

Anna dragged about dead tired from commuting three hours a day to school, doing her solfeggio lessons on the daily local, which "didn't make a hit on that crowded train at all."

As she was about to graduate she received a Fulbright scholarship, which her parents strongly opposed. Simultaneously she was offered a contract with Columbia Artists Management as the outcome of her senior recital at Curtis. They too opposed her going to Europe on a Fulbright, but she opted to accept the opportunity to study in Rome for a year. Her parents "were hysterical." The first night she ever spent away from her own bed was on the U.S.S. *Constitution* heading for her big adventure in Europe.

With that information revealed, Anna and I got down to discussing vocal technique. I observed that most singers of stature had begun singing as children.

"I was always doing solos," she said, "Flag Day, the Lions Club, Rotary, the Optimists' Club, and musicales, but I never studied. And, I hasten to say, if you're going to sing as much as I did as a kid, you really should study." She then expounded more specifically on the hazards of untutored singing during childhood.

"I thought the greatest voice was rich mezzo, so I began singing *Carmen* . . . all the Risë Stevens repertoire, because I just loved her. Without realizing it, I began gradually to do lower things: I had a real long voice, but I never used the top."

"Did any other problems arise before you began to study seriously at Curtis?" I asked.

"Somebody in my church once said to put two corks in the back of my molars, that the spreading of my teeth would open my throat. Well, I did that exactly once, and I said, 'If that's what singing is, I don't think I'm interested, because it hurts like hell.' I almost broke my hinge here."

"What did your early training at Curtis consist of?"

"I sang only Italian art songs and a little bit of Mozart for the first three years. Today the big tragedy is that the students start singing *Otello, Chénier* and *Gioconda* on their second voice lesson. They hate their teachers if they don't get to sing *Pagliacci* as soon as they're able to hit a B flat. Singing 'Tu lo sai' or 'Del mio amato ben' is much more difficult than singing 'Un bel dì.'"

"Anna," I said, "you are of Italian descent, have spent much time in Italy, and speak the language unusually well. What does the word *appoggiare* mean to you?"

"*Appoggiare* can mean 'to lean,' but if you say, 'I am going to *appoggiare* a candidate,' it means 'I will support the candidate.' If you say, 'I will *appoggiare* my friend,' if there's a crisis in his life, it means 'I will support him with help . . . money.' Whenever anyone said to me, '*Appoggia bene*,' it always meant support.

"With some singers," she continued, "the voices are naturally placed. Because of that, you do not quite get the message of *support* until you wake up one morning, and beautiful pear-shaped tones don't come out. That's when you are interested in how to do it. Your teacher will tell you, as mine did, but you don't really understand until you can't do it your way."

"I assume you have changed your thinking regarding support since your school days, Anna."

"I suddenly realized, in my new kind of study pattern, that what I thought was taking in a big breath was *locking* in breath. I sucked in a lot of air, kind of heaving the chest, almost gasping. When you make a pause or take a breath, the music should continue. A lot of people sing a phrase and stop . . . and kind of collapse . . . and start again. That is a big waste of breath and energy. I don't take those kinds of breath when I speak, why should I take them when I sing? I applied it to swimming. I used to try and exhale *all* of the air in order to come up and take another breath. I suddenly realized there's no need for that. Just come up and take what you need.

"I now do exercises where you take a breath, but you don't hear the air come in. Once I learned that, my speaking improved also. So now my exercises are based on . . ." Anna took a big breath, held it, and let it all out. Then, from the neutral position, she began doing *puh-uh, puh-uh, puh-uh*. This was a short puff out with an instant, automatic drawing back in of the small bit of breath that had been expelled. The instant recovery of that small amount of exhaled breath (the light puff) was simply caused by a relaxation of the breathing muscles; it was not a voluntary inhalation. She then demonstrated the wrong way of doing this exercise by a short puff followed by a quick gasping intake of breath, which was accomplished by a voluntary sucking in of the breath instead of by a simple relaxation of the diaphragm.

"When it's right," she added, "it goes right back in. Some people have a glottal attack because they slam into the breath. It's hard on the throat. My biggest problem is, if I know I have a big phrase, I must work *not* to take an extra big breath. I have found I have more breath than I think I have.

"I often read out loud. I don't say, '*Mi chiamano Mimi,*' gasp, '*ma il mio nom'è Lucia,*' gasp, so why should I when I sing? Sometimes for long, endless runs, I take a deeper breath and expand my back. To me, support is just putting the right amount of air under each note, and never letting it down, so it's all one piece . . . every note has the same energy. I feel as though a column of air is coming right out of the top of my head, but it starts at my feet . . . Naturally, it doesn't: it starts at the diaphragm. I breathe from the diaphragm and lower abdomen, along with the back."

"Let us move on to *open throat*," I suggested. "Do you associate it with a lowered larynx?"

"For me, the larynx is the home of my vocal cords, and that's all," she said firmly. "I don't ever feel anything in my throat. If I do, it usually means I've tightened up. For a short time I studied with [she mentioned a famous teacher] and she would say, 'Press the tongue flat, make it groove, lift the face and the teeth, so that you have more space in your throat.'

"By pressing the tongue, and making it go flat, I was tightening everything. She wanted a raise . . . terribly high. It's like opening the mouth of the lion when he doesn't want to. He will resist. That gave me terrific E's and F's, but rather tight G's and A's."

"How about placement?" I asked.

"You sing *ee, eh, ah, oh, oo,* it's all in the same place to me."

"What's this place you're talking about?"

"The place is the most forward, focused sound, complete with overtones."

"You say *forward*," I interjected. "What is forward?"

"Something that isn't backward," she laughed. "There are many singers who could get a much bigger sound if the voice was a little farther front."

"You're speaking of a sensation of a buzzing in the mask?" I proffered.

"Yes. On certain high notes I even get a momentary headache. You can tell . . . a note that doesn't carry too well is backward. I grew up with the term *throaty* . . . *ingollato.* Throaty, to me, is kind of backward, it's making what you think is an enormous, dark voice with no particular vibrant sound to it. It has no harmonics."

"You're really describing a somewhat breathy sound," I said.

"I feel no singer can spare unused air," she answered. "If I hear the teensiest bit of air escaping without being used, that's not the best I can do. It doesn't have *ping*, or *squillo* . . . focus . . . point."

"You're giving me terms like focus, ping, forward, et cetera. How does a student come to have a meaningful experience that brings him to an understanding of these terms?" I asked.

"Jerry, everybody has to have a second pair of ears during his whole career. If you don't, you're in a lot of trouble, because, no matter how great you are, you think you're doing something and you're not. It has to be someone who knows your voice . . . your vocal guardian angel."

"Anna, when you go up on a scale, or an arpeggio, do you think of more spacing in the throat as you ascend?"

"Yes, I give more space. But somebody once told me, 'When you sing arpeggios, think of opening an umbrella, going up.' That would completely undo me, because it means I have one opening for the open umbrella, and then I close it when I come down."

"Do you use *chest voice?*"

"I do, but I'm more inclined to use the mixed," she said. "The mixed voice has head voice in it. Chest voice has no head voice, no head resonance at all. I don't think it's very pretty. Chest voice I feel vibrate right here on my breastbone . . . as opposed to my nasal or head voice, which I feel right in the middle of my forehead, between my eyebrows . . . very high . . . a column of air going straight up through the top of your head, I guess. Basically, chest voice is not a good idea.

"They say people who use chest voice lose their top. Maybe you don't lose your top, but you get very wobbly . . . a hole in the middle, and you get two big breaks in the voice."

"Are there exceptions to this idea?"

"Jerry, there are people with extraordinary instruments . . . freak instruments . . ."

"I don't regard these as freak instruments," I said, "as much as freak techniques. We tend to limit ourselves by saying, 'That's a freak voice . . . I cannot expect to do that.'"

"No," she disagreed. "We should know what we can do."

I then brought up the case of a famous baritone who always had great trouble with his high notes, maintaining that he simply had never used the proper technique to arrive above an F natural.

"You're not going to tell me he didn't have a great technique," she cried. "I know him and he had a *great* technique!"

"No, he didn't." I was adamant. "He completely missed the boat on his high notes. He could have learned how."

"No," she said, "you're saying all people can be in the decathlon if they want. They can't. They really can't."

"Well, any *great* baritone, with a *great* technique, for my money, has to have a minimal ability to sing at least an A flat. They don't all have to have B flats like some. Naturally, there are voices that lie in the cracks between the notes. If a man has a good G, but no A flat, he should be called a bass-baritone and sing the corresponding repertoire."

"All right," I conceded, "I suppose we cannot expect any two singers to have exactly the same abilities. But when I hear someone doing something I can't do, I always strive to acquire it. I don't mean imitation of that person's sound, of course."

"You must be yourself," Anna said. "I may love a sound, but it is not necessarily *my* sound." (That took me back to Risë Stevens' influence on the young Anna Moffo, and I understood her viewpoint better.) "I think it's very important *not* to try and sound like somebody because she sounds great. To be yourself, it may turn out you're greater. Do what your voice was meant to do. Just as God made a million million different faces, He also made a million million different sounds. Isn't it wonderful that no two people really sound alike?"

Or look alike. I suppose that God was right in not making every young girl as pretty as Anna Moffo, what a madhouse it would be with all those protective fathers running around guarding their progeny. There would be no time for anything else, including singing.

Patrice Munsel

Patrice Munsel was born in Spokane, Washington. After winning the Metropolitan Auditions of the Air, she made her Metropolitan Opera debut in the coloratura soprano role of Philene in Thomas's MIGNON *in December 1943, while still in her teens. She was the youngest singer ever engaged by the Met. Other roles she portrayed at the Met were La Périchole, Adele in* FLEDERMAUS, *and Zerlina in* DON GIOVANNI. *Miss Munsel also starred in a film biography of Nellie Melba.* 🎵

"I LOST my first beau when I tackled him on the sidewalk during a football game and broke his collarbone. Of course," said Pat demurely, "I was captain of the football team."

I silently thanked kind fate that I hadn't gotten too fresh with this athletic diva when I dated her in the late 1940s, little suspecting she was a Charles Atlas alumna. I made a quick reappraisal of Pat's trim form, clad in an American Indian type outfit and hat as well as three or four beaded necklaces. That surely completed the picture of the all-American sportswoman.

"I've always been terribly physical," she continued. "My hubby, the kids, and I swim and jog every day. And when I am unable to do these things I spend twenty minutes with a jump rope, which is as good as jogging three miles. With that kind of routine you can forget diet."

I commented that I had never realized she leaned so heavily on the sportswoman's life, but I did recall hearing that her voice teacher, Mr. Herman, had his pupils do physical exercise as well as vocalises. Pat took it one step further.

"Why, he had us wear a large elastic belt during our lessons. We were supposed to push against it with the diaphragm while simultaneously singing our scales and tossing a heavy medicine ball about."

Considering Pat's gridiron background, she must have fit marvelously into Herman's approach to voice development.

"Pat," I said, "I remember a performance of *Lucia* you did on the Metropolitan Opera tour to Los Angeles. After the famous Mad Scene you had thirteen curtain calls! I know—I counted! You were still a youngster at that time. That was a mighty big load of stress and responsibility to bear at such a tender age. To be a coloratura soprano, having to maneuver your voice through such intricate passages and constantly brave your way to high E's and F's, must be a terrible drain on your nerves."

"It really is the decathlon of opera," she responded, "and for that reason it is terribly exciting. In those days I thought a great deal more about my voice and physical condition. On the day of a performance I wouldn't speak a word to anyone—that was very boring. But you know, getting married and having children put me much more at ease in my singing. First of all, it gave me much else to think about. I had no time left to be preoccupied with my voice, the condition of my vocal cords and things like that. It simply made singing much more fun. That and my physical background combined to give me a great deal of freedom.

"When I did *Coq d'Or* at the Met, the stage director asked me to run across that entire giant stage holding a high E flat. I saw no reason to balk, so I did it. Then there was *The Merry Widow*, in which I ended the cancan on a high C doing the splits with four ballet boys holding me over their heads eight feet in the air. And in one show I sang a song while being passed from dancer to dancer doing cartwheels in the air. As long as the demands of the director made sense I wasn't afraid to try anything. I've always had absolute freedom on the stage and have never balked at any feat."

"Now, Pat," I began, "you have successfully made the transition from Broadway to opera . . ." She broke in to correct me: "I sang both pop and classical from the beginning. When I first sang at the Met I got the 'Prudential Family Hour' with Earl Wrightson. I had to switch styles constantly at that time from classical to pop. When I had my own television show I would do 'Un bel dì' and a jazz blues routine consecutively with only one solitary minute to change clothes, attitude, and vocal technique. Such a routine is really a schizophrenic experience. You simply cannot mix classical and pop styles. I found the biggest problem was switching gears vocally as well as mentally."

"Isn't there an enormous difference in vocal techniques between the different styles?" I ventured.

"Not really. The production is about the same—except *belting* is much more relaxed."

"Now wait," I said, proud that I, as an opera singer, had even heard of *belt*. "For the unenlightened, just what is belt?" As Pat prepared to show me, I interrupted. "Don't demonstrate by singing. Put it in words. After all, I am producing a book, not a recording."

"But it's hard to put into words. I can't verbalize it."

"Yes, you can," I persisted.

"Belt is a flatter sound with no vibrato. It is high chest voice. I can belt to the C and D above middle C, but no higher without damage to my cords . . . and a possible heart attack. It has to be very forward—almost nasal (not French nasal). There is more space in the back of the throat. Oh, it's hard to verbalize."

"That's somewhat helpful," I answered, "but I don't think we have reached a gut-level feeling as to what belt is."

"Well," she went on, "take laughing. You can laugh with a silvery coloratura staccato laugh—or you can laugh with a belly laugh, right from the stomach and diaphragm. Yes, a belly laugh is a short belt. And belt is a sustained belly laugh.

"It is more relaxed in the throat," she expounded enthusiastically, "but requires more physical energy from the diaphragm than opera singing does. It's more animal. You can get really carried away by it, but you must be careful that the fun of it doesn't get in the way and you start singing on the cords. When you *belt* the whole body is in it."

"Don't you find a Broadway show is harder than opera?" I had done several productions of *South Pacific* and *Man of La Mancha*, and was always relieved to return to two or three opera performances a week instead of eight shows.

"I have done eight shows a week for as long as nine consecutive months," Pat said. "On such a run I have to keep the strictest physical and vocal regimes possible. It's like being in the army. I take such superb care of myself you would think I had been living in a spa. But if I didn't pamper myself healthwise I couldn't survive. I make all my friends understand that there will be no dinners before shows and before each performance I do the ballet bar with the dancers—as strenuously as possible. That warms up the whole instrument, the body, of which the voice is a part. If there is no ballet bar, I jump rope at least a hundred times, very fast. That gets your blood going.

"I eat little beef, lots of fish and chicken, tons of vegetables, and I have a juicer. I make all kinds of juices.

"But I do love to go dancing after the show and I can simply dance for hours. You know, dancing is great exercise."

"Now, that leads to another question," I said. "I've heard a few singers claim that learning to dance was important. How do you feel about this?" With this turn of thought, Pat really began to radiate.

"I think *all* opera singers should study jazz or flamenco dancing. It would free their bodies. Italian men don't need it. They are accustomed to throwing their arms about when they speak and act. They're very relaxed physically. But American men and women have a Victorian heritage which leaves them basically all tight and tied up. They are not accustomed to showing their feelings.

"But look at a flamenco dancer. Even without action you can feel all the way to the back row that his motor is running inside. He stands frozen. His arms slowly begin to rise. He is doing literally nothing but you can't take your eyes off him. There is a higher level of energy . . ."

My mind began to stray as the interview flew on. As I was an American opera singer of rather Victorian background, all of this was getting to me. As soon as I left Pat's apartment, I began looking for the nearest school of flamenco dancing.

Birgit Nilsson

Birgit Nilsson has long been acknowledged as the outstanding Wagner singer of her generation. Her repertoire has not been limited to Wagner, however, and she has been successful in a wide-ranging series of soprano roles in operas by Verdi, Puccini, Strauss, and Beethoven. Not content to build her career solely on a phenomenal natural voice of great size, beauty, and clarity, Madame Nilsson has in addition continually refined and developed her artistry over the years. Born in Sweden, she made her debut in Stockholm in 1946 as Agathe in Weber's Der Freischütz. *She became associated with the Bayreuth Festival in the 1950s, and sang there her peerless interpretations of Isolde and Brünnhilde through the 1960s. Her Met career began in 1959 as Isolde and has continued for more than two decades. In the 1979–80 season, after a long absence, she returned to the Met in a special concert and in a series of performances as Elektra in Strauss's opera, for which she received tremendous acclaim from audiences and critics alike.* 🎵

Have you heard the story about the farmer's daughter who wanted to be an opera singer? Well, her name is Birgit Nilsson.

The farmer's daughter exited from the Fortieth Street entrance of the Old Met just as my wife and I were being picked up by car.

"Would you like us to drop you at your hotel?" I called to Birgit as she emerged Victorious, with a capital V, from her spectacular Met debut in *Tristan*.

"No, thank you," she called happily, "I'll take a taxi."

With that, the Met's newest diva gracefully placed two fingers to her lips and with a whistle as heroic as any high C she ever delivered on the stage, hailed the nearest cab. Actually, it required two taxis to deliver her home because the first one could in no way carry her and all the flowers that had been delivered to her dressing room. As they pulled away from the curb the driver called back to her, "Hey, are you the one I read about in the paper yesterday . . . the gal that used to milk ten cows a day on the farm before she started her career?"

"Yes," said Birgit.

"Then you deserve all them flowers, lady."

It seems that overnight all of New York was in love with the farmer's daughter from Karup, Sweden, after that auspicious debut. It had been a night of mixed feelings for Birgit. "They told me that after the narration in the first act Martha Mödl got a big applause, so I was also waiting for applause after the narration, and I didn't get it. I thought, 'Oh, am I a flop, I've failed!' And then, when the first act was over, everyone in the house rose to their feet, and they were screaming their heads off."

I, of course, well remember how the evening ended, as I was singing the role of King Marke, and was privileged to hear that phenomenal "Mild und leise . . ." from a choice location on the stage, ten feet from Birgit. There is no need to expound further, it is operatic history. I also had the pleasure of singing in at least two more debuts for our diva: I was her Wotan in her first performances as Brünnhilde both at the Met and at the Festspielhaus in Bayreuth.

So it was a pleasant and nostalgic occasion for me as I prepared to interview Birgit for this book. We were seated in a cheerful apartment on Central Park South as I switched on my cassette recorder and began to question her about her early life.

"Did you sing as a child?" I began routinely.

"I sang before I walked." I did a double take on that one. "I walked very late," she added quickly. "And I sang very early."

"You're neck and neck in competition with Magda Olivero," I observed in a tone tinged with skepticism. "She claims she was only two years old when she began singing."

"I was younger," she said. "I was fifteen months! And then I could sing all the songs which my mother taught me. I spoke very clearly," she added, determined to convince me. I began to wonder if my next diva was going to claim a prenatal vocal career. "We had a very hospitable house," she went on, "and I sang for all the guests. I was singing sometimes seven or eight hours a day. My father was very proud of me."

"At what age did you begin to study seriously?"

"I was eighteen when I made an audition for my first voice teacher. After a few bars he turned around and said, 'Miss Nilsson, you are going to become a great singer.' I studied a little bit from him, then my parents sent me to school where I should learn to cook and sew and everything. I forgot a little bit about studying voice. It was many years before I got back. I really wanted to sing, but my teacher was sick. At twenty-three, I made an audition at the Royal Academy in Stockholm and came in as number one. It was the happiest day of my life. The night before I went to Stockholm for the audition I milked ten cows. I had to do weeding in the fields. It was hard work, and I hated it. I really wanted very much to sing . . . a whole new life began.

"My first teacher at the academy was a famous Scotch tenor who had sung at the Met. He thought I knew what a good impression I had made, so he tried to put me down under the floor. It was very easy to do that. He said, 'It doesn't matter if you have the best voice in the world if you have no brain, because it's really not for a farmer to become a singer.' I went home crying the first day. He was an impossible teacher. He had a poor technique and that was why he finished rather early."

"How long were you stuck with him?" I asked.

"I had him for three years. My voice became smaller and smaller. He had a right idea—so does everyone—but the way to come there—that's the difficulty. I had an incredibly big wooden voice, full of air . . . the voice didn't project. It was incredibly big in my head and to people close by. You have to have a voice which projects. So he wanted to take off all this unnecessary sound. He said, 'Oh, listen to Birgit. Now the ship is leaving the harbor.' He tried to get a concentrated tone, but he put the work in the wrong place. He didn't put you to work on the support or the resonance. He put the work directly on the vocal cords. I felt it was wrong; I got very tired, and I was very unhappy. Finally, the director of the academy said, 'You are going to ruin Birgit's voice.'"

"Why did you have to stay with him so long?"

"My parents had some money, but I didn't want to be supported by them, because my father didn't believe in me, he didn't want me to become a singer. So I wanted to take care of myself. I didn't have money to study privately . . . and I got so many other lessons at the academy, like languages, piano playing, everything . . . declamation.

"When I was finally finished with classes at the academy, I looked for another teacher, but he was not much better, he forced my voice in another way. I had to sing one high C after another for one quarter of an hour, and the next minute he wanted me to develop a chest voice . . . a very, very big, strong chest voice, and I rejected it. I said, 'It hurts when I do it.' After half an hour I couldn't speak. So I finished with him, rather quickly. After that I was so scared I didn't dare to go to a third voice teacher, so I was working with coaches, some conductors gave me tips, and I started to find my way.

"No teacher had been talking about *support* . . . how to support a voice, and how things work. I had to find out for myself. I always say the best voice teacher for me has been the stage. By experience you feel from one evening to the other how much you can give . . . how to sing in big rooms. I get very tired by singing in small rooms. I'm not particularly fond of small rooms."

"When did your experience on the stage begin?" I asked.

Birgit related how, at the age of twenty-eight, she was told there was a cancellation and she was to sing Agathe in *Der Freischütz,* but she didn't know the role and had to learn and perform it in three days. She got one small orchestra rehearsal—not with the conductor, but an assistant. Despite fabulous press, the conductor felt the one musical error she made in the entire evening branded her as unmusical. Because of his influence she did not get another role for a whole year.

Again, there was a cancellation, and Birgit had to learn the role of Lady Macbeth in just two weeks (if that's how farmer's daughters are capable of learning roles, opera needs more of them). The conductor this time was the famous Fritz Busch and the stage director was his son Hans. These two distinguished gentlemen were astute enough to recognize a great talent, and the next twenty-one days with ten performances constituted an extremely satisfying experience, in contrast to the one a year before.

"That was some feat, to learn such a role as Lady Macbeth and sing it in two weeks," I said admiringly.

"Well, I had willpower," she said. "Otherwise, I'm a little lazy . . . I don't like to learn new roles."

"Now, let's get down to vocal technique," I said. "What is your thinking on support?"

"I feel somehow I have my roots very low down, and sometimes I get a little bit sloppy or lazy, and I don't support quite right . . . at least now, at my age, the voice can be a little sharp on the bridge [passage] D, E, F. So one has to be even more conscious of support. The vocal cords you have to almost forget. They make the sound, but like the violinist you must have . . . the sounding board [she pointed to a spot on her forehead an inch or two above her eyes]. If one forgets the support it's like a flower without roots, after a while it begins to fade. It's the same with the voice. I hear so many young singers completely singing without the support. They are singing from the chest and up, and it doesn't sound well. It's like Sir Thomas Beecham, who said, 'Most sopranos sound like they've been living on seaweed.'

"I feel the higher the note goes, the lower the support. The support is as low as possible."

"No involvement with the chest, then?" I asked.

"No!"

"Some people feel that it is dangerous to take too much breath before singing," I said. "How do you feel about this?"

"I have not been thinking too much about it. The more you get distracted with details, the more difficult it is, and our singing shouldn't sound difficult or look difficult to the public. It should come easily and naturally. I haven't been thinking how much to breathe, how little. Of course, I know if I have a long phrase, I have to take a long breath."

"Now, how about the term *open throat?*" I asked. "Does it mean anything to you?"

"No. I don't think I want to think like that," she said as she pensively opened her mouth and dropped her larynx, as many singers do when they are describing an open throat.

"But also the root of the tongue . . . You can get a throaty sound. It's very individual. I don't like to think like that," she concluded.

"Then you leave the throat completely out of it?"

"I try, but after all those years by my first vocal teacher at the academy . . . what terribly hard work it was . . . I tried to relax my vocal cords, but I couldn't. They wanted to take part, because they were so used to *attack*. All of a sudden they were grabbing again, and it was so many, many years . . . It was so difficult.

"He opened my ears and my knowledge to make a beautiful sound. Earlier, maybe, I only made a strong sound, a big sound. He said I should sing like a violin and all of those things, but he didn't tell me how." She laughed. "And it took a long time to loosen it. I sang many years with a lot of pressure on my vocal cords. I remember the turning point in my vocal career. I went to Brussels to sing a Verdi *Requiem*. I had a terrible cold and it became worse after a few days' rehearsals. I was desperate. I was hoarse almost. I had a runny nose . . . throat ached and everything. So I locked myself in my room and I thought, 'Now you need to really know what you are doing. The vocal cords shouldn't work [or—work hard?]' I found a way to get the sound up in my head with the support, without applying pressure to the vocal cords. After one and a half, two hours, I found my technique. I had a very bad cold, but it all went beautifully." And Birgit claims it was through this experience she really learned how to sing.

"So, basically . . ." I prompted.

"I'm never thinking about the throat," was her firm reply.

"Let us explore *placement*," I said. "There are various opinions, ranging from 'no placement at all' to 'back, front, eighteen inches in front of the face . . .'"

"I think they all mean the same," she said. "It's just different feelings. I try to place my voice as far in the front as possible, without getting nasal . . . in the mask. There are different places which you can go *up* in the head . . . you can go *back* in the head. Of course, if one sings a high note, like a high C, the voice gets automatically a little bit back. That is quite natural, but you have to get this balance from a little bit behind, otherwise it doesn't work . . . at least for me. Still, to be able to project in big houses, you have to have your voice quite much in front.

"Another thing is what composer you're singing and how much you need from body sound. Say you sing Wagner, you need *much* more body sound, to feel much more open. To sing Strauss . . . a little between Verdi and Wagner, a bit in the middle. Verdi . . . a slender sound. Wagner needs the most of the body. That is a solid sound you cannot use for Verdi."

"Isn't the *tessitura* higher in Verdi?" I asked.

"Yes, Verdi, for sopranos, lies higher. Wagner has this deep middle voice which is not so often used for Verdi. For Lady Macbeth you really need three voices. You start first as a dramatic soprano. Then all of a sudden, you get a mezzo aria, and then you have to sing the Brindisi, which is full of coloratura. The last aria, which is the sleepwalking scene, ends with a high D flat pianissimo."

"As you sing higher," I said, changing the subject, "do you drop the jaw?"

"I look in the mirror and I take a high note, not a very high note, I see my jaw fall. I think there is a reason for that. There was a voice teacher who very much wanted to give me lessons. He said, 'When you sing a high note the Adam's apple goes up. It should go down with the high notes.' He started to push it with his thumb. My Adam's apple ached for fourteen days. That was the worst thing I ever have experienced. It goes automatically. It cannot go deeper for the high note."

"Sometimes, while demonstrating a tone," I said, "I notice your tongue is well forward. Do you think of putting it against the teeth?"

"No, but I don't want to have the tongue down in the throat. If I get it down in the throat it's a plug there."

"So you want it up against the teeth?"

"As relaxed as possible," she said.

"If you have no performance for, say, two weeks, how often would you vocalize in that period?" I asked.

"If I've been singing very much, and I don't have to sing for a couple of weeks, I at least rest one week or ten days. I think it's a very important thing not to sing too much, for the vocal cords need to have a rest in between, because they are under very strong pressure. Within ten days I begin humming a little bit."

"After ten days of rest, how long does it take you to get your voice back to normal, a day or two?"

"Yes, but if I have a vacation of two weeks, then it takes more time to get back, because you get tired, the muscles have been resting too long. I'm rather lazy when I have a vacation. I'm not thinking of my voice when I don't have to sing."

"On the day of a performance, how do you warm up the voice?"

"I start humming and I very often start with up to down [from high to low]."

"What time of day do you begin?"

"In the middle of the day, if I can, or sometimes only before the performance. It depends. If I'm staying in a hotel far away from the opera—I cannot sing in the hotel room, which is bad, of course, but there's nothing I can do. Ideally, it is good if I can warm up at twelve or one o'clock . . . to feel that everything's in place."

"Do you sing scales or phrases?"

"I do everything to get the voice placed in the mask. When I feel that the voice just bangs in the head, then I know that it is in place. I warm up before I go on stage."

"Any particular scales?"

"Not really. I sing some phrases from my part which I am singing which are very difficult. I sing *mnyee, mnyee,* and all . . . I have my tricks. I wouldn't tell you all my tricks. Otherwise everyone would take my secrets." She burst out laughing.

"Come on, what are your secrets?" I coaxed.

"Oh, I'm just kidding."

"I have some crazy, trick sounds I use to test or warm up the voice," I admitted.

"Me too," she said. "I was down in New Orleans warming up, and the police came and said, 'What's going on, here?' They said, 'We have a concert here,' to which the policeman responded, 'For me, that woman sounds like an elephant who somebody tramped on the foot.' They weren't very much impressed with my warming up. It doesn't sound very nice."

"I take it you don't believe in a great, strenuous amount of vocalizing?"

"I had one colleague," she said, "a Wagnerian singer, and she started singing at a quarter after seven A.M., and she went on like that until twelve o'clock. If I would have done that, I wouldn't have anything left for the evening. One has to be very calm and not let the nerves run around. Sometimes you can feel very poor, but you have to calm yourself down, because the nerves can really kill you. I cannot point out enough . . . I think singers are singing too much . . . vocalizing . . . not letting the voice rest before a performance. If you *think* more and sing less, you know, think how you want the voice to sound, then half the work is done," she concluded.

"Now, some people say they sing every day," I began.

"You can hear it, sometimes," she cut in ironically. "The day after a performance I usually keep my mouth shut."

Our conversation moved to her recent return to the Metropolitan in *Elektra*. She admitted that she had had qualms about it, not only because she would be competing with the Birgit Nilsson of the past, but because, she observed wisely, time makes memories grow sweeter.

I had been told that the opening performance had ended with a forty-five-minute ovation for her. She modestly corrected this to a mere half hour.

Pretty good punch line for a story about the farmer's daughter!

Magda Olivero

*Magda Olivero's career has been a remarkable one. The soprano
made her debut in 1933 in Turin as Lauretta in Puccini's* GIANNI
SCHICCHI. *Then, after achieving fame in her native Italy, she retired from the stage in 1941. Ten years later she was convinced by
the composer Francesco Cilèa to return to opera as the heroine in a
production of his opera* ADRIANA LECOUVREUR. *Her renown in
Europe grew, particularly as an interpreter of verismo operas, and
her long-delayed American debut occurred in Dallas in 1967 in the
title role of Cherubini's* MEDEA. *She made her Metropolitan Opera
debut as Tosca in 1975, when she was in her sixties (!), a performance considered by many to have been one of the best sung and
acted Toscas in recent Met history.* 𝄢

"SHE has no voice! She has no musicality! She has no personality!
She has *nothing!* Change profession."

This was the verdict of the combined staff of VIPs from Italy's
prestigious RAI concerning the young soprano from Saluzzo. Since
Magda Olivero had come to RAI with a glowing recommendation
from a most important magistrate, the staff agreed to hear her a
second time.

Again the same verdict! In this second audition there was one
slight difference: in an obscure corner of the room was Luigi
Gerrussi, who did not agree with the fatal verdict. He stopped one
of the auditors and asked, "What did you think of this girl?"

"It's not even worth discussing," was the sour response. "She's a
complete *nothing.*"

"You're wrong," he protested. "This girl has everything: great
musicality, a personality, and also a voice, and her teachers had the
ability to destroy it all. I'd like to try . . ."*

* This interview was conducted in Italian, and the English translation is mine.

"Gigino, if you want to waste your time . . . waste it!" was their sarcastic reply. Luigi Gerrussi shrugged it off and offered to teach Magda. Her response was, "I've already changed teachers three times . . . Number four? I'll think about it."

First of all, Magda had to convince a skeptical father, a judge in Torino, who already felt his daughter had wasted enough time with her three previous teachers and should go to the conservatory and pursue studies on the piano. Father finally conceded and gave her one more chance, since her background all of her life had been singing.

"I remember at the age of two years I stood in front of this window, gripping the grillwork with my little hands, as a lady sat down at the piano . . . and the first song I learned was 'Torna a Sorrento' . . ."

"You mean you sang publicly for the first time at the age of two?" I asked incredulously.

"Two years." I shook my head in disbelief, but she was persistent. "However, my official debut in public was at eight years. There was a priest in our parish who knew that I sang, and he signed me up," she laughed. "It meant a great deal of work for my mother, a wonderful woman who knew how to do everything well. She made the most beautiful costumes for me, and the performances, which were held in a theater in the church, were always sold out. I had a strong voice. If anyone had heard but not seen me when I was a child of nine, they would have said it was the voice of an adult."

"What sort of things did you sing?" I asked.

"Oh, all of the songs."

"And operatic arias?"

"Yes. Then, unfortunately, I have to say that at thirteen years of age I began to study seriously. The first teacher was a singer who knew nothing and left me unchanged, in the primitive state. The second was the sister of an important Torinese critic.

"The passage in the voice is the most important part and she would not admit it even existed. Instead she made me strike, '*pum, pum, pum,*' always with a glottal attack. After a little while I was in bad shape.

"Then I changed teachers again and studied with an important mezzo-soprano from La Scala. She had me sing some scales and then put me to singing arias *and* arias, but how can a person sing them when she knows nothing about singing?"

"And," I observed, "these were your three teachers before you auditioned for RAI. Then you began studying with Luigi Gerrussi."

"In that moment my eyes were opened!" she exclaimed. "I understood what technique was! No one had ever spoken to me about the diaphragm . . . sustaining the sound . . . nothing! This maestro . . . he had such energy. With his fists clenched under my face he would cry, 'Sustain, sustain!'

"One day I said to him, 'Maestro, I can't do it. It fatigues me so . . . all these muscles I've never used before . . .' He said to me, 'This is the last time you are going to say *I can't*. Those words must not exist! If necessary, I'll see you dead to get what I want! Die, afterward, if you wish, but first *you must do what I want!*'

"I passed those hours in the studio in terror, but slowly, slowly, after six months of studying every day, I changed completely . . . an absolute metamorphosis. Another voice came out. Then we began to study arias and scores. He made me use my imagination, which I already had by nature, and I have always used it.

"He said to me, for example, 'To have this sound well placed, think of some object there, in the distance . . . far, far off. Your sound must arrive there.'

"One day, I happened to be listening to a record of Ponselle singing the first act of *Gioconda* . . . in that phrase 'Enzo adorato' . . . that high C, taken piano . . . reinforced, diminished, I was so enthusiastic I ran to my lesson and said, 'Maestro, I heard Ponselle today in that phrase "Enzo adorato." I want to be able to do that.'

"He laughed at me and said, 'That will be the *last* thing that you will learn to do. To do something so difficult you must have such a mastery of the breath that you can play with it.'

"But Ponselle had given me this immense desire to be able to do it, and I succeeded. It was always my dream to do pianissimi. And I achieved them by studying."

"Then you did not have pianissimi by nature?" I asked.

"No! I didn't have them at all. I do it all with breath, breath,

breath. When you do pianissimi you must support twice as much as when you sing forte."

"And you continued your studies with Gerrussi?"

"My career began very quickly and I continued to study with him another eight years. I started with *Rigoletto,* then I did *Traviata,* an opera that came to me naturally; I had no difficulty with the first act . . . or any act. I studied *Don Pasquale, L'Elisir d'Amore, Lucia,* and finally arrived at Philine in *Mignon.* I sang easily to the high F. My maestro said, 'Remember that the composer must be respected. To sing Verdi, operas like *La Forza del Destino, Trovatore* . . . you must have a voice of profound color and power. You do *not* have the color of voice and power to do these operas. Therefore, do not profane Verdi.' Even after my voice grew stronger, I still had this complex that I shouldn't do these other Verdi operas. But today I no longer have this reverential fear. I sing everything. I feel that when one has reached a certain age and position in a career . . . and knows how to sing . . . she can permit herself this luxury. One can say, 'All right, if I ruin myself, and my career is finished . . . goodbye.' But the young people beginning their careers—*Aïda, Trovatore*—it is not good. When they are just beginning they must 'let their bones form themselves.'"

"I have seen opera management push a young singer to do roles too heavy for him," I said, "and then when he collapses under the load he is dropped from the roster instantly."

"They don't realize their misdeed," she agreed. "They say, 'He is of no more use to us' . . . a kick . . . and he is out. No, no, no. When I began I had no illusions about the theater. Humanity and gratitude do not exist. I have no illusions. I have always said, 'All beautiful things that happen in the theater are the exceptions.'"

"Let us get down to your vocal technique. With Gerrussi. You began working on scales?"

"The five notes," she said, "do, re, mi, fa, sol, done slowly, and returning slowly. Then, other exercises with the sound held long . . . mi, do, mi, sol, mi, do, beginning with the *ee* vowel, then to *meh,* which helps carry the sound into the mask. When you arrive on the sol [G] with the *ee* vowel, you pass to the *oh* vowel in such a way that you relax all the muscles of the throat, and keep the sound forward . . . in the position of the *ee*.

"When I began with him I was accomplishing agility by use of the glottis. Instead, I had to forget all that and do it with the breath. Then I would do do, re, mi, fa, sol, fa, mi, re, do, re, mi, fa, sol, la, si, do, re, do, si, la, sol, fa, mi, re, do, very fast." She demonstrated, singing this five- and nine-note scale.

"But he said, 'Remember, the five-note scale is the best medicine for the voice.' And I do it to this day."

"On a day that you are not performing, how long do you vocalize?"

"A half hour," she said. "But tranquilly, slowly, slowly."

"Beginning lightly?"

"Yes, yes! Always."

"And on the day of a performance?"

"A little in the morning, around noon, a half an hour of exercises, and then, according to the opera—if it's one of the lighter ones I practice the agility to lighten the voice. If, instead, it is something like *Tosca*, at the very end I still practice my agility a bit so the voice won't get too heavy. First I make the sustained sounds . . . slowly, with the breath. Then another exercise that is very good:

sung with *ah, ee, eh, oh,* and *oo,* but all done in one breath."

I understood that she meant to do the entire scale, up and down, five times, each time on a different vowel.

"At one time in my life," she continued, "I was able to repeat the whole thing twice with only one breath."

I was impressed. It is interesting that many singers feel that being able to sustain very long phrases in one breath is very good for the technique. I personally have observed many singers who, when they are in vocal trouble in a performance, take twice as many breaths as one would expect.

"Then," she continued, "an important point is the breathing dur-

Magda Olivero

ing the exercises . . . it must be slow and always deep in the diaphragm. People speak of modern technique. No! The technique was the same in the ninth century as it is now! Everyone must come to know themselves . . . their own organism.

"I sometimes have the impression of seeing my breath with inner eyes. When I breathe, I am aware of my diaphragm. If I breathe and am aware that my diaphragm has not moved, it is a sign that there is something in my organism that is not functioning. But when I feel right, the mouth relaxed, the throat relaxed above all . . . breathing lovingly, gently through the nose . . . I feel this breath going down . . . Beautiful! The thorax enlarges, and then, at a certain point at the end of the inhalation, I feel my diaphragm do . . . *tac!* It raises and blocks [resists?]. Naturally, you take the breath according to the phrase. It would be ridiculous to pump the lungs full of air for a short phrase. Instead, reserve the long breath for the long phrase, or for high notes.

"Suppose you are going to attack a high A, B, or C. You breathe and the note is already made in the imagination. The breath arrives . . . *pam* . . . the same moment in which the sound comes out. It is not necessary to do anything other than produce the breath. The sound is already made. To attack the sound on the breath is the most difficult part of all.

"Many times I would find myself getting dizzy because I would attack . . . No, it's not right! Attack again . . . No, it's not right. I was attacking with a blow [a stroke] instead of *on the breath.*" She then demonstrated by floating a beautiful sound. "That is the sound you can crescendo and diminuendo. On the breath . . . that is what is difficult."

"Returning to the diaphragm," I said, "there are those who advocate pushing down, like giving birth to a baby, or . . ."

"No! That is excluded for me. I have this sense of height [*alto* in Italian]." She then demonstrated with a one-octave descending scale. "Think as if you were ascending the scale, not descending . . . to maintain the diaphragm, the breath *up.* Everything beautifully *up.* Think of going down without changing the sound. Many people say that the stomach area expands. No! Not the stomach, not the abdomen. The rib cage enlarges like a bellows, and then . . . *pam* . . . the diaphragm goes up, and *vooo* . . . the column of air is already in the mask. In front [she indicated the stomach area] the diaphragm goes *up*, and the stomach and the abdomen go in."

I summed up, "It's the ribs that expand as you breathe . . ."

"And my back almost as if it were arching," she added. "When I go up to a high C, I feel inside as if I were completely empty. There is only this column of air that vibrates. I almost have the impression that it shakes me internally.

"The throat does not exist. The throat must always be like gum rubber [*gomma*], completely relaxed. You can make any movement without interrupting the sound . . . sing with the head laid completely back . . . in *any* position . . . because it is independent. The breath works by itself. The muscles of the throat don't exist.

"Now, this is important. We have a throat full of muscles. The vocal cords are embedded in some of these muscles. If, in singing, you tense these muscles, the cords will vibrate for a while, but in the midst of all this rigidity they will tire. They will get swollen and pink. When, instead, the vocal cords vibrate in a relaxed, soft mass [of tissue] they never tire, they never get pink. When we sing there must be an abandoned feeling . . . only in the throat. The strong muscles are those below the shoulders." She indicated about a hand's breadth beneath her shoulders, on the sides of her chest wall.

"Do you use chest voice?" I asked.

"My maestro said, 'On some occasions you might have to, but support it as much as possible. Use it once in a while, but don't abuse it. At the end of your career you may permit more of such luxuries.'

"Sometimes now I permit myself this luxury, but in the moment I do it I have a sense of remorse, because my teacher's words remain with me . . . 'Don't do it' . . . and I feel I am betraying something."

"You spoke a while ago about your second teacher, who ignored the *passaggio* in the voice," I said.

"Three notes, D, D sharp, and E, those are the notes of the *passaggio*. When I studied with her she made me push . . . *pum, pum,*

pum . . . those sounds no longer existed . . . it was an empty sound without color. I had to find them again . . . with the breath. The arc of the breath helps you to pass over [the *passaggio*]. You should not feel the *passaggio*."

"What is a good exercise to use for this?" I asked.

She demonstrated with a slow

"You pass slowly from the *ee* to the *oh*, keeping the breath the same and the *oh* in the same position as the *ee*, without doing eeyyoh. You do it slowly and all the muscles relax as you feel the tongue sliding from one position to the other. This exercise is tremendous."

"And the throat, on this transition to *oh*, must be . . ."

"Abandoned," she replied. "The head should be a little bit back. When the head is forward [or down] it is a bad sign."

"Now that we're speaking about the throat," I interjected, "what does *open throat* mean to you?"

"What I have explained up to now *is* open throat."

"You don't think of things such as a lowered larynx, or . . ."

"No! If you teach a young student to push down the larynx . . . goodbye! That he should do automatically. If he does it with force, he will have troubles. When things happen naturally, when the breath is right, the problems are resolved. Singing should be a *massage* . . . not a violence . . . not a trauma. The breath massages the vocal cords."

"When you sing, do you use the lips?"

"For pronunciation, yes. *Ah, eh, ee, oh, oo.* But this *oo*, it is necessary to press the lips, but not to press on the throat. To do this is a great secret I learned from Tito Schipa. At the beginning of my career he told me, 'The vowels are little and they fall from on high over the lips, and the breath makes the vowels run into the theater.

Magda Olivero

The vowel does not form itself inside the mouth or the throat. The vowel drops from above. The words drop from above onto the lips.' This is a great secret.

"So, when your technique is right, even if you're not well, you'll still be able to do it. In fact, Cottogni, the great baritone, said, 'A singer cannot permit himself the luxury of saying he doesn't feel right this evening and won't sing.' He said, 'No, the singer is at the service of the public.' So one must study and obtain such a technique that he can sing even with bad bronchitis. The only time when he must not sing is when he has laryngitis. He must stop immediately. But with good technique he will sing even with handicaps.

"Also, above all, one must have such a technique that the voice can be put at the service of the character being portrayed. Then the character can come alive without having to say, 'Oh, heavens, here comes a high C' . . . or this note, or that passage.

"No! Go on stage and think of performing, not singing!"

"Signora," I asked, "do you feel you need an extra ear, outside of yourself, for control of your own voice?"

"I have found this independence, to be able to listen to myself. I have a second pair of eyes, as I said before, to see myself inside. I am like two persons: one lives in the character, and the other vigilantly watches, saying, 'Why did you do this? Why did you do that?' It's all brain, like an electronic machine that perceives all . . . absorbs all. Fortunately, I have this. All orders come from the brain . . . also, for the sound, coordinated with the breath. At the attack the brain perceives the note already, has given its orders. But there must be *no* fracturing of this process. To breathe, then, after a moment of emptiness, to attack the sound—that would already be some form of rigidity with its immediate consequences. That kind of suspension [before the attack] can be dangerous."

I sat there in a Detroit hotel room, looking at this enthusiastic, distinguished diva, my memories of past performances flooding in: television appearances I had caught in Italy; performances she had stolen from me and the rest of the cast in *Mefistofele*, both in Italy and the United States; memories of her lying flat on her back on

Magda Olivero

the stage singing floating high B's, a voice and personality that took one's breath away . . .

That's the girl who had "no voice . . . no musicality . . . no personality . . ." Perhaps the VIPs from RAI should have changed *their* profession, instead.

Luciano Pavarotti

Luciano Pavarotti has become one of the most popular and well-known of all operatic artists to the general public, both as a superb singer with a superb tenor voice and as a warm, friendly man with an infectious, charming personality. He was born in Modena, Italy, and made his debut as Rodolfo in LA BOHÈME. *Early in his career he was engaged by Joan Sutherland and Richard Bonynge to appear with them on an Australian tour, and has since continued with these colleagues in a series of outstanding operatic recordings, as well as in live performances in many opera houses. Mr. Pavarotti made his Metropolitan Opera debut in 1968 as Rodolfo, a role he also performed in the Met's first live telecast in the "Live from the Met" series. He has appeared yearly in this TV series since then.* 🎵

I PUSHED my way through the stage door of the Met and walked briskly to the desk to see if there were any messages or rehearsal slips for me. As I turned to go to my dressing room, I saw a burly figure standing before me and recognized the distraught face of our new tenor, Luciano Pavarotti. He had canceled his Met debut in the previous performance of *Bohème* because of a serious windpipe infection.

Luciano's face lit up with his usual quick, easy smile when he saw me.

"*Ciao*, Hines, how are you?"

"More important," I responded, "how are *you*? I hope you are fully recovered from your cold."

"I am still very sick." A harried look came over his face. "I shouldn't sing, but I must! I have already canceled once, and if I cancel a second time they will never give me another chance." He shrugged fatalistically.

Luciano Pavarotti

He had my sympathy. I was in a similar situation when I debuted in *Boris Godunov* in Moscow in 1962. My throat was so bad I could hardly speak. In an operatic career there are the crucial moments which one must face with a judicious combination of wisdom and guts: wisdom to make the right decision, and the guts to see it through.

After wishing Luciano well I hurried to my dressing room and attempted, through the wiles of makeup, to transform myself into a twenty-year-old college student. A little while later we four Bohemians assembled on the stage.

The entire cast had been won over by Luciano's warm, humble personality, and we were all pulling for him from the start. Indisposed or not, he sounded great to my ears. When the moment of truth arrived with "Che gelida manina," the Marcello, Schaunard, and I all listened intently from the wings. He sang the aria very well, taking the perilous high note quite securely, and there followed an enthusiastic reception by the audience. At the end of the act, despite our congratulations and assurances, he was justifiably tense; there were still three acts to go. Now my chance to cheer up Luciano had arrived.

A critic for the *Tribune* had once written: "Jerome Hines' scene stealing in the second act of *La Bohème* would be grand larceny in any court of law, and this reviewer will gladly volunteer as attorney for the defense." My scene stealing in Act II consists of consuming one and a half chickens, five salami sandwiches, and Mimi's ice cream between my singing cues. In attempting to lighten the evening I stuffed myself into a week's indigestion, but it was worth it. Even Luciano, known for his prodigious appetite, seemed impressed and my antics seemed to cheer him up.

Our tenor's voice held up very well to the end of the opera and he was very simpatico on the stage, but he was not happy about his performance. When the final curtain fell and it was time for Luciano's solo bow, he took a deep breath, mustering his courage to face that ultimate critic—the public. As he stepped in front of the curtain, he was greeted with a roar from the audience, and deservedly so.

At first he did not bow, but stood there looking dazedly at the people while slowly the overwhelming accumulation of nerves and tension manifested itself in the tears which began running down his cheeks. He remained immobile amid the storm of applause for at least half a minute—just crying. Then, after one quick, humble bow, he hurried into the wings to find us all waiting with tears in our eyes too.

Surely, every great career is fraught with such challenges and, I suppose, this is what separates the men from the boys.

And now, in the winter of 1979, I was about to interview Luciano, who was fast becoming such a popular figure in opera. He had insisted that, before the interview, I must attend the first of two master classes that he was giving at Juilliard.

I found myself in the front row of a jam-packed auditorium reverberating to the clamor of Luciano's wildly enthusiastic fans, many of whom were vocal students, all convinced that they were going to learn to sing like their hero in two short hours. If the theater was jam-packed, the stage seemed even more so, what with bright lights, TV cameras, crew, and managerial VIPs abuzz with such confused activity that one wondered how our famous tenor would even be able to find the audience when he arrived.

Finally Luciano was introduced and, after confiding to the audience that he was scared to death, promptly sat at a large table. There followed a parade of young, talented opera aspirants, each of whom sang two arias as Luciano conducted with a pencil as a baton. After some excellent singing, punctuated by Luciano's constructive comments, there came the question-and-answer session.

"Mr. Pavarotti, how do you get your high notes?" The questioner got what he deserved. Luciano promptly sang an ascending scale ending on a beautiful high A flat.

"There," he said emphatically, closing the subject. The student sat back with a glazed look in his eyes. That scale was a voice lesson in itself, not only for the excellence of the high note, but also for the flawless transition in the *passaggio*, around the F and G, which was technically so well executed that it was imperceptible. Here was the accumulated skill of years of study, not explainable in a few short sentences.

Luciano Pavarotti

"Mr. Pavarotti, if a mezzo-soprano has a problem in the passage from the chest to the head voice, how does she overcome it?"

"I just showed you."

And this was true in a sense. The passage from a woman's chest voice to the head voice is identical to the passage that is such a challenge to the male singer when he goes from the upper middle range to the high voice. The only difference is that this *passaggio* lies low in the female voice and high in the male voice, but the problem of the transition is the same, and Luciano's demonstration was valid for both cases.

These students, unable to imitate Luciano's sounds, were seeking a verbalization of the sensations he felt in his throat. From there on their questions began to penetrate more deeply, and Luciano responded clearly and intelligently, but there simply was neither time nor coherence of questioning to produce proper material for my book. A week later I had the opportunity to ask my own questions.

As I entered Luciano's apartment on Central Park South, a visitor was being outfitted in the tenor's own scarf and hat.

"You must be warm when you go. It is very cold out there," Luciano said as he wrapped up his departing guest like a mummy. I wondered what he thought of me coming in from the freezing elements garbed in a sport jacket and open collar.

As Luciano ushered his friend to the elevator, I wandered about the living room taking in dozens of paintings strewn about on tables, chairs, and every location possible. There was as much paint splattered on the carpet as there was on the canvases.

"You paint these?" I asked as he returned.

"Yes. You like?"

I'd better like . . . he outweighs my modest 225 pounds by a considerable amount. But seriously, I was impressed. It reminded me of my dear, late friend Salvatore Baccaloni, who was also quite skilled in painting.

"I like. But what are you going to do with that carpet," I asked, "cut it up and sell it for modern art?" After a little more small talk we got down to business.

Luciano told me that he began his formal vocal studies in Modena at the age of nineteen, working with the tenor Arrigo Pola. Before that he had sung several years in church, starting at the age of eight.

"How long did you study with Pola?" I asked.

"Two and a half years, and I remember the six first months . . . they were pure vocalizing . . . nothing else . . . to learn to open my jaw. Still now I do not have an enormous mouth. And Pola taught me very well the *passaggio*, very clearly."

"Let us come back to that," I said. "Did you study more after your two years with him?"

"Pola left to sing in Manila and then I went to Campogalliani in Mantua and studied another four years."

"Again doing scales as well as—"

"More than scales," he broke in. "I began to do antique arias, as well as 'Che gelida manina.'"

"But you still included scales in your study?"

"Oh yes, yes. But always, always, always . . ."

"Did you use any particular books of scales?"

"Sì, sì . . . four or five of them.* I would do two slow scales and two fast scales . . . always. And I used to do one of the most difficult scales for any singer . . ." He demonstrated.

"Do you still do scales?"

"Of course, every day!"

* I don't know if he is referring to four or five books, or scales. It could be that he misunderstood my question.

"Do you have a certain discipline or routine you employ?"
"I do:

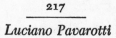

and then I do":

"These scales that you now use," I said, "you do them throughout the entire range of your voice?"

"Oh yes, yes."

"If you were singing a performance tonight, would you vocalize during the day?"

"Oh yes. I sleep until eleven or twelve the day of the performance. I trust very much in rest for the voice. The moment I get up I vocalize about two minutes, and then, I don't care how it goes, I stop. Then I eat. I vocalize two hours after breakfast . . . a quarter of an hour. Then five minutes of scales a half an hour before I go to the theater. Then, in the theater, another five minutes and I sing through the first romanza of my performance, full voice."

"Luciano," I said, "it has been forty-one years since my first voice lesson, and I find as I get older I must keep a stricter discipline . . ."

"Oh *sì, sì, sì, sì!* There is no doubt that when you are twenty the voice is there; when you are thirty . . . mmm; when you are forty . . . always more and more . . . If you play tennis you get going on the court immediately at twenty years of age. But now when *I* go on the court . . . the first five minutes I am ve . . . erry quiet."

"Now that you mention tennis," I broke in, "do you feel that exercise and sports are good for the voice?"

"I play tennis just the day before a performance. In my case," he went on, "there are only two things I have to be careful of . . . never to let my feet get cold—strange, isn't it?—and not to go out in the cold when I am perspiring. When I come off the tennis court I must cover up, come right home and take a hot bath. Then I go to bed until I feel normal."

"Otherwise you feel your voice would be affected?"

"I think so. Of course, we're all different," he said, taking in my light clothing. "A strong change in temperature is bad . . . a change to either hot or cold."

"Now, let's get down to vocal technique," I said. "What part does imitation play in the learning process?"

"From a recording, or by singing for someone," Luciano said, "you can demonstrate the critical sound . . . the crucial part of the voice . . . which is the *passaggio*. By hearing you become aware of the change of sound—let's call it covering. If you don't do this [cover], the voice becomes white, white, and whiter . . . and more tired . . . and you don't reach the end of the performance. If you cover the sound, the position and the voice are solid."

"Now this *passaggio*," I cut in, "is the transition from the upper middle voice to the high voice, and I know that students are interested in your approach since you have such a flawless *passaggio;* it is so smooth a change one is not aware of it."

"It took me six years of study," he said, "and one must be convinced of its importance from the first day . . . never change ideas. You know, the first five or six months it is very depressing because it does not come out right, and you become cyanotic, red in the face. Then some students begin to think this approach is wrong, and they try the other way, but it will never bring them security of voice."

"Let us try to translate this word *cover*," I said, "as it is used in the *passaggio*, into sensations in the throat. What is the difference in feeling in the throat when you make the change from middle voice to high voice?"

"I think there is a kind of tightening . . ."

"A little more muscular strength in the larynx?" I prompted.

"Yes, nnnn . . . not really the muscles. The opposite. I think the muscles must be very relaxed, like you're yawning. But you must really make the voice more *squeezed*. At the beginning of study the sound seems almost sacrificed. This changes the color." He then demonstrated, using a scale going up into the passage, exaggerating a squeezed sound, even to the point of breaking the top note as a novice might do.

"In the beginning," he continued, "you always crush these notes . . . always. And when they begin to come out correctly, they are very secure, even if not yet very beautiful. More and more they take on body and become really . . ." He broke off to demonstrate with another ascending scale, distinctly going from an *ah* vowel toward *oo* as he went through the passage.

"Do you make more space in the throat as you go up to the high notes?" I asked.

"Nnno . . . I think I give less space when I go through the *passaggio,* and then more space after I've left it. The normal space I give before and after it."

"Then it's only the *passaggio* that is squeezed?"

"Yes! More squeezed inside me. It doesn't mean the sound comes out like that. The sound should be even, but inside there is a kind of . . . almost a suffocation of the sound. Also, you use very much the resonance in the *passaggio*—more than usual."

"Then you're saying that when you enter the *passaggio,* you put the sound a little more in the mask . . . ?"

"A little. But remember, not enlarging, but squeezing."

"When you go up into the *passaggio,*" I asked, "do you think deeper?"

"No," he said positively. "I think that the position is the same. For me the position never changes . . . it is high, even when I sing a low note."

"A while ago you mentioned a relaxed sensation, like yawning, when you sing. Now, some singers speak of the beginning of a yawn . . ."

"*Sì!*"

"In other words," I continued, "they are saying the larynx should be down a bit . . ."

"I think *so!* No doubt about it."

"And this is what you consider an open throat?"

"Oh yes, no doubt . . . *awe* . . . *awe* . . ." He demonstrated on this vowel.

"So that the back of the tongue is a little bit down," I continued. "The larynx is down . . ."

"Give a look," he said. "I don't know . . . but give a look . . ." He assumed the yawning position of the throat and sang an *awe* vowel, gesturing for me to look into his mouth.

"Yes, yes," I said, as I distinctly saw the back of his tongue depressing and his Adam's apple lowering.

"*Awe* . . . *awe* . . ." he said, "not *ah!*"

This, of course, was the pure Italian *awe,* which is a deeper sound than *ah.*

"For me, the voice begins in the brain," Luciano went on, "like every thought . . . goes to the diaphragm and must be formed here in the throat . . . not in the nose . . . not in the other cavities. It must be *awe* . . . *awe* . . . *awe.*" He demonstrated with a mezzoforte tone, using a sharp, almost glottal attack.

"It starts in the cords," he said. "You must make the cords vibrate immediately. For example, most students reach the note late, after they have made two or three other notes."

I didn't understand this point until Luciano sang a phrase imitating a poor student.

"In other words," I said, "an unprepared attack. The student slides into all the proper functions during the first part of the phrase, rather than starting the first note right on.

"What sensation do you have when you take a breath before singing?" I asked.

"The sensation is very simple. I don't know how you are going to describe this," he said in a discreet tone of voice, "but you take a breath and stay in the position as when you are in the bathroom . . . and you keep this position until the phrase is finished. You'll have to explain this, perhaps . . . with other words . . . You must push, like a woman in labor, giving birth . . . it is the same thing. When you push like that, the diaphragm comes up."

"In other words," I added, "you're basically working to keep the feeling down?"

"Because," he broke in, "*up* will come by itself. As the breath goes out, it comes up by itself, slowly, slowly, as you sing . . . as you speak. The great secret is to have the patience to let the diaphragm go down again before beginning the next phrase."

"You mean," I said, "the bad tendency is to let the diaphragm stay up between phrases?"

"The balloon is not full again," he said.

"I've heard other singers speak of the sensation of a balloon in the stomach . . ."

"Yes! I think it is like that! It is a balloon with air . . . going up and down . . . up and down. Sometimes, according to the phrasing, you make a little balloon, or a bigger balloon."

"Now," I said, "let's talk about head voice, chest voice, and placement."

"For me," he said quickly, "I don't know, because I don't think I prepare my voice in the nose and the mouth. It comes from the throat. And I don't think I make chest notes. I don't think I am this kind of singer. And I generally don't think men do . . . it is more the ladies . . . they do . . . [he proceeded to make a yodeling sound] I am not aware that men do this."

"In your master class, you stated you do not believe in using the falsetto . . . You're against using it?"

"Totally."

"When you mark, or *accenni*,* it is very beautiful. Do you always mark when learning new scores?"

"I always mark . . . but I do it on the diaphragm. With the falsetto, the diaphragm is not working. I believe that if I let my diaphragm be lazy for five or six days, it will not be ready when it's time."

"When you Italians speak about the diaphragm, you employ the word *appoggiare*, which is used when one speaks of leaning on something. In English we use the word *support*. Some people insist that support, meaning *hold up*, is a bad choice of words."

He answered, "It is right and wrong at the same time. *Appoggiare* means . . . lay that thing down . . . lean something against the wall . . . put this on the table . . . But in the sense of singing,

---

* *Accennando* is using a tiny, light sound, just above a whisper.

it is *push down the voice* . . . in a way that it doesn't move anymore. You understand? Not *aaah* [he made a flaccid, open sound] but *huumph* . . . *humph* [with each of these sounds he compressed his diaphragm and pitted his breath against closed vocal cords . . . compressed air against closed cords, with hardly any audible sound]. That's *appoggia*," he said emphatically.

"Then support has a different meaning from *appoggiare?*"

"But it's still the same because, if you put something down, it will go up by itself. The result would be the same."

I was confused by this until a picture came into my mind of trying to keep a rubber beach ball pushed under water. My push was the *appoggia* and the beach ball's buoyancy was the support. One exists because of the other.

I switched to another subject.

"Luciano, when you go from *forte* to *piano*, is there any change in your vocal production?"

"No, it is the same, with less breath . . . less pushing . . . unless it is a *piano* phrase ending on the notes of the *passaggio* . . . then [you must] use a little of the suffoc . . ."

"In the *passaggio* you must squeeze a little bit," I added, as he hesitated.

"A little."

"And years ago, when I had great trouble with my high notes, I found I couldn't hum those notes. I kept trying and when I began to succeed, I felt as though I was strangling, until the muscles grew strong."

"Exactly," Luciano agreed, "because the muscles, they bite. We say in Italian, *mordere la voce* . . . bite the voice. When you do a high note the muscles must bite . . . *aiing* . . . *aiing*."

"Back to mezza-voce for a moment," I said. "Was it always easy for you?"

"To sing 'Parigi, O cara' on the stage, it took me one year. The first year I always sang it *forte*. Singing *piano* it is very easy for this piece to be flat. Then I said to myself, 'I cannot sing *piano*, why?' One night I said to myself, 'Let me pretend to have lost my voice.' It was there just like that . . . incredible, natural pianissimo . . . same position . . . same diaphragm."

"You felt as if you were *accennando* . . ."

"Yes!"

"A final question," I said. "Do you think it is important always to have somebody around who knows your voice . . . to act as a second ear?"

"To judge us? I think, to be honest with you, the best judge of me is myself. I know very well what I am doing. Exactly! Because I am very honest. You must be very honest . . . almost cruel. I learned this after many years of career. They come to me and say, 'Tonight you were fantastic.' I say, 'How was that note?' 'Oh, well . . . last performance was better.' You see? It was terrific, but . . . the other performance was better . . . I understand . . ."

As I left Pavarotti's apartment, I understood very well. How many performances I have done in my life where they said, "You were terrific" but I knew . . . I felt the difference. Earlier I said that the ultimate critic was the audience. Let me amend that. Luciano has reminded me that the ultimate critic should be *the artist*. And the way his career is skyrocketing today makes one believe he has no critics out there at all, only fans.

Jan Peerce

Jan Peerce, in his seventies, is still an active singer at the time this book is being published. He was born in New York City, and early in his career he played violin in a dance band and sang as soloist at the Radio City Music Hall. He made his operatic debut in Philadelphia in 1938, as the Duke in RIGOLETTO. Alfredo in LA TRAVIATA was his debut role at the Metropolitan Opera, on November 29, 1941. His tenor voice was heard at the Met for over twenty years in a variety of roles including Rodolfo in LA BOHÈME and Don Ottavio in DON GIOVANNI. ❦

JEROME HINES CALENDAR 1979–80 SEASON:

November 10, 1979: Interview Jan Peerce. Call day before. Canceled. Peerce has unexpected engagement. Call Peerce November 13.

November 13, 1979: Peerce won't be available until December 1–9. I will be in Memphis. Will call again in mid-December.

December 15, 1979: Peerce on tour. Call back early January.

January 14, 1980: Peerce leaving for California. Call back . . .

So it had gone for the previous nine months and so it went on until the end of June 1980. I have never seen a busier singer . . . and Jan has passed his seventy-sixth birthday. Many great artists have sung professionally until their late sixties, but this was one for the books—especially *my* book. Jan and I finally agreed that the only way to make it work would be to do the interview *on the telephone* on June 26.

As the day approached, I had the opportunity to reflect on the years I had known Jan. First of all, I made my debut in opera with him in the fall of 1941 in *Rigoletto* with the San Francisco Opera. I was singing Monterone, Lawrence Tibbett in the title role was attempting his first unsuccessful comeback after losing his voice, and

Lily Pons was Gilda. Jan had a great success with the Duke, which resulted in a contract with the Metropolitan Opera.

Over the next few years I often heard him on the Met broadcasts. In fact, he performed there so often during the war years that people were calling it the Jan Peerce Opera House. After my own debut at the Met in 1946 we sang together many times.

In July of 1952 he was rehearsing *La Bohème* in Cincinnati with the beautiful redheaded soprano Lucia Evangelista. Came the morning of the dress rehearsal and all went well until the cue for Mimi's entrance. She didn't appear. The conductor, Fausto Cleva, threw down his baton and shouted angrily, "Where is Evangelista?"

"She got married," came an anonymous voice from backstage. Cleva was not a man to joke with during an orchestra rehearsal, and it took several minutes of heated exchange to convince him that Evangelista had indeed eloped with Jerome Hines at 1:30 that A.M. She showed up in time for the second act, and got a tongue-in-cheek chiding from Jan (who is one of the funniest men alive) for marrying a bum like Hines, especially without first getting his permission. Finally, I said, "Jan, take away my extraordinary size and physique, take away my handsome face and my glorious voice, and what have you got?"

"Yeah, what have you got?" he said cockily.

"Jan Peerce," I replied. From that day on I never won another battle of wits with Jan, but it was fun trying.

The last time I sang with our indestructible tenor was at the Met in *La Forza del Destino*. He was about sixty years young and finished each performance fresher than when he began. Since then he has been seen constantly in *Fiddler on the Roof*, television, synagogues on the high holidays, and in countless concerts. He is indeed an extraordinary man, enjoying an extraordinary career. And during December 1980 he performed in Carnegie Hall to celebrate his fiftieth year singing tenor (he sang alto as a child in the synagogues). So it was with much nostalgia that I picked up the phone and dialed his number. His high-tenor speaking voice was as fresh as ever, and his spirits soaring as usual.

"Jan," I said, "to what do you attribute your enormously long and successful career?"

"Being religious, I am very thankful for the little endowment that I have, but," he warned, "we must have respect for our limitations. God doesn't expect us to do everything. What you do, do it with love and respect; love your fellow man, love your audience. Take care of what you have to the point of not overdoing, not going beyond your natural capacity, like singing wrong things. One should be able to sing hours and hours without fatigue. Cantorial work is a marathon and you shouldn't get tired. You become fatigued when singing because you're singing wrong . . . the wrong things."

"Whom did you study with during your career, Jan?"

"At seventeen I studied with Martinelli's teacher, Roxas. Then Samuel Rothafel discovered me . . . you know Sam Rothafel, who created the Roxy Theater.* He heard me fiddling and singing and offered me a scholarship with Eleanor McClellan, and I studied with her for three and a half years. Then it was Alfred Martino for two and a half or three years, followed by Giuseppe Boghetti, the teacher of Marian Anderson, Helen Traubel, and Blanche Thebom. I studied with him for four years. Then I became my own teacher. At some point you must become master of your own destiny. Does Mischa Elman study? Does Heifetz study? Oh, sometimes one needs a professional ear to listen. Once I got in trouble. My mother died; I was very close to her. I suffered and my voice suffered. My wife, Alice, pointed it out to me. She said, 'Your voice is not projecting. Study!'

"I worked with Alex Lorber and in 1945 with Robert Weede. But basically, I spent hours and hours at the piano by myself, and we have God above directing us. He's a critical director. He guides us through."

"Jan, you seem to have a marvelous balance of respect for God's part in our lives as well as our own part. I, too, am a firm believer, and I feel we have to use our physical, mental, and spiritual gifts all to their fullest to achieve what God intends for us."

"If God gives a voice," Jan said, "it's good fortune if he gives a

* He also conceived Radio City at Rockefeller Center.

bit of brain to go with it. You have to become the master of your voice. You must be musical and desirous of certain sounds. You have to decide whom you'd like to emulate."

"Who were the singers that influenced you the most?" I asked.

"Gigli, John Charles Thomas, Lawrence Tibbett, and Richard Bonelli."

"They were all great singers, Jan. Now let's talk about some specifics in technique, beginning with breathing."

"Well, you take a breath in the most natural possible way, usually through the mouth, which is fastest. However, outdoors, try to avoid it so as not to dry the palate and larynx. For the larynx, hot or cold air would be bad.

"Also, you shouldn't be a clavicular breather. Such singers lift their shoulders and upper chest very high, which limits your range, because your diaphragm is not functioning. The air space is small and the opening to your larynx is small."

"Some singers say support should feel like giving birth to a baby with a downward push," I prompted.

"That is the German school," he observed. "I agree to a certain degree, but every part of the body should function. That idea would help in making a strong sound. But proper use of the diaphragm keeps everything free in the chest."

"What does an open throat mean to you?"

"The throat must be left alone," he said. "Throaty singers think they're making a big sound, but it's a choking sound, and it will not be heard."

"How about the change in the voice as you go through the *passaggio?*" I asked. "Isn't there a change in the larynx?"

"Well, by nature I always got a *misto* (mixed) tone on F (first F above middle C). I cover on F sharp, but the F is not left open either."

"In other words, the F is preparing you for the covered F sharp, and is not completely open and not completely covered," I added. "But the sensation in the throat that accompanies covering . . . ?"

"I don't believe in any manipulation of the larynx."

"All right, then, let's approach it from the point of view of vowel sounds and the use of the jaw and the lips . . ."

"Some singers believe you mustn't start singing without a smile on your face," he said. "For instance, a tenor sings 'Una furtiva lacrima,' and you say, 'What the hell are you smiling about?' It makes no sense."

"Not when he's singing about crying," I laughed.

"How about the lips . . . do you use them to form your vowels?"

"No, I don't believe in using the lips, as a habit, for making vowels. Oh, for special effect . . . you can use your lips if you wish to be secretive, to sing *scuro* [darkly], or even for soft singing. But you don't make faces when you sing."

"Now, how do vowels change with register? Say you're singing an ascending scale . . . do you modify the vowels or not?" I asked.

"You've got to dress up a vowel to protect yourself as you go up," he said. "*Ee* goes to *ih*, like a little umlaut. *Ah* goes to *awe* and *oh* goes toward *oo*. Also, your jaw opens loosely as you go up. When I vocalize, I put my hand on my chin to see if I'm down. It's amazing how many singers have a terrible chin wobble. They're confusing it with the vibrato. It's a dancing tongue and a quivering chin."

"I've noticed it's much more common in women, and I don't know why. What do you think is the cause of this chin wobble?" I asked.

"I think it's a lack of diaphragmatic support," he said.

"They are probably trying to make the sound with the throat and jaw muscles instead of with the breath," I interjected.

"But that's wrong, a beautiful tone is not *made*, it's *emitted*. But that brings us back to God again. It's what's there. Don't go beyond your natural capacity."

"What about placement?"

"You should use all your resonance chambers," he said. "The sound must be forward in your cheeks. You should sing *by* the nose . . . not *in* the nose. If the voice is nasal it is not a pleasant sound. It should be in the cheeks and in the upper part of the head, but it should be natural and pleasant. When you sing you've got to think *beautiful*. That means an unconstricted, free, projected sound.

"And don't overdo on emotions. That can become force and can cause damage. I always strived for beautiful sound. You see, I was a violinist, and that was important, because I learned what a beautiful sound should be. It was also great for phrasing. Don't look for size, look for beauty. I was never a *shvitzer* [one who works up a sweat].

"Well, Jan," I said, "you certainly have been an inspiration to many, including me. What, to sum it up, is your advice to singers who desire a long and successful career?"

"You must be blessed with good health, and be kind to the little things you have been given. Every morning I do bending exercises and run in place. That keeps you flexible. And watch your diet . . . do everything in moderation. But most important is to be blessed with a bit of good health and a good bit of technique, which gives you an assured attitude—you know your voice is going to function for you as you want it to. Be the master of it. Your technique must be made second nature. You can't stand on the stage and plan it.

"Age has nothing to do with your singing; the larynx is the last organ to show age. The Talmud says this too. The proof is found in those men who at thirty-five and forty can't sing anymore. Why, De Luca made a record at sixty-eight. When I heard that, I said, 'If he can do it, so can I.' So did Battistini. Why shouldn't I be able to do this?"

"And now you're seventy-six and still going strong," I marveled. "When's your next engagement, Jan?"

"I'm opening in Westbury tomorrow in a variety show. You know, it's already sold out! The last show, according to the impresario, was a bust. As he put it, 'God wasn't with us.'"

"Well, Jan," I observed, "God was obviously with you all of your life, and still is." I thanked him and wished him well, and as he hung up the phone, it was quite easy to picture him bustling off to his rehearsal, wisecracking all the way . . . that is, when he was not praying or vocalizing.

What a beautiful combination he is of all the vital factors essential to such an impressive career: faith, intelligence, humor, and hard work. Jan's deeply religious orientation turned my thoughts to the Book of Proverbs in the Old Testament. Solomon constantly spoke of knowledge, understanding, and wisdom. Think of the *knowledge* Jan has gleaned regarding his instrument in his fifty years of singing. Think of the way he has applied himself to the *un-*

derstanding of that knowledge, which is, of course, technique. But do not fail to think of the third part of the trinity of truth, which is *wisdom*. Any man can acquire knowledge and understanding, but few have wisdom, which only God can give. And Jan surely appears to be amply supplied.

Roberta Peters

Roberta Peters achieved instant fame with her sudden debut at the Metropolitan Opera in 1950 as Zerlina in Mozart's DON GIOVANNI. She was very young and a last-minute substitute. She was also very good, and created a sensation among music-lovers and with the media. Born and raised in New York City, Miss Peters was also completely American-trained. She has maintained a long association with the Met, and has sung many roles there, including Zerbinetta in Strauss's ARIADNE AUF NAXOS and the Queen of the Night in Mozart's THE MAGIC FLUTE. Engagements abroad extended Miss Peters' popularity, and she has become as well known in Europe as in America for her lovely coloratura soprano voice and adept characterizations. 🎵

"I CAN'T believe it! You look just like the pretty young thing I used to date in 1951. Excuse me, I should say, 'double-date,' because every time I took you out to dinner and a movie, your mother had to come along. It was quite frustrating, because I have to admit my intentions were not honorable." I was sitting in a Met dressing room with Roberta Peters, international star of opera, film, television, radiant housewife, and mother of two grown children. If nothing else she surely was the very picture of a screen star.

"But you haven't changed one iota from the time of your debut . . . when was it?"

"November 17, 1950, and this is now my twenty-eighth season," she said pertly. I began reminiscing.

"Do you recall that concert in Syracuse that we did in the early 1950s? I dragged you along in my informal clowning style and next morning's review had the headline, 'Les Enfants Terrible of the Opera.' Hurok wouldn't let you do another recital with me for the next twenty years."

I studied her young, trim face and figure, wondering what was the outstanding feature about her that had assured this long and successful career.

"You've been at the Met a heck of a long time," I observed. "What do you attribute it to?"

"I don't see an end," was her enthusiastic reply. "I feel wonderful. I'm still doing a lot of the coloratura repertoire, expanding *slowly*—vocally, that is . . . which is one of the reasons I feel I have lasted. I have not changed my repertoire or my whole feeling about my voice as some people do in mid-career and then *that's it*. I have just started to do *La Traviata* and *La Bohème* after all these years. That's the heaviest I could do. I would never do any other Puccini except *Schicchi*, of course. All the other stuff . . . I'd kill myself, and why should I do that? I love to sing. I enjoy my work, and I'm glad people still want to deal with me. It's a responsibility for us to maintain our voices and bodies as long as we can.

"Another thing, beside the repertoire, which is important . . . your physical feelings at the time you sing . . . you must not be tired. If you start tired you're going to give a lousy performance."

"You're saying that energy is extremely important," I observed.

"Energy and the know-how to handle it, and inner poise on the stage. I always feel I stand outside myself and look at myself as objectively as I can. We cannot be completely objective, of course. That poise on the stage . . . knowing what's coming next . . . preparing for it. And mentally it comes because you've done it, and you started it early. That's where I credit my teacher. When you're young you can do a lot of things. As you grow older, if you don't take care of yourself . . ."

"What is the secret of your perpetual youth?" I asked.

"My husband doesn't even know. I just run him out of energy. My mother had a lot of drive. I may have inherited some of that. But I'm talking about an inner energy . . . to be able to go and do. My husband says to me, 'You're crazy.' But I don't know how to live any other way. I need that for my own self-preservation. I have a tremendous energy."

"But I suspect all this is not just hereditary," I said. "How about personal habits that may contribute to all this energy?"

"If I don't sleep, I'm a wreck. I cannot perform and function correctly. I need at least eight hours."

"You must eat carefully."

"Well, Jerry, all my life I've had the worry about gaining weight. My mother was heavy; my grandmother was heavy. One cannot abuse one's body, and that goes for food, very definitely. I know that if I started to let myself go, I would feel I was dying. It would be because I was in a depression. That would be the end."

"I get the feeling you can't stand to be depressed, which is healthy."

"I try very hard not to let myself get depressed. Over the years I've tried diets . . . Weight Watchers . . . Dr. Atkins . . . I've tried them all, and I've maintained my weight. We don't keep candy in the house. We don't keep cake in the house. It's not always easy. We're under tremendous tension, and that tension is what makes you eat or grab something. You must take care of yourself.

"Let's get down to basics," Roberta said. "William Herman was my only teacher until I made the Met. His way of teaching was very unorthodox. He was a very physical teacher. He would ask me to put the palms of my hands against the piano, feet about three feet away . . . leaning . . . that's what it was . . . *appoggio* . . . and that's what you have to feel, which is leaning. I was singing in that position as I was leaning.

"Then he would have me sing bending down, so the blood rushed to the head a little bit. Also, I would lean over, when I stopped singing, when I needed a little rest."

"That forces blood to the vocal cords and the brain," I said.

"It relaxed the whole throat area. The other thing we did—it was in *Life* magazine, because it was so picturesque—was a man standing on what looked like my stomach, which was really my diaphragm."

"I remember seeing that article."

"I used to go to a gym on Eighth Avenue, Joe Pilates Gym. It was an exercise place, and had terrific contraptions . . . even a wind machine, a little windmill. You'd take a straw and very slowly exhale to see how long you could keep that windmill going. It helps for breath control, for longer phrases.

"Herman always said, 'Breathe low. Don't breathe too high, because then you get tired, all your muscles start to contract.' Very often, when I was singing, he would whack me right in the diaphragm . . . I mean unexpectedly. So I developed a terrifically hard spot here."

"Did you do the medicine ball routine too, as Pat Munsel did?" I asked.

"Oh yes. Holding it out in front of you."

"How much did it weigh?"

"Ten pounds, I would say. It's almost like holding weights."

"What about your early background?" I digressed.

"My mother and father never knew one thing about opera. Nobody, as far back as I could trace, ever sang in my family."

"At what age did you begin singing?"

"When I was ten. My mother took me to a lot of those kiddie shows . . . *The Children's Hour,* radio shows, et cetera. Jan Peerce knew my grandfather, who asked him to listen to me, and he did. Jan Peerce was the one who recommended Herman. At thirteen, fourteen, and fifteen I studied Bach, Handel, and French art songs. I took five lessons a week; I was drinking in the whole atmosphere. I studied French with a French lady who was a friend of Caruso. I studied Italian with a diseuse.

"It sounds like Cinderella. The Met was my first professional engagement, because Peerce came to my lesson and said, 'I'll bring Hurok up to hear you.' Hurok signed me. He said, 'We've got to go to Bing.'

"I sang for Max Rudolf at the Met, and I came all prepared to do arias. Max said, 'Which duet do you know? Let me hear this ensemble.' I was flabbergasted! I didn't know he wanted that. I did it and he was very impressed that I knew my operas. I knew twenty operas by the time I got into the Met."

"I knew twenty operas by the time I turned twenty," I said, surprised by this coincidence.

"We have so many things parallel," she said. "We've been very fortunate. You were ready and I was ready."

"It took plenty of hard work," I mused.

"I didn't know anything else," she said. "I wasn't with my peers! I didn't go to proms. I never had a date."

"Again, it sounds like my story," I exclaimed. Once more I digressed. "You know, you and Pat Munsel not only studied with the same teacher, but you have one more thing in common: after all these years, you both look great . . . trim, healthy, young . . . I think it was your basic training with Herman, where you found joy in the physical attributes of life. I believe this was the basic source of your energy."

"I didn't have it before I started with him," she reflected. "My big thing is tennis now. I love tennis and swimming. When I can't do those two I take my jump rope on the road with me."

All of this convinced me more than ever that basic habits in a singer's student days are of supreme importance in later life, especially when it comes to that basic energy which is so essential to a long, full career.

"Let's get down to basic technique," I said. "What discipline of scales did you use?"

"Would you believe that I sang clarinet parts. Klosé is a clarinet book, and we went through all the clarinet things. Herman was a real bug on agility. I studied the García books, the three-note [triplets] and the four-note and every combination of scales up and down . . . and arpeggios . . . everything. I used the Mozart piano sonatas . . . I'd sing them with the pianist. Anything that would have me do phrasing, agility, coloratura work. The first half hour would be just vocalizing. I always had trouble with triplets. I never could get them even and fast. You do them slowly first, as pianists do, then pick it up. My first opera was *Lucia*, when I was sixteen years old.

"We did the *messa di voce* almost every lesson, because he felt that if you can produce a very small note, and crescendo it, and then come back, your cords are working. But if you couldn't do that, there's a certain hook, he used to call it, you'd hook into that top voice."

"What do you mean by *hook?*"

"It means getting more into the head voice."

"Well, then, do you use chest voice?" I asked.

"No, I don't use chest voice. He always wanted it extremely even. He never believed in registers. You have to keep it as even as you can up and down. You're not going to have the exact same position of the throat on the top as you have on the bottom. You can't have that. When I was descending a scale, he would tell me to think *high* . . . think *up,* as I was going down, because if you think down, then you dig, and you're pushing, you want to make it bigger and bigger.

"When I first started with him, I used to sing A above high C. Until recently I vocalized up to high G. If you're going to do a high F in public, you've got to have a G. I vocalized a lot. The hard thing when you have performances is not to vocalize too much before, and not to vocalize too little."

"A bit ago you said 'Think high.' Did you mean in terms of a high sensation of vibration?"

"I guess it would be vibration."

"As you go up on a scale, what difference is there in throat setting?"

"On the E, F, and G below high C . . . that's the *passaggio.* Something changes there. Sometimes it can get very thin, but I've always been afraid of making it too big, because at that point, if you give too much, you lose the top. And that's been the whole thing, all these years: hang on to that coloratura. Don't dig, don't push, because I love the coloratura singing. It's the only thing I have known from the very beginning."

"As you go from the middle to high, do you think in terms of more spacing in the throat?"

"No, never," she replied. "I never think of anything, I take a good low breath, *not* a high breath. I feel it in the back and the diaphragm area . . . an expansion. There are some people who speak of this pressing down. I've never had that feeling. I *think* low, around the diaphragm and rib area, take as much breath in as I can, and know how to adjust it so I can sing a long phrase."

"What do you mean by *adjust it?*"

"I'm talking about letting it out sparingly as you're singing."

"And what do you use to accomplish this?"

"Support of the breath."

"It has nothing to do with the larynx?" I asked.

"Nothing. I never think of the larynx. I've seen pictures of what the larynx looks like and it confuses me. I don't really think that way."

"Do you think in terms of placing the voice?"

"It's a hard question. I know it's basic and very important. To me *placing* means *don't push*. I know when I'm pushing. I have to think high, keeping it away from the cords, keeping the breath flowing evenly, not to *dig*."

"You constantly use the word *dig*," I observed. "By dig, do you mean getting the larynx into the sound?"

"That's right. It's tight. Try to keep the throat as loose—out of it—as possible. Yet," she reflected, "your throat is doing all of the work. All singing is breath coming through the cords."

"So the trick is . . . ?"

"Knowing how much to give, how much not to give. How much breath to apportion so that you can do what you do well. Don't dig! Don't force the air into your cords. Don't force anything *up*.

"European singers come to this theater. They say, 'What a big house!' I haven't got such a big voice, but you can hear me in every single place in this theater. Some people call it projection. I say, 'What is this project, project?' I don't know what 'project' means. I know what I do. I take a breath as low as I can, and I try to apportion my breath so that I can finish my phrase without anything getting in the way. Not tightening up those cords so that you're pressing. I would say this is technique . . ."

"What does *open throat* mean to you? Do you ever think about it?" I asked.

"Not really. I think of pure vowels . . . *ah, eh, ee, oh, oo*. I also think the words have to mean something to you. You must know the language you're singing in."

"Some singers say that to smooth out the *passaggio* you must have a more narrow feeling in the throat, even a feeling of squeezing it down in that range," I said.

"I don't feel that I have to squeeze it," she responded, "but I feel . . . *small*. Otherwise, if you let it spread, you're not going to get above. You've got to guide it very carefully through a narrow passage around E, F, G, A [in the upper middle voice]. And then you can open up on the top."

"Now, on the lower *passaggio* just above middle C, some sopranos and mezzos say that thinking slightly *nasal* helps smooth it out," I said.

"When you say nasal, that means keeping it forward. If I sing D, E, F, G above middle C, I can get into chest voice, and I have to be very careful. That's when I say think high . . . lighter . . . so I don't wham into it and give it chest voice, because the chest voice, for me, is disaster."

"How about your vocal habits?" I asked.

"I don't vocalize every day."

"Let's say you're not performing for a month or so. How often would you vocalize?"

"Oh, twice a week, if I were working on something new, which I am most of the time."

"If you're going to study a new role, do you vocalize first?"

"Yes. I always vocalize, even if it's five or ten minutes. I love to do scales. I vocalize in different ways. Sometimes I start low just to warm up lightly . . . the eight-tone scale, starting on a low D . . . mostly on *ah*, occasionally going from *ee* to *ah*. After I've done that for a while, I like to do the *staccati arpeggi*, descending:

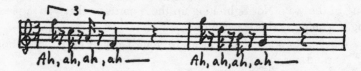

to keep the voice high . . . starting at F below high C."

"Would you go all the way up to the top at first?"

"No! I'd go maybe to A, and then I'd go back to my scales. I try not to warm up too fast. Then I start to get into a little bit of what I'm going to sing that night. Usually when I warm up for a specific performance I don't sing anything from something else. I like to sing what I'm going to sing that night."

"On a performance day, how do you warm up?"

"I use my voice hardly at all. I hardly talk. I try to keep the lowest profile I possibly can."

"When do you vocalize?"

"About an hour before I leave for the theater. I try to get my energy down, relaxing, because the performance is going to be the top of my day: at eight-thirty it's going to be my twelve noon."

"So you vocalize around six . . . for how long?"

"Not long. I do ten-fifteen minutes. I like to vocalize in the bathroom of my hotel. I put the warm water on . . . the steam going. It may be a quirk, but I do it. Then I go back and start to make up, and then another fifteen minutes of vocalizing, to keep it up."

"And after you go to the theater?"

"I try not to vocalize in the room. I get to the theater dressed in my gown, or costume, and I like to get there late."

"Most of your colleagues do something similar," I said. "They feel that hot showers and brisk walks tune them up for their performances."

"And you feel good physically," she said. "I maintain that these heavy singers cannot sing so long, because their muscle tone, their energy, is not good . . . it's all fat! It's the worst thing for you. If your muscles and your body tone are good, your vocal tone is going to be good."

Well, I felt like cheering after that rousing dénouement. We have both endured for many years at the Met, and I think our mutually shared views on health, just sheer vital energy, have had an enormous amount to do with our vocal longevity. Think it over, youngsters, and start today.

Paul Plishka

Paul Plishka, born in Pennsylvania, made his debut with the Metro-politan Opera National Company in 1966 as Colline in La Bohème. *When that company was disbanded, Mr. Plishka joined the parent company, making his debut in 1967 in a small role in* La Gioconda. *In the following years his sonorous bass voice graced a number of small roles and an increasing number of leading ones as well. His beautiful voice has been heard to good advantage as Procida in* I Vespri Siciliani *and Giorgio in* I Puritani. *A "Live from the Met" telecast in 1980 featured his Philip II in* Don Carlos.

"THAT was the most beautiful high F I ever heard from a bass," Lucia said.

"You dare say that to me," I cried, "me, your husband!"

Why did I react so? It's very simple! My wife was not talking about *my* high F, but Paul Plishka's.

"You want me to tell you lies?" she retorted. "No! I always tell you the truth."

That's what comes of being married to another opera singer, es-pecially one who sings better than you, and never lets you forget it. Every night when I go home after a performance, it's like going to bed with a critic from the New York *Times*.

"Okay," I said, "I'll be interviewing Paul in about two weeks and I'm going to discover his secret, and then . . ."

"And then . . ." Lucia said with a syrupy smile, "we'll see!"

The interview took place at the Regency Hyatt in Atlanta during the Met tour, and Paul and I were alternating in *Aïda* and *Eugene Onegin*. I pretended to be interested in his background and tech-nique in general, but I wanted that high F. (Drat it, I've got a good high F, but Lucia has given me a thing about this.) So here's how it went.

Paul was born in Old Forge, Pennsylvania. (Maybe it was the water in Old Forge that did it. I could have it bottled and make a fortune.) His kindergarten teacher told his parents that he should have voice lessons, but fortunately (according to Paul) they did nothing about it. In the eighth grade he took up guitar lessons and he and his teacher would play and sing together. Later he was sent to a voice teacher at the conservatory in Scranton, where he sang songs but didn't really work on his voice. Paul liked singing, but he wanted to be a farmer or a football player.

During his junior year in high school his family moved to Paterson, New Jersey. While singing in the school chorus he made such an impression on the teacher he was invited to do the role of Judd in *Oklahoma!* He then joined Armen Boyajian, who was forming an opera workshop in Paterson, and Paul performed in excerpts from such operas as *La Bohème* and *Otello*. Soon thereafter he did Don Basilio in *The Barber of Seville*, Padre Guardiano in *La Forza del Destino*, and Philip II in *Don Carlos* (at the age of twenty-one). He did more than sing with the company; he drove the truck, painted the scenery, and worked on the stage crew as well.

Paul had two years of college in Montclair, New Jersey, where he was a voice major and also studied piano. It was there he met Judy, who soon became his wife. Not satisfied with the academic approach to opera, he quit school and went to work driving a truck for an ice cream company. After each day's work he hurried to his voice lesson or opera rehearsal.

At the age of twenty-three he entered the Metropolitan auditions and made it to the Eastern Regional Finals. Later that year he was accepted in the Metropolitan Opera's National Company. When that company folded, Rudolf Bing auditioned all its soloists and Paul was among those hired by the Met. He began with a contract to do buffo (comic) roles, learning Melitone, Dulcamara, Pasquale, and Bartolo. He spent a lot of time observing and understudying Fernando Corena.

"To be a buffo, you have to be musical. The music is fast; you have to be sharp and alert. I learned so much from Fernando, I can't tell you."

After three years the management realized that Paul had a voice more suited to serious roles and began to give him the opportunity to move in that direction. The training he received on the job at the Met was what he had sought and not found in college.

"You train your voice for so long," he said, "but yet you don't have that total professionalism that you acquire from working with great coaches. I started off doing the tiny, tiny roles, and I worked, five hours a day for five years with them! If I had to pay for the hours I spent with these coaches, it would cost me a hundred thousand dollars. On my first coaching with Masiello, we spent a whole hour on the first page. It was a great way to learn, if you have the patience. Not only that, you rehearsed with the greatest people in the business, listening to the language, the phrasing, the diction, the way the words come out of their mouths. Then, in the evening, in a role like Sam in *Ballo*, you're three hours on stage. You have all the opportunity to try things . . . movements . . . et cetera. If it doesn't work, it doesn't matter because the audience isn't watching you, it's watching the tenor or the mezzo-soprano do their thing.

"Some of the buffo things were good for the voice. They got it to sail up easily to the top. But my teacher [Armen] was clever enough not to let me bring all the weight to the top, and even though I said sometimes, 'Gee, I sound like a lyric baritone,' we didn't care. It's where the voice belonged . . . and we did it that way.

"In that period," Paul said, "they asked me to do the Grand Inquisitor, and Boris when I was twenty-six. I just wouldn't do it, and I believe in that. I didn't do my first Méphistophélès in *Faust* until I was thirty-three. I think that's helped me a great deal. Richard Tucker didn't do *Aïda* until he was in his fifties."

"We Americans have an especially great challenge in having to sing a vast repertoire in five languages, with a great diversity of styles," I said. "I don't know how you feel about it, Paul, but I do alter my technique somewhat from one role to another."

"You change," Paul observed. "Basically you shouldn't, but you do. I really think it should stay in the same line, but that's one of the problems I have with the German repertoire. When I go to the coaches, they want certain sounds . . ."

"I sympathize with you on that," I said. "And I do not sing Ger-

Paul Plishka

man with the pure German vowels; I round them out a bit in a more Italianate way. In that sense I don't change my technique. I always use, more or less, the same vowels.

"But since we're on the subject of technique," I said, "let's discuss yours."

"Well," he began, "Armen believes, and so do I, that every voice has three or four notes in it that are the natural sound. I think, for the bass, it usually is from B (the second below middle C) to G (the first below middle C), right in the very middle of the voice. And you could do anything; you could be standing on your head . . . and those notes always seem to be nice. So the trick, going up and down, is to make the rest of the voice match that as evenly as possible, without having the clicks and the bloops, and drastic changes of technique to get to the top.

"So, what Armen did in the beginning was to start . . . in the vocalizing . . . with very close simple progressions. You would do . . . [he sang a slow five-note chromatic scale, up and back down, and repeated it higher] so that you could feel the closeness of one [note] to the other, getting from one [note] to the other without losing the step. The relation is so close to the one before that it's hard to lose it. In other words, not to go . . . [he sang up and down an octave arpeggio]."

"You feel that with the big leaps of the arpeggio you could inadvertently make a big switch," I added.

"Yes, and you wouldn't realize you were doing it. But this way you can feel where you were before, and you can slide, and connect them. When you start with a young voice, no matter how much intelligence you put into it, the throat itself, is just not ready to do it, so it's a very slow process. You just have to let the voice find its way.

"Say you've got the voice lined up even from the low A to the middle C, and you're singing a piece where you've got to sing an E flat (above middle C). So what do you do if the voice isn't ready to make that smooth transition? You sacrifice! You let it do it the way it does naturally. You go up to the C with the evenness and the smoothness and the cover, and then the E flat comes out blatant and loud. Just let it be wide, or spread, or open . . .

Paul Plishka

"You take what comes. That's why a voice at that age shouldn't be exposed to something that's going to hurt the singer professionally later on. Instead of making bad impressions [in important places], do it in your local opera workshop . . . do it out somewhere in the sticks. Don't come to New York City with an incomplete voice at the age of twenty-one and make a bad impression. Two years later they won't even listen to you. They'll say, 'I heard him.' Especially with heavier, more dramatic voices, you have to be patient. I don't believe that my voice really reached its final maturity until I was thirty-three or thirty-four.

"Over three or four years, as we worked the voice from the middle, it began pulling and pulling, and it got longer and longer. When I first signed with the Met . . . for me, E flat and E natural were hard . . . very hard."

I was pleased to hear that Paul had to acquire that beautiful high F. Perhaps he could describe how. I tried to be patient.

"But," he continued, "having to do that buffo repertoire, and taking the weight out to get up there and sustaining all those high notes . . . you're singing Ds and E flats all the time . . . somehow it came, because I dropped the weight out of it. We are very quality-conscious and also very high-note-conscious. So Armen and I worked very hard with the quality . . . smoothness and evenness of voice, and we worked very hard at developing a good top. We never really worked the bottom of the voice, because I think it's one of those things with the bass that come later in life . . . the mature sound. It's a terrible thing to say, but basses are not paid for low notes, they're paid for high notes and quality. The roles that had a few really low notes were roles I really wasn't interested in, like Sarastro.

"One thing that's very important with a young voice is that you don't try to make it anything that it really isn't. When I was twenty-four, we added a little color, a bit of darkness. But when you get a little older, in your middle thirties, the voice naturally gets darker itself, so if you don't take away that artificial thing you put in, then you have that thing you put there *plus* the natural darkness, and it sounds like a record going slow.

"When these changes happen, you have to be ready to think

changes in your technique. That's why I believe in *two* people . . . the person with the voice and the person with the ear . . . because you can't really hear these things happening.

"Often when Judy and Armen are the most satisfied with my voice, I'll say, 'I'm sounding like a tenor.' 'No,' they say, 'you're sounding too dark, too covered. You need more point to the voice, more ring.' And finally they'll say, 'That's good.' It can't be, but it is. It's important that you can put your faith in someone else."

"In your early years, did you do any scales besides those chromatics?" I asked.

"One we did was connecting the vowel sounds. That exercise was:

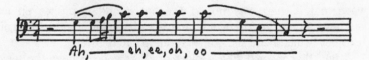

making them [the vowels] connect smoothly instead of going . . . [He repeated the exercise, exaggerating the change from vowel to vowel.] It is basically the same position for all the vowels. Somewhere there is a common denominator, you might say: one sound that holds throughout all the changes of the vowels, and that's your vocal point which you hang onto. That gives you the smoothness of the sound . . . that all the vowels connect without any break. And that was achieved through that kind of exercise."

"What does support mean to you, Paul?"

"I'm big. I basically have a muscular stomach. Apparently, because I was a physical person, we really never discussed support. If you were going to take a trip to New York, you'd have to put a certain amount of gas in the car to know you're going to get there and back. It's the same thing with your breathing, it's a natural thing. But if you know you have to get to the end of this phrase, all it takes is doing it three times, and you know how much air it's going to take. So you take a deep breath, and you sing the phrase, and that's it.

"I believe in the evenness of breathing. I've always avoided jogging, because I think in jogging you use a different kind of breathing technique. It's shorter breaths. Even swimming . . . you have the strokes and you put your face in the water, and you hold your breath. Then you blow it out. It's a perfect rhythm, but we don't use a perfect rhythm in singing. You take a long breath, and you use it. Sometimes you use a shorter breath in a phrase. You've got all these phrases; how many phrases are of equal length? So you have these different lengths of breath. The important thing is that it's smooth, and I breathe from the chest . . . low . . . the stomach seems to be going in and out . . . the chest doesn't move . . . it's the stomach that moves.

"You take a good breath and it pulls in as evenly as possible. It's a release. It's like the waves in the ocean. Sometimes it's a big, long wave and it goes way up on the beach and it pushes up and swishes around the top evenly and goes back into the water again. It comes in again and sometimes it doesn't go that far.

"I find that when I sing a piece, and it's good, I have the sensation of having a line the minute I start the piece to the end of the piece . . . an unbroken line. It's constantly moving, and there's no stopping or starting . . . even when there's a pause in the music. There's maybe ten measures of music in between, before you sing. Somehow the emotion picks up where you've actually physically stopped singing. You're emotionally involved . . . it carries that line . . . just a movement of the head or something. So, from the beginning of the piece to the end, it's one long line, not only vocally, but physically."

"That is a beautiful concept," I said. I was sorry I had to return to the mundane world of technique after this rather poetic excursion. "Now . . . what does an open throat mean to you?" I asked.

"I don't know."

"That's a good, honest answer," I chuckled.

"I know the vocal cords are in the throat," Paul said, "but when I'm singing I have no sensation in my throat at all. The only sensation I have is around my upper teeth, and my nose."

"Then let's go to placement," I suggested.

"I've done some master classes, and I've dealt with students who have been studying voice for four years, and my son, who's never had voice lessons, can sing better. It's because they have no concept of this forward placement. Sometimes I give them a hum, and when you hum naturally you vibrate up in your nose."

"Humming on an *m* or an *n?*" I asked.

"It's really an *n*," he said reflectively. "I get them to hum . . . [he hummed and slowly opened his mouth to an *ah* vowel] and not lose that sensation here [in the mask]. Let the mouth open and don't change anything. It's hard for them to do when they're not used to it. This is the very forward, Italianate sound my teacher worships. To me, everything happens here in the nose."

"A very difficult phrase for me is 'Ella giammai m'amò' . . . the attack of the 'Ella' is deadly for me. Deadly! I'll do a little hum, almost to myself . . ." He attacked "Ella" with a hint of a hum before opening his mouth.

"I use a slight impulse, like a half *h*, on that attack," I said.

"That's dangerous," he replied, "because then I get too airy."

"Pinza used a lot of that," I countered.

"I've only heard him on records, and he crooned a lot."

"Paul," I said, "my wife thinks you have the greatest bass high notes in the business, so I warn you, I'm out to steal your secrets for myself. So let's talk about that."

"A friend of mine was listening to a recording I was doing, and he said, 'When you hit the high notes, there is something about them that reminds you of a tenor. They're dark, yet they have the ring of a tenor.'

"I have a great admiration for tenors," he continued. "I think I approach my high notes the way a tenor approaches them, more than the way you traditionally hear a bass approach them. It's a very forward, high placement . . . a ringing sound."

"You mentioned getting rid of the clicks and the bloops as one goes up to the high notes," I said. "Of course, that means you shouldn't have major transformations as you go into a certain range."

"They are there. When I go from the middle into the top, I cover . . . C, D, E flat, depending on the vowel, depending on the pianissimo, or whatever."

"Can you easily sustain an open E flat (above middle C) on an *ah* vowel?" I asked.

"I cannot sustain it for long."

"With me it tends to be spread," I reflected.

"Yes, very spread. Sometimes I cover a C sharp, even a C, depending on the vowel."

"On a scale up to the top, what do you do to make that passage smooth?" I asked.

"Again it's the half-tone progression. As you go from the C sharp, then the change comes here in the throat, but the nose position never changes: this is locked. The only thing it might do is move a little higher up into the nose. And that is your connecting. To the listener it stays the same. They hear a sameness, whereas you know you're covered."

"You mentioned that as you covered, something happened in the throat," I said. "What happens?"

"Like a flip."

"What flips?" I zeroed in on the sensation. "What does that really mean? Is it a feeling of a little more spacing in the larynx?"

"Yes! A column of air that comes up from the stomach . . . [he held his forearm straight up from the elbow, with his hand bent forward at the wrist]. You've got it straight coming up. As it gets to the throat, there's a little bit of turn, and it comes up off your nose somehow. Now as you go up to the other thing [the passage], the bend there straightens out, which allows the tone to go up straighter . . . [he straightened out his wrist and hand so his fingers were pointing directly up] and higher into the nose. The air column comes up and passes through the vocal cords, and turns, and goes out through the nose. As you go higher you've got to get a higher point in your nose."

"The column straightens out on the high notes," I said.

"It just goes higher."

"Some singers," I continued, "maintain that as you go up to the high notes, the sound has to go back. Maybe that's like straightening out the column."

"Probably so. Yes. If it's bent, going out forward, it can only go so high. When you're aiming a cannon out there, and you want it to go farther, you've got to lift the trajectory a little higher. So you're lifting it [the sound] a little higher so it can go up into the head. Sometimes when I hit a really high note I get so dizzy . . . I've almost lost consciousness. I always feel if I have any trouble with high notes, it's almost ninety-nine percent of the time because I've taken too much weight up. It's too thick in the middle."

"It's easy to make that mistake in the Grand Inquisitor," I said. "It's written in such a gutsy way that by the time you get to the first high F, you're pushing too hard and heavy. I think Verdi deliberately wrote it in an anti-vocal way just to make the old man sound about ninety-three years of age," I remarked.

"I think so too," he agreed. "I've sung many Filippos in different theaters, and when *you* started going up, I said to myself, 'He's never going to make it. No way is that sound going to go up.' But you did, and I was shocked. The credit there, I think, is to your physical condition, which is excellent, and a very secure technique . . . confidence in your technique."

"Well, Paul, it's your technique we're interested in for this interview, not mine, and I feel it has been most enlightening."

As I took my leave of Paul and his charming wife, I clutched my notes to my chest and scurried back to my hotel to study them at my leisure.

"Watch out, Paul, I've got the secrets of your high notes on paper. Now all I've got to do is get them into my head and throat. Drat that Lucia."

The truth can be so painful.

Rosa Ponselle

*Rosa Ponselle is considered one of the greatest of all American
opera singers. Born in Connecticut, as a young teenager she sang
with her sister Carmela in vaudeville. Later she made her Metropolitan Opera debut, in 1918, as Leonora in LA FORZA DEL
DESTINO, opposite Caruso. Her opulent dramatic soprano voice was
heard for almost twenty years at the Met, in roles including Norma
and Violetta in LA TRAVIATA. After her retirement, Miss Ponselle
taught at her home in Baltimore and was also director of the Baltimore Civic Opera. Miss Ponselle died on May 25, 1981.* 𝄞

"I AM terribly sorry, Mr. Hines, but we will have to cancel your appointment with Madame Ponselle; she is very ill."

My heart dropped to my toes, as I had very much anticipated interviewing the diva who, at the age of twenty-one, created the role
of Leonora in Verdi's *La Forza del Destino* in the Met's premiere of
that work, with Enrico Caruso playing Alvaro.

"Shall we set another date for me to come to Baltimore?" I asked.

"I'm sorry, but it is so serious that we are afraid Madame Ponselle
will not live through the summer."

Rosa had suffered a stroke and was in a precarious suspension
between life and death. It was to my happy surprise that I received
a call exactly one year later that she had, thanks to her strong constitution, pulled through in spite of the odds and wanted to see me.
I was warned that speaking was difficult for her, but we would find
a way, because she was enthusiastic to share her great vocal heritage.

As I drove to Baltimore, I had qualms about what sort of interview I would obtain, considering the circumstances, but surpris-
ingly, the afternoon turned out to be extremely fruitful. Upon my
arrival at Villa Pace I was immediately impressed by the warm,

generous hospitality of Rosa and her coterie. I was wondering how I was going to conduct a detailed interview by a swimming pool with the several guests sitting about sipping drinks and partaking of a feast of crab claws, cheeses, and other delightful tidbits, until it finally dawned upon me that these were no ordinary guests, but a carefully selected team to aid and abet the interview.

Igor Chichagov had been the accompanist in Rosa's studio for most of the years she had taught in the Baltimore area, and had come down from New York just for this occasion.

Kira Baklanova was a longtime student of our famous diva and, indeed, I recalled we had sung together in a concert version of *Boris Godunov* with the Baltimore Symphony. She had been my Marina. Kira had enjoyed a bright career in Europe and also with the Baltimore Opera and NBC Opera tour.

The gentleman seated at my right, by the pool, with voluminous books of notes under his arm, was Hugh Johns, Rosa's greatest fan, who had compiled a most exacting collection of information pertaining to her illustrious career.

These three and Rosa provided me with one of the most rewarding interviews I have had the pleasure to conduct.

Rosa Ponzillo was born in Meriden, Connecticut, on January 22, 1897. She sang as a child and also studied piano and violin. She was so proficient on those instruments and in sight reading that her grade-school teacher often sent her in to teach the other pupils. Although she never formally studied voice, her early professional jobs were always as a singer. Her first job was in the local dime store singing songs behind the music counter. After that she went to work in the local silent-movie theater singing illustrated songs while they were changing reels during the show. From there it was Cafe Mellone in New Haven, where Rosa did a classical program with piano and violin accompaniment.

She came from a musical family: her mother sang, and so did her brother Tony and her sister Carmela, who was already in vaudeville and had made a hit in the musical show *The Girl from Brighton Beach.* Tony was a spinto tenor, and Carmela (I believe a mezzo) later sang for ten seasons at the Met (some family). Carmela's agent thought that a sister act in vaudeville would be great, and two weeks after Rosa auditioned for him the two girls opened in the Bronx at the Star Theater. The Ponzillo Sisters were an instant success and were soon headliners at the Palace in New York, which was the "Met of Vaudeville." The hit of Rosa's act was Victor Herbert's "Kiss Me Again," which she first played on the piano and then sang. The act closed with a rousing rendition of the *Faust* Trio done as a duet with Carmela.

At the height of her success in vaudeville, Rosa sang for Caruso, who took her to Gatti-Casazza, resulting in a contract for the next fall at the Metropolitan. Before her historic debut, Rosa's only contact with opera had been a pair of Met performances she had attended. She was assigned to do the Met premiere of *Forza, Oberon, Cavalleria Rusticana,* the world premiere of *The Legend,* and the Verdi *Requiem,* quite a task for one who had never had a formal voice lesson. Rosa says, "It just came naturally," but she did have a profound musical background, and was even able to read orchestral scores. How else could a twenty-one-year-old girl tackle a complete recital program, four operas and the *Requiem,* and be ready to perform in eight months?

On November 16, 1918, Rosa Ponselle became the first American-born singer to debut at the Met with no previous training or experience in a foreign country, opening the doors for all her fellow countrymen who have followed. She was a familiar sight bicycling from Riverside Drive to the Met (with a chauffeur following close behind). Gatti put an end to that eventually, because her weaving in and out of traffic made him too apprehensive.

It is unbelievable to consider that this wonder girl of twenty-one not only made her auspicious debut at such a tender age, but also, within six weeks, had added *Oberon* and *Cavalleria* to her triumph in *Forza.* There is no need to elaborate on her glorious career, since it is well-documented history. But it is interesting to note that after her marriage and subsequent retirement, this self-taught diva went on to become one of America's most famous voice teachers, working with Beverly Sills, Raina Kabaivanska, William Warfield, Lili Chookasian (who was so kind as to arrange my belated interview with Rosa), James Morris, Richard Cassilly, and countless others.

Surely Rosa had an extraordinary mind, and here was I to glean all I could for the good of future generations.

"Rosa," I began, "where do we start on vocal technique?"

"Keep a square throat," she said laboriously. I thought at first I had heard wrong because of her difficulty in speaking. I turned quizzically to Igor and Kira.

"That's right," Kira said. "Rosa always told us to keep a square throat."

"Caruso taught me that," Rosa said. "He kept a little stretch in the back of the throat to keep it open . . . open in the back and relaxed. It feels like a square, but only on the high notes."

"But this square," I said, somewhat in the dark as to what it meant, "what . . . how . . . ?"

"The square is in the back of the throat," Igor ventured. "She used the term all the time with her pupils."

"But is this square sensation vertical or horizontal, lying down flat, standing on end . . . ?"

"The palate is high and the back of the tongue flat," Rosa said. "This is the square."

"Ah . . ." I said, "then the square is standing up on one of its sides like . . ."

I described it as in this picture where the two upper corners of the square represent the forces lifting the soft palate and the two lower corners represent the flattening of the tongue in the back. Rosa et al agreed that this description was valid.

"I suppose," I ventured, "that what we're really talking about is what is commonly called an open throat. But you are basically applying this, you said, to high notes. How do you approach the concept of open throat in general?"

"Keep the tone dark," Rosa stated positively.

"Her favorite vowel was *oo*," Igor said. "Her Latin voice tended to be too bright, so her only coach, Romano Romani, insisted on this school of Ruffo and Stracciari: use *oo* to keep a cover on the tone."

"I used *moo*, in the lower register . . . pure *moo* . . . then gradually to *mah*," Rosa said, and it was evident that this was the Italian *awe*, not the brighter *ah* used in French, German, or Russian, "but with a slight smile."

Kira demonstrated what she meant as Igor quickly added that it was not a real smile, showing the teeth, but only a hint, or trace, of a smile. That was logical, as I do not associate the high, toothy smile, advocated by many, with a dark, round sound.

"None of you seem to use the protruding lips to form the *oo*," I observed.

"No, you can't if you have a slight smile," Igor said, and then I understood the meaning of this "trace of a smile": it was the insurance against putting tension on the lips when making the *oo* vowel, which would have to be formed deep in the larynx. It was the dark round *oo* that is related to the Italian *awe* simply by the opening and closing of the loose jaw.

"No lips for the *oo*," I concluded.

"Always round," Rosa added. "And don't let the top get away from you with high *tessitura*. It's a low, round sensation, the *oo*, and all vowels are based on it."

"Okay." I got the picture. "That's the basis of the open throat, the tongue flat in the back, which drops the larynx a bit, and a raised palate . . ."

"Giving the square throat," she added.

"Early in her career," Igor said, "she was having a little problem with some high notes and not with others. She realized one of the good ones was on 'Mia *madre*.' That's the darker *awe* vowel."

"I started with *m* and a relaxed throat," Rosa said. "When I was not in good voice, and could not get a good *awe* from *oo*, I would work on it until I got it."

"How about the other vowels?" I asked

"Going to *ee*, the back of the tongue raises a bit," Igor said, "but the throat stays always open with the . . ."

"With the same square," Rosa added. "If you cannot sing the *oo* with a slight smile, the *oo* is wrong."

"What do you feel about support, Rosa?"

"It's a rubber band," she said. After a bit of discussion, my impression of a rubber band gave way to a rubbery cushion, or diaphragm. "You breathe through your nose and mouth," she continued, "*not* nose alone!"

"Do you raise your shoulders?" I asked.

"No! Not raised . . . you widen your chest, upper part of the body relaxed, straight spine, abdomen expanded, back included, all around."

"When you breathe, do you go immediately and rhythmically right into the phrase or do you pause in the moment of the breath, like a sharpshooter holding his breath as he aims the gun?"

A bit of round-table discussion affirmed that one should breathe and sing rhythmically without hesitation or interruption of the breathing cycle.

"The purpose of the support is to maintain even flow [of breath] . . . *appoggiare* . . . lean on it . . ."

"Wait," I said. "Do you mean lean into the sound with the vocal cords, or lean deeply upon the diaphragm?"

"The diaphragm, not in the larynx," she said. "Always push out with the stomach and abdomen during the phrase, *not* in."

"How about placement?" I asked.

"You use the mask . . . forward," she said. "You get the feeling your face is going to come off."

"From the vibrations?"

"Yes!"

"Did you use chest voice?"

"Only when necessary, but always in the mask."

"Now," I said, "how about the transition in the throat or jaw as you go up in range from low notes to high notes? Is there any change?"

"In the middle register just talk, don't mouth words . . . don't make too big a spacing," she said. "But as you go up you need more spacing . . . mouth more open, jaw dropped, relaxed."

"One more point on technique, Rosa: you had such a beautiful pianissimo. Some people say you have to be born with it. Did you always have it or did you acquire it?"

"I always had it," she replied.

"Is there any imagery you could give those that are not so fortunate that might be of some help to them?"

"In pianissimo you almost feel as if you're pulling a thread through your nose . . . and don't let it ever stop."

I asked Rosa what sort of vocalizing she did during her career. She said she vocalized in the shower, or when she felt like it. At first she tested her pianissimo and did a scale or two to see if the voice was there. Her vocalises were simple; for agility, for example, she used the classic

But she maintained she did next to nothing of vocalizing, just *moo, moo, moo.* All was based on this vocal conditioner and scales on the Italian word *addio* [goodbye].

The round, dark sound based upon *moo,* with a trace of a smile, was so fundamental to her technique that I asked Igor if he had anything to add to it.

"We used to have cattle on the estate and it is a fact that the cows came to listen to Rosa when she sang. They used to push against that fence," he indicated the nearby one, "and they always got their heads caught in it trying to get nearer."

Thinking of a similar circumstance with Louis Quilico (see the chapter on him, following), I decided that it was not the *moo* exercise, but that these gentle beasts have an affinity for a beautiful human voice.

At this point it was announced that dinner was served, and that alone was worth the trip to Maryland: the delicious food, the serene beauty of Villa Pace, and the warm hospitality. Before I left I was given two records of Rosa, who, since she could no longer write easily, autographed them with a kiss, leaving the impression of her lipstick on the covers. I was deeply moved by the occasion. I am sure that her performances on the stage must have been made of the same stuff. Imagine what she accomplished without a single formal voice lesson! But she also made you unaware of her excellent technique, because she lived the text of every role she sang: she breathed the breath of life into her art.

Suddenly, I became aware of the central quality of Rosa Ponselle: she loved life intensely, and that love shows in everything she has done. I will be reminded of this every time I take out her album to play it, and see her special autograph. I am reminded of the famous thirteenth chapter of the book of I Corinthians, written by St. Paul. Read it and get a glimpse of the heart of Rosa Ponselle.

Louis Quilico

Louis Quilico is a Canadian who was born in Montreal. His debut as Germont in La Traviata *occurred at the New York City Opera in 1956. In 1972 he made his Met debut, as Golaud in* Pelléas et Mélisande. *His smooth, beautiful baritone was later well displayed at the Met in the role of Coroebus in Berlioz's* Les Troyens. *Other roles New York audiences have enjoyed include Rigoletto in the Met's 1981 television broadcast of that opera.* 🎶

"Blast it, Mr. Quilico, I can't put up with this any more. Go below and *sing*."

"Aye, aye, Captain," was the quick reply, hardly out of his mouth before he was hastening below to sing a concert for his noisy, boisterous audience. When Louis arrived and promptly began his first number, he could hardly be heard over the din, but his resonant baritone finally began to get through to even this unruly crowd. Little by little the sheer beauty of his voice began to sway his listeners, and finally silence reigned as they attentively listened to his second selection. When Louis Quilico, one of the finest young vocalists to emerge from Montreal, finished his brief recital, there was a breathless hush . . . not the sound of a single handclap. Cows don't clap.

Louis was working his way across the Atlantic to Italy on a cattle boat, for which he was paid fifty dollars. Soon after the sturdy ship had begun its sixteen-day voyage it was discovered that no one in the crew had the courage to go down and clean the bull but Louis. One day when the sea was quite rough, the cows became very nervous and began lowing uproariously. Louis began to sing while he was cleaning the bull, and his audience of 149 cows and 18 chickens was calmed to abject silence by his golden tones. After this was brought to the captain's attention, it became Quilico's job to do a concert in the hold every time the noise became unbearable.

After he arrived in Italy, he was constantly heartsick because he had left his fiancée behind. She was a concert pianist and they both concluded by letter that she should continue her musical studies in France. All that was sidetracked, soon after her arrival in Europe, by their marriage at St. Peter's in Rome.

In a short time they ran out of money and were forced to return to Montreal, where Louis worked a year and a half for his father, who, incidentally, was completely against his son's career, because he wanted him in his business. But music was in Louis' soul, having sung in the school and church choirs from the age of six.

"I always felt you're not supposed to get paid when you sing," he said, smiling. "My soul would sing . . . it was an exultation. Kids today need dope. I did not need dope. I didn't know what liquor was, what cigarettes were. My great joy was singing."

After another year and a half of working 104 hours a week in his father's bicycle business, Louis had had it. Music won out and he and his wife left for New York, where he worked as a tinsmith while attending the Mannes School, studying voice under Martial Singher. Two years later, in 1953, Louis went back to Canada to win an important contest called "The Singing Stars of Tomorrow." Then, in 1955, it was the Met auditions, and again he won. He was offered a Met contract, but the Met's musical adviser, Max Rudolf, told him to refuse it, because he was not prepared for it. The offer with its $175 a week, compared to the $85 a week he was making as a tinsmith, made it hard to refuse, but with his wife's urging, he did.

That year he got a contract with the New York City Opera, singing only one performance in seven weeks. Then from 1956 to 1960 he auditioned for the Met roughly three times a year.

"I got very fed up after this," he said. "In 1961 Roberto Bauer called me and said, 'Mr. Bing would like you to sing for him.'

"I said, 'To sing for him an audition . . . no more! That is the end. Tell him I am singing a performance in this city [Louis was in Italy at the time], to come, buy his own ticket, and listen to my performance.' Afterward my agent asked me what I had done to Mr.

Bing. He had said, 'As long as I'll be the general manager of the Metropolitan, never is he going to sing there.'

"I made him a liar. I sang at the Met before he left the house."

This took place in 1972, when Louis made his Met debut as Golaud in *Pelléas* after having had successes as one of the greatest baritones in Europe's major opera houses.

"Louis, let's talk about technique," I said. "How did you go about learning to sing?"

Louis told me a most unusual story. Right after he turned down his Metropolitan Opera contract in 1955, he got an offer from the San Francisco Opera. He had six months to prepare for the engagements and decided that he'd have to really learn how to sing in the interim. There was an empty room where he lived and every day for three months he went into that room and stood about three feet from the bare wall and meditated for at least five or six hours on how to sing. And he claimed that this is how he learned the basics. As a result, Louis said, "The less you're going to sing when studying, the better it becomes." I was curious as to why he said this. "The reason is," he went on, "you have to discover inside of you. The mind does everything. The voice will not do anything by itself. It has to be commanded. As a teacher, I never talk about sound, because for me the sound is the least important of all. You have muscles that are obstructing. You have to eliminate these muscles. How? There's only one way we can do it. Thinking [knowing] where they are and eliminating them, because we should be master of our body. I call my way of teaching 'Nine Laws.'"

"What is the first law?" I asked.

"The way to stand on your feet. You don't stand right, you create tension. Never stand on two feet. Either you create complete tension, or you transfer the whole tension to one place."

Louis demonstrated by standing on both feet, drawing attention to his tense thorax and body. As he shifted his weight to one foot only, his shoulders seemed to settle and relax.

"I see. You stand on one foot, and the tension transfers to that foot," I said. "Very good. Now, what's the second law?"

"Support." He demonstrated by placing my hand on his abdomen. As the lower abdomen pressed in, the stomach area came out.

"We have two sets of muscles here. The lowest muscles of your abdomen, that's—"

"The support," I said.

"It's a small action . . . very supple. The reasoning of support is like the shock absorbers of a car—you know, the bouncing.

"You don't take the breath . . ." He demonstrated how not to take a breath by using the chest. "There's only one way of breathing. Whenever you breathe you go down there." He indicated his lower abdomen.

"You obviously are used to breathing properly," I observed, "because, in spite of your weight, you do not have any hernias, which are so common among male opera singers."

"The reason that I don't have a hernia is because I'm using that muscle," he said.

"Instead of pushing against that muscle, you are using it as a protective floor . . . Now, what is the third law?"

"How to breathe. The thing that is most important for a singer is his mental approach. If a student wants to study with me, I tell him, 'Maybe from the next three to six months you might not make one sound.'"

"Then you feel the concepts must come first," I said. "How you should breathe . . ."

"The way you take the air," he agreed. "You don't *take* the air, you *shoot* the air. Not that you intake [inhale] the air. Always believe that the air goes toward the brains, not that you take the oxygen into the lungs. The terrible thing about singing is . . . you emphasize, you emphasize, you overdo. If you do the opposite, you don't emphasize, that means the right amount of air will come in. Otherwise you emphasize so much that automatically you take too much.

"For instance, when I teach, I always say you have to believe that you have a little pipe right between your two teeth." He indicated his two upper front teeth. "The air goes just behind the teeth. You don't *take* the air! Don't swallow the air!"

"By that do you mean don't take too great a quantity of air?"

"You can take three times more . . . but you don't emphasize!"

"Ah," I said, comprehending, "you mean de-emphasize the process of taking the breath. Taking the air through the little pipe makes the process gentler."

"Now," he continued, "never think that you are going to inflate your lungs. No feeling of expansion. They will inflate themselves. Another thing, never breathe only by the mouth, and never breathe only by the nose."

"Okay. Now, what is the fourth law?"

"How to open the throat. Now, everything has to be done with a certain amount of flexibility. To bring down the larynx is not a natural thing."

"The larynx must be brought down, though?" I asked.

"Yes!" With that he demonstrated with an up and down jiggling motion of his Adam's apple, absolutely independent of his jaw, which did not move. "The point is, when you start to move other things, like the jaw, with it, you make an obstruction. It's like a child. You say, 'Make a wink.' What does he do?"

"He squeezes both eyes," I said. "Similarly, instead of everything around the larynx, like the jaw, pulling down with it, you must learn an independent motion within."

"Yes, yes! You have to come to the point where you can move muscles. You see a man who becomes like Mr. World. He can move all different muscles, one at a time. A person like that can do it. Why not me?

"At some one point everything becomes one action, but you know that each one is an individual action. Later in life, when you start to have trouble, you have to be able to understand where *is* the trouble. Everybody gets in trouble, but it's to be able to come out of trouble . . ."

"Anything else on the open throat?"

"Not only that it's a movement up and down," he continued, "but you have to try to feel the expansion." He demonstrated this by turning his hand palm up, with the thumb and fingertips touching, and slowly expanding the fingers open like a flower blossoming.

"What you're doing reminds me of an expanding pipe," I said.

"Exactly. And a pipe that will go up and down."

"But a pipe that feels as though it's expanding in the area of the larynx . . . the Adam's apple . . . *not* in the back of the throat [the pharynx]," I added.

"Exactly. But what the student does when you ask him to bring down the larynx . . ." He pulled down his jaw and his head. "Your head cannot be up, cannot be down. You bring it down, the throat cannot function anymore, because you collapse the larynx. It collapses, not only down, but also up. If you want a pipe to give you a tremendous jet, make it straight. Bend it . . . what happens? The jet won't be the same. You have to eliminate obstructions. It's vertical. You want to sing to the balcony." He leaned back with his body, not moving his head.

"What is the fifth law?"

"The tension of the cords," he replied. "The thing is to make people realize 'When are you using the cords?' There is a very simple thing that can be done with the slightest sound." With that, Louis made a tiny, raspy, scratchy sound. "The tickling that you feel . . . it irritates. It's exactly the irritation that will give you an indication where the cords are. Using the muscles alone, you don't know where they are. You come to the point where you have to find a certain feeling for them.

"And my feeling with the cords is to never sing with the air going through the cords, but with the cords going through the air . . . that you're compressing the air. You have to have the feeling that the cords are going down, but one thing . . . it's got a suspension in it. It's elastic.

"It's the cords that make the pressure, not the wind [breath]. But the voice is the most flexible part of ourselves. That pressure is never a great pressure. It's very flexible. Remember, the cords have to go down into the air. The cords have to be tense like a violin string, with air for a bow."

"What is the sixth law?"

"Broadness of sound in the cheekbones. There's the upper part of the face . . . we're taught that we sing with the resonance. What makes the resonance? Collapse the cords . . . where is the resonance? There is none. You tense the cords a little bit . . . there is more resonance. Naturally, there is a certain cavity . . ."

"But you don't *put* it there . . ." I anticipated.

"But you do! You know, the upper palate lifts. It gives more space. At the same time, in your imagination, you have to think that you are giving more facial space. This is elasticity, more than getting space. It's kind of imaginative. You have to feel that you become very, very broad in the face. The actual sound is a little point about eighteen inches in front of your nose, and you sing into that little hole. Except, everything has to be very spacy.

"My feeling is, like you have a concrete cavity here. I'm not talking about the nose. The nose for me is a piece of meat."

"You're speaking of the teeth," I said.

"Exactly. It is the bone cavities that you have to reach, as much as possible. How do you take out the meat you've got inside of your palate? Inside of your nasal passages? The meat for me is a restriction. You have to reach, as much as possible, the bone cavity . . . *not* the meat cavity."

"How do you do that?"

"Add the sensation . . . broadness of the cheekbones."

"And that's the sixth law. Let's go on to the seventh."

"Seven and six . . . they are about the same thing. If I bring my eyes down, I don't have any sensation of the ceiling. But when I take a breath, I am aware that I take the air from this whole roomful of air. With the eyes, for instance, just a lifting of the eyes makes me aware . . . awareness with the eyes . . ."

"You want awareness of the space around you," I said.

"Exactly."

"That's the seventh law?"

"Yes. You can put it, if you want, 'lifting of the eyes.' "

"The eighth law?"

"It's a combination of the intake of air and sensation."

"Explain."

"The sensation is . . . while I take the air, instead of swallowing the air, I absorb the air, which goes toward the brains. Oxygen goes into rotation and at the end of the rotation, goes out. There's a suspension. A *cycle* and a *suspension*. The air that goes in is being suspended in your whole body, blood stream . . . everything. Tremendous circulation. It creates in the human being a tremendous force. You know, it's part yoga."

"Yes, like prana," I added.

"There is a suspension between the intake [inhaling] and exhaling. It transfers itself into a tremendous power. If I push it out, I lose what I want. If I'm not pushing it out, I'm using the actual strength of it. That gives me the power of my voice."

"You always achieve this suspension . . . equilibrium . . . before you attack," I said.

"Think of a tightrope walker. When he starts to walk on the wire, what does he do? He touches the wire with his toe . . . his feet. Why? Does he go . . . gazooom?"

"No," I said.

"He touches it. Then he slides. He wants to know exactly where it's supposed to be touching. Because there's only one place that he knows . . . that the wire touches. He's safe. He's like a blind man. He doesn't have eyes. He has feet."

"So this pause of concentration is the eighth law," I said in summation. "What is the ninth law?"

"Make the sound," he said smiling.

"That has made for a most interesting interview," I concluded. "You are a very unusual person—with a deep, mystical nature—that is enthralled by singing. It shows in your powerful artistic achievements."

Louis summed it up: "We as human beings have great moments in life. But I think the greatest moments in your life are the most intimate moments . . . to make love with the woman you love, and it becomes sublime. Well, when you make the right sound, it becomes the same ecstasy as the intimate moments of your life."

Leo P. Reckford, M.D.

FROM DR. RECKFORD'S DIARY OF THE YEAR 1959:

Monday, March 30, 1959: 4:30 p.m.   J. Hines in my office. Diagnosis: tracheitis. Local treatment and antibiotics. Informed Met for possible replacement for Saturday matinee of *Don Carlos*.

Tuesday, March 31, 1959: 12:45 p.m.   J. Hines in my office. Continue local treatments and medication.

Friday, April 3, 1959: 12:30 p.m.   J. Hines in my office, great improvement noted, but still some insecurity about next day's performance. Suggested ultrasonic treatment before performance the next day.

Saturday, April 4, 1959:   I was in Mount Snow in Vermont, watching my children skiing. Listened in my car to the opera broadcast. Was delighted with Hines's performance.

"How could you sing so well with the condition you were in? Did you use the ultrasonic?" Dr. Reckford, one of the most highly esteemed throat specialists in the world, was questioning me on the phone.

"Yes, I tried the ultrasonic and it helped me enormously," I replied.

"Hmm . . . you'd better come in and we'll discuss it further."

A month before I had been visiting with my best friend in New Jersey, Dr. Arthur D'Alessandro, a renowned surgeon. He was acquiring an ultrasonic vibrator, which was supposed to be effective in reducing swelling (edema) in traumatized tissues.

I asked him if these high-frequency waves could penetrate the cartilage of the larynx, reaching the vocal cords and the trachea, and he affirmed this. I theorized that the main cause of not being able to sing with a windpipe infection was the edema in the tissues and muscles under the cords, and that if the ultrasound could reduce that edema, even temporarily, it could be most useful. He said he would be willing to try it on me the next time I got in trouble. As luck would have it, I came down with a fierce windpipe infection five days before my most important performance of the season, doing the role of Filippo in *Don Carlos* on the Saturday broadcast from the Met.

Dr. Reckford, on Friday, said that it was quite possible I would not be able to sing the next afternoon. I persuaded the Met to let me withhold my decision on canceling until twelve noon the day of the show, explaining I intended to try this new experimental treatment at eleven forty-five.

The next morning I could hardly speak. At eleven-thirty I drove to Dr. D'Alessandro's office and took the ultrasonic on my larynx for ten minutes, at the end of which time my speaking voice seemed to be restored almost to normal. I decided to go on.

I did quite well in the first two acts, but felt that the stimulating effect of the treatment was beginning to wear off just before my most important aria, "Ella giammai m'amò." I was forced to use all the know-how that fifteen years of operatic experience had given me. I feel that the know-how and the treatment together made the performance possible. I was made well aware of the fact that no scientific miracle can take the place of experience and knowledge, but it can be a great supportive tool in emergencies.

Dr. Reckford heard the broadcast and was very pleasantly surprised, especially in a performance where I might not have been able to sing at all. This aroused his scientific curiosity and prompted his phone call to me, after which he went right out and ordered an ultrasonic machine for his own use.* He has now employed it as a therapeutic tool on most of opera's and Broadway's stars with great success for a period of more than two decades.

Dr. Reckford has been my throat doctor since January of 1948. He has a rare combination of qualifications that make him unique. Leo Recknitzer—that was his legal name—graduated as a medical doctor from the University of Vienna in 1928, but he had already made his operatic debut in 1927 as Dr. Falke in *Die Fledermaus.* He also sang Sarastro in *The Magic Flute* and describes himself as

* Dr. Reckford's version is given later in this chapter.

being "terrible . . . a baritone with a low D and no high notes, who didn't know how to sing." He had been a good pianist from childhood, playing school concerts, etc., until he was sixteen. He also composed music. At the same time he went to medical school, he also attended the New Vienna Conservatory as a vocal student.

He emigrated to the United States in 1939. In 1944, when he became a citizen, he intended to enlist in the U. S. Army, and changed his name so that if he were captured by the Germans they would not know that he was a German Jew. After such a meticulous preparation for an Army career, he was rejected because he was forty-one years old and had a duodenal ulcer.

His subsequent writing and teaching (he is Clinical Associate Professor of Otorhinolaryngology at New York University), as well as his vast experience in treating ailing opera and Broadway stars, have made him one of the leading authorities on phoniatrics* in the world. So now I sat in his office on the upper West Side of Manhattan on a pleasant fall evening (made all the more pleasant because I was not there as a patient) to learn something that I could share with my readers.

First, Dr. Reckford gave me a brief history of his field from the time of Demosthenes up to the present. Some facts, such as García being the first person ever to see his own vocal cords in action, were familiar to me. Other facts were not. I was told how the field of vocal physiology was founded by Antoine Ferrein, who wrote about his experiments on an excised dog larynx in 1741: "I approximated the lips of the glottis and blew strongly into the trachea; the organ seemed to become revitalized and produced, not only a tone, but a real voice, which was more pleasant to me than the most beautiful concert." It was he who coined the term "*cordes vocales.*"

In 1837, Johann Mueller suspended an excised cadaver larynx in a frame, which permitted measurable changes in the position, tension, and vibration of the vocal cords, as well as the use of various air pressures. He subsequently demonstrated that in order to maintain a particular pitch as you increased the air pressure, you had to

---

* Phoniatrics is the science that deals with the research of voice physiology and pathology, and with the rehabilitation and habilitation of disturbed vocal functions.

Leo P. Reckford, M.D.

reduce the tension on the vocal cords, otherwise the pitch would get higher as the pressure increased. These results were amended about forty years ago by Dr. Deszö Weiss, who demonstrated it to be the opposite for the chest voice: there is a tendency to flat with increased air pressure. In the high voice, above the pure chest range, where the falsetto is added to the sound, the "compensation of forces" is still valid.

This concurred with my own practical experience. I had found that too much pressure of breath, when trying to make a big sound, tended to make the tone sharp on high notes and flat on low notes. I found I could avoid the tendency to sharp on the top, for example, by not making the tone overly bright, but letting a bit more air pass the cords, giving a slightly darker, rounder sound, which, of course, corresponds to less tension. Also, instead of trying to make big, black low tones, which tend to flat, I learned to keep the sound more focused, brighter and higher, which corresponds to more tension on the cords.

I then questioned Dr. Reckford on what happens physiologically with regard to the vocal cords when we sing variously with falsetto, mixed voice, and chest voice.

"In a falsetto," he said, "you only let the edges vibrate. In the mixed voice more than the edges vibrate. In the chest voice the entire width of each vocal cord vibrates. In the falsetto, muscularly we only *pull* on the cords, lengthening them with the crico-thyroid muscles, and air passes, only vibrating the edges. I'll show it to you on your fingers." He had me hold my hands out toward him, palms down. He then grasped the tips of my index fingers, which were close to each other, and pulled them gently but firmly toward himself.

"I know the cords open like a V," I said. "The opening is . . ."

"In the back," he supplied. "They [the cords] are always closed in the front—the *anterior commisure*. There are muscles outside here"—he indicated the front of the larynx—"the crico-thyroid muscles, which pull on the vocal cords."

At this point he decided to clarify the function and anatomy of the crico-thyroid muscles, saying, "It's not complicated and I am sure you will understand it." He began sketching the larynx as follows:

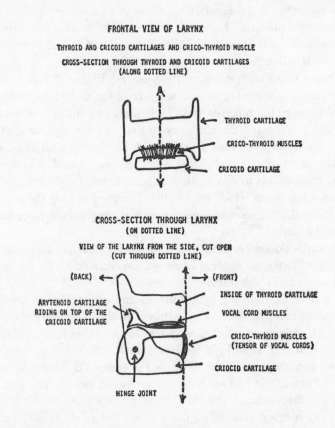

FRONTAL VIEW OF LARYNX

THYROID AND CRICOID CARTILAGES AND CRICO-THYROID MUSCLE
CROSS-SECTION THROUGH THYROID AND CRICOID CARTILAGES
(ALONG DOTTED LINE)

THYROID CARTILAGE
CRICO-THYROID MUSCLES
CRICOID CARTILAGE

CROSS-SECTION THROUGH LARYNX
(ON DOTTED LINE)

VIEW OF THE LARYNX FROM THE SIDE, CUT OPEN
(CUT THROUGH DOTTED LINE)

(BACK)   (FRONT)

INSIDE OF THYROID CARTILAGE
ARYTENOID CARTILAGE
RIDING ON TOP OF THE
CRICOID CARTILAGE
VOCAL CORD MUSCLES
CRICO-THYROID MUSCLES
(TENSOR OF VOCAL CORDS)
CRIOCID CARTILAGE
HINGE JOINT

This was his explanation of the diagrams of the laryngeal cartilages and muscles:

"When the crico-thyroid muscles contract (shorten), they pull the cricoid cartilage upward toward the thyroid cartilage, in the front. The back part of the cricoid cartilage, with the arytenoid cartilage, which rides on top of the cricoid cartilage, moves or turns in the hinge joint backward, pulling on the vocal cords, trying to

Leo P. Reckford, M.D.

lengthen them, thinning them out and increasing their inner tension passively. At the same time, the thyro-arytenoid, or 'vocal muscles' (inside the vocal cords), may contract too and try to resist the cords' lengthening. This increases the tension of the vocal cords, this time actively. The proper coordination of these two muscle groups, working together as far as the tension is concerned—"synergists"—and against each other as far as lengthening is concerned—"antagonists"—this coordination is one of the basic principles of vocal technique in the changing of pitch. Like all coordinated muscle actions, this technique can be learned and practiced. A little skill or talent might help to do it with ease, smoothly, and in the end automatically.

"For the mathematician, Jerome Hines, I add here the formula for pitch (frequencies) for the human voice:

$$N = \frac{1}{2\pi} \sqrt{\frac{E}{M}} \ .$$

N is the frequency, E the elasticity coefficient or tension, and M is the vibrating mass.

"When we stretch our vocal cords only through the action of the crico-thyroid muscles, without the contraction of the vocal muscles (thyro-arytenoid), we produce the so-called 'falsetto' voice. The vocal cords are actually elongated or thinned out, and leave an oval chink open between the adducted cords. The airflow passes easily through this opening and sets only the inner edges of the cords into vibration. At the same time we might feel a sensation of release through the relaxation of the vocal muscles. By the most subtle and intricate coordination of these two muscle groups in connection with a gradual increase and decrease of air pressure, the change from one register into another can be achieved. High, middle, and low registers should smoothly flow into each other by the skill of the artist, like the automatic shift in an automobile or like the fine coordination of our eye muscles, when we accommodate to distance or light difficulties."

"How," I asked, "does this fit in with the common slogan 'Think low when you sing high'?" But it struck me then that there might be another meaning to it apart from its application to the larynx. "Or does it mean think low in terms of breath support?"

Leo P. Reckford, M.D.

"It might have some explanation in the low placement of muscular action for well-supported tones," he observed. "I am inclined to consider it a very helpful image to distract the attention of the singer from his larynx to a lower place on his anatomy. Any concentration on a certain organ will eventually result in a subconscious overexertion, and might lead to unnecessary tensions. I do not fight helpful images if they produce good results, even if they lack anatomical or physiological justification. Caruso's ideas about his own vocal technique were full of misconceptions. How wonderful that nobody tried to correct them."

"We just touched on the subject of support," I said. "Let's pursue it further. How do you describe it?"

"Breath support . . . *appoggio* . . . *Atemstütze* . . . The scientific, rather dry definition," he said, "is: the stimulation of inspiratory muscles during singing, which is voiced expiration, in order to counteract a too fast loss of breath, and to increase the air pressure, or modulate it at will. The chest is kept in inspiratory position, and so is the upper part of the abdomen. '*Appoggio* is a conscious retardation of expiration' (Winckel 1952). 'Any tone that oscillates with rhythmical breath pressure is well supported' (Hartlieb)."

"What does that all mean in singers' language?" I asked.

"You buy yourself a balloon," he smiled, "and you blow it up, standing undressed in front of a mirror. You don't do it very fast. You will see that the chest remains lifted for a little while, and also the belly, or abdomen, remains extended for a while. Of course, the diaphragm, which is a muscular plate, moves up and down. When you move it down, you contract. When it is moving up, you relax it. It separates the thorax from the abdomen. The term 'diaphragmatic breathing' is very frequently wrongly used. Many singing teachers say you have to pull in the abdomen to support the diaphragm. It isn't pulled in right away. You start with the pressure low down, in the lower part of the abdomen, and then gradually the abdomen goes in, and finally also the chest goes down.

"When you contract the diaphragm, you do it for inhaling. You widen the chest,* and the abdomen is pushed out. When you ex-

---

* Note that he did not say raise it!

Leo P. Reckford, M.D.

hale, you relax the diaphragm, and the abdominal wall pushes the diaphragm up *gradually,* not suddenly."

"You are saying there are two opposing forces," I asked, "the diaphragmatic muscles in opposition to the muscles of the abdominal wall?"

"That's right."

"Is there any relationship between this state of two forces balanced against each other and the idea of keeping too much pressure from building up directly under and against the cords?"

"Yes," he said. "In case you do it wrongly and squeeze *in* the abdomen in order to support better, which some singing teachers, in misconception, teach . . . or when you want to sing a high tone, you might (*ugh*) pull in fast, and in this moment you struggle here [he indicated his throat], and you feel it immediately as a closing of the larynx.

"I asked Mr. Titta Ruffo once, 'What is *appoggio?*' He said, 'Very simple.' He did a little trick: while he was singing a high F sharp, he pushed the piano away with his abdomem. He said, 'Why can I do it? Because this [the abdomen] is still bulging and tight.'"

"You mentioned a 'closing of the larynx,'" I observed. "What does an *open throat* mean to you?"

"By an 'open throat' we understand that no voluntary unnecessary muscle tensions should be used on the larynx . . . external muscles, and even internal muscles. Still, you bring the vocal cords together, right? in order to phonate. The inner vocal muscles, which are inside the vocal cords, must be tense, of course. But they are very small and you don't know when you are tensing them. When you use the pressure in adduction you squeeze the cords together, and that means the throat is not more *gola aperta* (open-throated), but it's a squeezed throat . . . a pressed throat."

Once again he had me hold my hand out. This time, instead of pulling my two index fingers toward himself, he pressed them together at the knuckles.

"When you press them together, you get the pressed sound."

"And that squeeze comes from the internal muscles inside the vocal cords," I said.

"The adductors and the internal and external thyro-arytenoid muscles. That you should never do." He demonstrated with a tight squeezed sound. *"Gola aperta* [open throat] means . . ." He again demonstrated, but this time with an easy, floating sound. "You pull [with the crico-thyroid muscles], and the tension inside will be increased passively, and, as a counteraction, also actively. The so-called vocal muscles will become tense just by pulling on them."

"Most singers say an open throat is a depressed larynx," I observed.

"No! I've heard about this also, very, very much. When you lift your larynx up, that is not helpful for your vocal production. But when you pull it down with force, you can only do it with a pressure, usually a pressure on your tongue. Both are wrong. Pulling it higher or pressing it low down is wrong."

"How about simply dropping the larynx loosely, as in singing the vowel *awe* instead of *aah?*" I persisted.

"The larynx should make minimal excursions up or down. It should rather stay more or less in a relaxed position. As long as you don't use pressure and the sound is good, you're okay. I'll accept everything that makes the sound good, and doesn't hurt you, and doesn't make you tired, and doesn't make you hoarse."

"And the larynx?"

"When you sing an *ee*," he continued, "it goes a little way up. When you sing an *oo*, it goes a little way down. This is a natural thing. But the excursions are measured in millimeters, and not, as some teachers stress, in centimeters or inches. It's definitely wrong!"

"Now, what do you think about placement?" I asked.

"That's a very important question," he said. "You can *place* a beam of light to a certain place, because it's straight. But the sound goes in concentric waves from the source. It goes in hemispheres away from you, so the placement of an airwave is impossible. You can't focus it; it goes and vibrates anyplace where it fits. This means it resonates in the resonating tubes, resonating chambers: the pharynx, the nasopharynx, the muscles, the bones of the head, everywhere. It doesn't only resonate up in the head, it resonates also down in the chest. We call it chest voice, because a singer has the feeling that more vibrations in certain tones are in the chest than in the head.

Leo P. Reckford, M.D.

"And then there are the very difficult expressions of 'head voice' and 'chest voice.' It doesn't exist that way, because the sound vibrates in the head *and* chest. But what do the singing teachers mean by placement? They mean that there is a place of strongest vibration somewhere in the head, or somewhere . . . When you sing an ideally free tone, it will vibrate somewhere more than another place. It depends on the pitch, the air pressure, and the person . . . the formation of his head and bones and so on. So it will never be the same place for Mr. Hines and for Mr. Corelli. But there will be a certain place of strongest vibration felt by the singer. If he feels it on a certain spot, and the next time he feels it again, then he can speak of placement. In a way it is a help for him. So the next time he feels it there, he knows he has the same place . . . and apparently the right thing again, but the placement of the tone is only the result of the good sound. You can't say there is no such thing as placement, but you cannot direct the placement. It is the result of good singing, not its origin, and not the cause."

"Earlier in the interview you spoke about how only the edges of the cords vibrate when a singer uses pure falsetto, part of the cords when he uses the middle or mixed voice, and all of the cords when he uses the chest voice," I began.

"García was deeply interested in what happens when you sing in the high register and when you sing in the low register," Dr. Reckford observed. "He explained at that time, 'A register is a sequence of tones which are produced by the same mechanical principle, and have a specific quality of sound, in contrast to another sequence of tones which are produced by a different mechanical principle, and have also a different quality of sound. If I sing in a high register and a low register, these two registers might overlap, and that's what we call the mixed voice.' This was one hundred forty years ago. In a way it was accepted until very recently, when I started to question it. What I question is the 'different mechanical principle.' It is entirely different only in the extremes, as in the extremes of falsetto, or high voice, and the chest, or low voice.

"*Chest voice* and *head voice* are singing teachers' expressions which mean, in one case, more vibrations in the head, and, in the other, more vibrations in the chest. But these expressions don't say anything about the formation of the two 'voices,' or the production.

"So far, García is right: two different mechanical principles, one method is only the edge vibrating, the other method is the entire width and the entire body of the vocal cords vibrating, moving up and outward, and back again. How can you mix two different mechanical principles? You cannot! And that's where I came in and said, 'Something is wrong!' You cannot mix two entirely different mechanical principles."

"What muscles are being used to produce the low, or chest, voice?" I asked.

"The thyro-arytenoid muscles—call them the vocal muscles—internal and external. Now, what happens in the so-called *mixed voice?* The more air pressure you put under that falsetto, gradually the falsetto becomes a little bit more full. It becomes a full tone of the head voice. A tenor, especially, can start with a falsetto on B natural and gradually increase and make it more forte until it becomes a brilliant, half-mixed tone . . . the full tone of the head voice. Also a baritone can do it, but with a tenor you sometimes don't know if it is a falsetto or isn't. When he sings a C sharp or a D, he definitely starts with a falsetto, but he might be able to put enough pressure on it that the vocal cords come closer and closer, and much more than only the edges vibrate.

"When you can finally mix it to the degree that half of the width of each vocal cord is vibrating, you have the ideal mixed tone. But it is still only a quantitative difference between the falsetto and the full tone of the head voice, and between the full tone of the head voice and the mixed voice, and from the mixed voice again only a quantitative change into the full chest voice. More and more of the width of the vocal cords is engaged for vibration. That means that it is only the quantity of vibration which changes. It is not the quality of the whole production."

"What causes more and more of the cords to vibrate? Doesn't one then have to consciously put into play the internal muscles in the cords?" I asked.

"The stronger the air pressure, the more they [the vocal cords] will come together automatically. That is the correct way. When you have to press them together in order to make more sound,

Leo P. Reckford, M.D.

that's wrong . . . Let us go to the trumpet player. The human voice is a musical instrument very similar to the trumpet, only that a trumpet player uses the lips instead of the vocal cords. The lips vibrate and make an ugly, not very musical tone."

"And so do the cords probably," I interjected.

"Probably it's not a very musical tone if you cut off the head. In some cases I have the feeling it would sound better," he observed humorously.* "When you blow air into a trumpet, nothing comes out but air. But if the lips make an ugly little sound, it is transformed into a beautiful trumpet tone. Now, in a singer, the lips are the vocal cords. These lips make the sound and from here on [he indicated from the larynx up] is the trumpet . . . the resonator. When the trumpet player wants to blow louder, he doesn't bend the trumpet, he doesn't squeeze it, he holds it the same way he held it before. He only blows harder, but leaves the trumpet alone. It is the air pressure which increases the sound. All you do is blow a little bit harder, pressing the lips a little bit tighter, otherwise the tone will break. You have to coordinate the tension of the lips to your pressure."

"Then," I began, "regarding falsetto, head and chest voice . . ."

"Call them high register, middle register, and low register. Actually these are all produced in the same way, and—this is my idea—the change from one to the other is only quantitative, with more and more, or less and less, vibration of the width of the cords."

Dr. Reckford and I discussed many other details of the relationship between vocal technique and physiology. I personally would be most happy to see Dr. Reckford's vast experience of over half a century of treating vocal problems put into book form, and I am personally grateful for the thirty-three years of advice and help he has given me. I am sure an incredible number of great performers would willingly join me in this accolade.

In contrast, there are a few singers I have known who couldn't abide the man after one visit. They complain, "He tried to tell me how to sing!" When a singer goes to a doctor with red, swollen vocal cords, he wants a quick miracle cure through pills, sprays, and glittering electronic devices; he doesn't want to be told he is

---

* Dr. Reckford admits saying this but later added, "I repent."

doing something wrong, that his cords are being abused. He much prefers being called a postnasal drip! His ego gets in the way, leading to an early vocal demise.

I have endured thirty-six years as a leading singer at the Met, breaking Antonio Scotti's all-time record. I believe that one of the major factors in my survival has been a willingness to listen to criticism of my vocal technique, and Dr. Reckford has handed me plenty of it over the years. Thank you, Leo.

Gail Robinson

Gail Robinson has been associated with the coloratura soprano rep-
ertoire since her debut as Lucia di Lammermoor in Memphis in
1967. Miss Robinson was born in Mississippi and American-
trained. She obtained a Metropolitan Opera Studio contract and
later debuted at the Met in 1970. Lucia, Gilda in RIGOLETTO, *and*
Pamina in THE MAGIC FLUTE *are among the roles she has sung at*
the Met. 🎶

PROLOGUE: JUNE 1978

It was a warm June night in Central Park. The Sheep Meadow
was jammed with a hundred thousand opera fans who had come to
sit on the grass and listen to *Rigoletto,* munch sandwiches, sip wine,
follow scores, conduct, or smooch. We artists, seated on a giant out-
door stage, are always treated to one of the most interesting, and
oftentimes distracting, shows that New York has to offer. For us the
real performance is the one taking place on the grass below: half-
dressed gays entwining in time to the music, children and stray
dogs ambling aimlessly about, erstwhile conductors melodramati-
cally cueing in the soloists and instruments, and music lovers
cozily wrapped two by two in their blankets. All this is the singer's-
eye view of "The Met in the Parks."

The performers on the grass took time out from their activities to
listen and stare in rapt attention as our tall, slim Gilda from Mississippi began the opening phrases of "Caro nome." A serene peace
settled over the giant mass of humanity that carpeted the meadow,
a peace induced by the gentle brushing tones of Gail Robinson's
voice. I was as spellbound as the rest of the audience, perhaps even
more, because being up so close I could fully appreciate the tranquillity on that gentle, expressive face, observe at first hand her
smooth, effortless technique. After the aria came to an end the ova-

tion almost didn't. I wholeheartedly shared the audience's enthusiasm and decided then and there that Gail would have to be included among the artists in this book. True, she had not yet had a long career like most of the others I had chosen to interview, but she had such an exceptional quality of repose in her singing that I was intrigued. I asked her to write her own story, and it came out as follows:

JUNE 1980

GAIL ROBINSON: God gave me a voice. As a child I sang all day . . . making mud pies or building sand castles. Even now if I'm in a taxi or doing grocery shopping, I'm always subconsciously humming. (It drives my husband crazy!)

I had a natural ability to harmonize, and I played the piano by ear, picking out hymns by age four. I had no background for classical music. In fact, no one in my family as far back as we can remember was musically inclined.

By the time I was a teenager, I was well known in our small town as a pop singer, doing songs Connie Francis style for local civic clubs, et cetera. Since I was brought up in a Baptist church, there was never an opportunity to sing the well-known liturgical literature . . . it was mostly gospel singing. So it was somewhat a surprise to discover that there was another voice somewhere inside me.

I had studied piano for several years before beginning voice lessons. My first teacher was herself a mezzo, and because of my well-developed chest voice, she tended to guide me toward a dramatic style of singing. I think the first aria I learned was "Dove sono."

Singing pop music for so long had left me with a not so uncommon vocal problem. I had a strong chest voice from C below middle C to B flat above middle C . . . and a strong head voice from G below high C to C above high C. In between, however, was practically nothing but air. So the task in that early year of study was to try to blend those two voices into one. The agility, the staccato, the trills were there, though, from the very beginning.

I had pneumonia when I was fifteen, and my father brought the radio and put it beside my bed. I heard a beautiful high, floating voice singing a song I'd never heard. The words I couldn't understand, but the melody never left me. I went to the music store days later, told the man I wanted that song from "Rig-a-something" that went "La-la-la-la-la-la-la," and was off to my voice lesson that day with "Caro nome" in my hand.

That started a new adventure for me. I didn't dare let the cat out of the bag, though. What would my friends think if they knew I was going to become an opera singer? Everybody knew opera singers might as well have two heads, they were so strange!

I later got a voice scholarship to Memphis State University, but I had never yet seen an opera! My first experience on stage was in the chorus of the school's production of *Mignon*. I was given a beautiful purple velvet costume, and I was so spellbound that at the dress rehearsal all I could do was stand there with my mouth open. The stage director stopped the rehearsal and stormed down the aisle. "Miss Robinson," he shouted, "do you intend to sing, or are you just going to stand there?"

After debuting in the role of Fiordiligi (quite a part for a nineteen-year-old), I entered the Met auditions. Much to my surprise, I won the regional competition, and the National Finals in New York. I was awarded the Fisher Foundation Award and an invitation to join the Met Opera Studio. From there, I joined the Met in 1970, doing Papagena, Barbarina, et cetera. Then came the night in Detroit when I stepped in at the last minute and sang *Lucia*.

So the road to success was very short for me . . . not quite four years from the time I sang my first role at the university. The pitfalls, however, were inevitable.

For the first time, I seemed to be confronted constantly with the word "technique." My colleagues in the Studio would sit for endless hours and discuss "technique," "placement," "support," "resonance." I didn't know what any of those things were. I just sang. (Once after listening to a discussion about "tongue placement," I couldn't sing for days because my tongue kept getting in the way!)

As a result of *listening* constantly to other singers, I began unconsciously to imitate different vocal sounds. I would go for a voice lesson, and my teacher would be able to tell whom I had heard the night before.

Gail Robinson

The greatest realization of the word "technique" came to me during a period of serious illness in my early twenties. I found that my body would not respond to what had always come naturally. I was forced to develop and fully understand my instrument, and learn, not just how to make a beautiful sound, but how to sing in adversity.

It was a blessing in disguise, for I find now that I can sing under almost any circumstances. Just this season, I did Gildas at the Met with a broken foot in a cast, and once with laryngitis so bad that I could hardly speak . . . but I could sing.

There are only a few basics that I believe in for myself. First and foremost, I never push. My voice is not large, but, if properly produced, it carries well. I strive for a clear, bell-like, almost ethereal quality. Looking back over reviews one word pops out at me so often . . . "effortless." I'm not sure if that's good or bad. Sometimes I think the audience would rather see someone strain and push than to see someone who looks as if she's not working. After a performance of Constanza in *Die Entführung aus dem Serail* last season, a woman came backstage and said, "I watched you with binoculars, and you never breathed!" Well, I did breathe, and I was gauging how much breath to take and how much to let out. But that's my job, and I don't feel that the audience, which is there to involve itself in a plot, should be distracted by such things. Let me say just a few things about breath. When I sing, I'm aware of everything from my shoulders to the pelvic bones. That is to say, it's not just a matter of the diaphragm. The whole rib cage, front and back, must be filled with air and continue in an outward motion till the end of the phrase. One has to be careful, especially with a voice like mine, where sometimes long runs are involved, not to let out too much air. If you sing a scale with a slightly exaggerated h between notes resulting in ha-ha-ha, not only is the run choppy, but you run the risk of not finishing the phrase! The phrase "open throat" doesn't mean much to me. I just don't think about it. If I have any feeling in the throat at all, then I know I'm doing something wrong.

I try to keep the sound very frontal . . . sort of between the top teeth and the eyes. Some singers talk of feeling the sound in the back of the head, or other such places. I just think of singing in the mask. Sometimes a slight smile which raises the cheeks will put my voice in just the right spot. The sound starts there and ends there.

The jaw is also very important, and I'm always conscious of keeping it back out of the way. If not, I lose some of the sound behind the bottom teeth.

I'm not a very academic singer. I hate doing scales, even though I make myself do them occasionally. I find, as I said earlier, that the fact that I'm always singing or humming *sotto voce* keeps the voice flexible. I'm fortunate. I can wake up at eight A.M. and the voice is there. But then I'm fortunate for so many reasons. God gave me the voice and the determination. But he also gave me the chance to sing on some of the world's most exciting opera stages and has inspired me with wonderful colleagues, coaches, and teachers. I'm so grateful.

EPILOGUE: JULY 1980

Gail Robinson's story was indeed informative, but I had the feeling it was not enough in depth: perhaps some penetrating questions could elicit more pertinent answers. Also, the source of her ethereal repose was not evident and this was possibly the most outstanding quality about her performing.

I called Gail and we discussed the problem and decided we might be able to finish this interview on the telephone. We set a date for a week later, when she would have a little more free time. As the week passed I reflected on what factors could have contributed to her air of tranquillity. Was it just living in peaceful idyllic surroundings? Was it her deep, abiding Christian faith which she had at one time shared with me? It certainly was not the case of one untouched by the harsh hand of hardship, as she obviously had had her share of physical suffering. Finally the day of our telephone appointment arrived.

Gail answered my call in her usual pleasant manner. She left me holding the line a moment, while she shooed the kids out into the yard to play.

Upon her return, I asked, "Gail, is there any aspect of breathing you've ever had to give special attention to?"

"Why, yes. I guess my main problem is to keep my shoulders down. Sometimes I would take a shallow breath up in the throat, rather than down below. I have to think constantly to keep the breath down. If I take my breath too high and let tension get up into my shoulders, then tension gets into my throat, too."

"Do you take your breath through your mouth, your . . ."

There was a sound of commotion on the other end of the line and Gail quickly asked me to hold the phone. After three or four minutes, during which I heard various children's squeals and cries, she returned and coolly explained that Jennifer, her three-year-old, had just fallen off the swing and bumped her head. There went my picture of Gail the ethereal singer living in peaceful idyllic surroundings. Any mother of two normal little indians has learned to "endure hardness." We resumed our discussion after she got her breath.

"When you are singing, and not chasing your toddlers," I resumed on my original tack, "do you take your breath through your mouth, your nose, or both?"

"I take air through my mouth and nose. But if I have time, I prefer to breathe through my nose, because it opens all the resonating chambers and gives a reserve of breath which I just don't get through breathing with the mouth. Breathing through the nose also avoids cold air and dryness of the throat. Everything seems to open up when you breathe through the nose."

"All right," I said, "you've taken the breath, now what happens?"

"I try initially to take my breath deep down in the abdomen, then the feeling of support comes in the ribs and the back. You see, after breathing in, there is a sort of clamping of the rib cage . . . the bottom ribs sort of close in . . . trying to keep everything down. I have to think of that constantly."

"You say, in your article, that 'open throat' doesn't mean anything to you," I recalled. "Try an experiment right now. Sniff through your nose as if you were smelling something faint and beautiful, and describe to me if you feel any accompanying sensation in the throat."

I waited patiently as I heard sounds of sniffing and inhalations over the phone. She said, "I tried sniffing through the nose, and I do feel space going down the back of the throat."

"You said before that everything seems to open up when you breathe through the nose. You see, that *'everything'* you spoke of included the throat as well as the 'resonating chambers.' Actually, you have not been aware of the opening of the throat because it is so gentle. It is not that exaggerated spreading of the pharynx and pinning down of the larynx that so many singers indulge in. They try too hard."

"For me it's just the opposite," she went on. "Singing is such a pleasant sensation, it gives me physical pleasure. It is very soothing, better than taking a tranquilizer. As a student, when I was upset, I'd play the piano, and it would dispel all my problems, and singing does the same. Singing is the thing I do best. I was born a singer, it is part of my body chemistry, it's in my blood."

There was a silence. It seemed like a betrayal to return to the mechanics of singing. The betrayer in me won.

"Let's talk about placement," I suggested.

"Sometimes I try to get a picture of a pipe going from my diaphragm through the throat into the head. A voice like mine is not big, but it projects, because . . . up in the area of my nose . . . right between my eyes . . . I feel like there's a ball of sound, and it's spinning, like your hands rotating around each other. That's what gives my voice its projection . . . The sound comes up and shimmers as it goes out," she added.

"You have said you strive for an almost ethereal quality," I noted. "Your striving is in the spirit rather than in the body. *That's ethereal* . . . a spinning ball . . . the sound shimmers . . . It's a radiant concept like light filling space, like a whirling galaxy showering its vibrant sparks of energy out into the cosmos . . ." I brought myself up short. What was I doing, trying to posture as a cosmic poet and philosopher rather than a vocal technician?

Yet, a singer is first a poet, artist, or philosopher, else his or her art degenerates into a cold, mechanical system of impossible rules. But without that keen and cool intellect, that delicate, controlling touch of the understanding that is needed to maintain the steady course, one could never achieve the goal of total freedom, the supreme joy of unfettered vocal expression.

Suddenly, our interview was interrupted by another domestic emergency, and Gail and I were forced to sign off. As I reflected upon our conversation, I realized that, in these discourses between the older and somewhat scarred veteran and the younger blithe and wonderfully gifted chrysalis, it was essential for each to behold the other, taking what was needed. I am reminded of Arkel's beautiful words in *Pelléas et Mélisande:**

"An old man feels the need, now and then, just to touch his lips to the brow of a maid or the cheek of a child, to keep on trusting in the freshness of life, and drive away for a moment the menaces of death."

But that is only half the message, the other part should be:

"A child, unknowing, has the need, now and then, to feel the touch of the ancient's hand, a guide through the maelstrom of life, and a beacon to the shores of immortality."

End of epilogue: July 8, 1980.

* English translation by Henry Grafton Chapman, A. Durand & Fils, Editeurs.

Mario Sereni

Mario Sereni made his Metropolitan Opera debut in 1957 as Gérard in ANDREA CHÉNIER, only a year after his operatic debut in his native Italy, as Wolfram in TANNHÄUSER. His rich baritone voice has been heard in many roles, particularly those by Puccini and Verdi, including Sharpless in MADAMA BUTTERFLY, Amonasro in AÏDA, and Miller in LUISA MILLER. ❦

"Cos' è quel esercizio che fai?" Mario Sereni had poked his head through the door of my dressing room at the Met, asking me what was the vocal exercise I was doing.*

"Oh, you heard me vocalizing . . ."

The baritone's dressing room is adjacent to the bass's and he had heard me through the wall.

"That is very interesting what you are doing." Mario went on questioning me about what scales and arpeggios I used to warm up. He tried everything I showed him, asking very sharp questions about voice placement and technique.

All this took place during a Met rehearsal; what the opera was escapes me because it took place long ago. Since that time Mario has often dropped into my dressing room to discuss voice. Over the years he has proved to be an excellent technician who was always unusually cautious as to his choice of repertoire. He constantly maintained that he was a lyric baritone and had to vigilantly fend off tempting offers to do operas that were much too heavy for his voice. He always seemed to husband his resources wisely and I was looking forward to our interview. I knew he had an open, inquiring mind and I anticipated tapping it.

The most obvious furnishing in his hotel room was his recording

* This interview was conducted in both Italian and English.

equipment, not for its sophistication, but for its accessibility. Obviously, it was in constant use and an integral part of his vocal life.

"Every singer should buy a recording machine," he said, noting my interest. "It is not only the greatest critic in the world but also the greatest maestro.

"Listen to this," he said, turning the tape on. It was "Di Provenza" from *Traviata*. He constantly broke in with comments approving or criticizing his performance.

"You hear that phrase? It took me twenty years to learn to do that."

"But surely the tape recorder has not been your only maestro," I said, "so let's go back to the beginning."

He related that his vocal debut was at the age of six, when he sang Schubert's Ave Maria in church. He continued to sing in church, off and on, until he was twenty. At that time he met the opera basso Giuseppe Flamin, who persuaded him to study voice. He worked with him two or three times a week for three years until Maestro Siciliani heard him and immediately took him to Florence to study at the Maggio Fiorentino.

Mario had learned the trade of precision mechanic in Perugia and Torino, and took up this profession while studying in Florence. By so doing he paid for his own training. But his two years of study in Florence were considerably diluted by enjoying life in the big city.

Finally he debuted at the Maggio Fiorentino in the opera *Diavola in Campanile* under the baton of Tullio Serafin. He was then sent to study in Siena and Rome and then to Milan, where he came under the tutelage of the well-known baritone Mario Basiola, who had also sung at the Met. Six months with Basiola "put his voice in place."

At the age of twenty-seven Mario did his first performances of *La Favorita* in Marseilles, but due to severe trouble with his wisdom teeth, he was forced to withdraw after the second performance. He had been paid so little for his role that he could not meet the payments due for rent and hospital bills, and had to work for twenty days as a precision mechanic to get out of debt. This, he claimed, was the only misfortune of his career.

Mario Sereni

His first big contract came with the Teatro Colón of Buenos Aires, for *Faust, La Traviata, La Bohème,* and covering *Nabucco.* The baritone scheduled for the title role in *Nabucco* was taken ill and Mario debuted there in that role, doing it eight times, and then fulfilled the rest of his contract, all this at the age of twenty-seven. ("I have always been very lucky," he said.)

After singing in various major Italian opera houses on his return, he was taken to Milan to do an audition for Rudolf Bing, and was offered a contract for the Met.

Mario's debut was to be in *La Traviata,* but when Bastianini canceled *Andrea Chénier,* it was offered to him. The cast included Zinka Milanov and Mario Del Monaco ("I tell you I am lucky"). But during the rehearsal period Mario was constantly in the theater hearing his new colleagues, Robert Merrill, Leonard Warren, George London, among others, and was overwhelmed by their enormous voices. ("Four times the size of us Italians.")

He went to Max Rudolf, the assistant manager of the Met, and confessed that he was afraid to debut with such *vocioni* [big voices]. Max Rudolf assured him that the Met had plenty of others to replace him in case of difficulty. This little bit of reverse psychology made him pull himself together and fight back, resulting in a successful debut.

Subsequently, the Met management began to push him to do more dramatic roles, but he steadfastly resisted the temptation. He said, "I was not born with a big voice. I was associated with the big, great voices like Tucker, Warren, Milanov, you, Siepi, but I never had a voice like that. I'm not being modest. I consider myself to have a good voice, but not a big, great voice. But I have sung many important things. I told you I am lucky."

With this I interrupted, "Mario, I am convinced that people who are always lucky *make* their *own* luck by having what it takes and being well prepared. I have always considered you an excellent technician; not only were you a precision mechanic but you are also a precision singer as well."

"But," he responded, "I studied voice without intellectualizing too much; I did not approach it mechanically. I didn't follow any particular singing teacher's advice. When I left Basiola, I learned from then on by listening to other singers and questioning them. I was much influenced by Robert Merrill, and you remember, years ago, I heard you singing scales in your dressing room and I came in and asked what scales you used and why. I still do those scales . . ." He began singing:

and:

Naturally one cannot sing with the voice of another, but there are things one can learn by listening. Technique . . . there is only *one!* But there are many ways to approach it. But the sign of good technique is a long career. We have all heard stupendous voices that last a few years only. Obviously something is wrong in their approach. They did not go about searching—researching.

"When I sang with Richard Tucker, for example, I questioned him about his technique.

"I was singing *L'Elisir d'Amore* at La Scala and a few phrases were not going well. I went to Carlo Bergonzi's house and asked him to listen to these phrases. I found him to be one of the greatest pedagogues in the business."

As Mario went on, I realized how humble he was about his own gift and how complimentary about others. This is not common among opera singers.

"Now, let us talk specifically about technique," I said. "Some singers don't use scales when studying. They sing opera scores. How about you?"

"No, no, no, no! I absolutely believe in a strict discipline of scales. And I vocalize almost every day for about a half hour. Now, I am in a period at the Met where, for a few weeks, I don't have much to sing. This is the time when I am more careful to maintain the tonus of my voice. When you are singing a lot, the voice stays up. But you must never go for an extended period, such as two weeks, without using the voice. I don't say vocalize hours and hours. Ten or twenty minutes would be better than that. But Björling once told me that it is not necessary to vocalize every day of your life, either.

"When I begin vocalizing, I do it with the first scale you showed me years ago. I do it many times until my voice wakes up. When I used to listen to Tucker, he did all the vowels. So do I."

"Do you use other scales?" I asked.

"I do the second one you showed me, which opens the throat for me. Then I do:

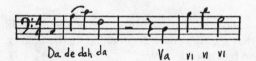

This I do for pitch."

"Now, Mario, you have a very smooth passage going into the high voice, and you obviously know what you are doing."

"There are two passages in the male voice," he said, "the first, for baritone, around the G, A flat, and A just below middle C; the second around E flat, E, and F."

"You use a mixed tone on the second passage," I broke in, "giving you a perfectly smooth passage with no sense of change. Did you always have this?"

"I had a smooth passage in the room studying, but lost it a bit in performance through emotion. It took years to overcome this."

"Consider a singer who does not instinctively have this ability; what would you advise?"

Mario continued, "The greatest baritone in the world, Mario Basiola, taught me this smooth passage. At the piano, he had me do three notes at a time:

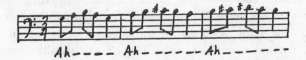

You do this up through the passage without changing anything in the position of the throat. Of course I do open up a bit here," he said, indicating the area of his larynx with the palm of his hand up, bunching his fingers and thumb together above the palm, like a cone, point up. Then he slowly opened the thumb and fingertips like a flower. This struck a familiar chord with me.

"Look," I said, bunching the thumb and fingers of my right hand similarly. Then I lightly wrapped the thumb and fingers of the other hand around them. As I expanded the fingertips on my right hand like a flower opening, I gently resisted with the fingers of my left hand.

"It feels as though I had a rubber sleeve about the fingers of my right hand that gently resists the opening of the fingers," I said. "Is that what you feel in your larynx?"

"Exactly."

"With the accompanying feeling of anchoring the larynx firmly down in place as you go up the scale into the passage?"

"Exactly," he went on, "but you must support the voice . . ."

"Wait a moment," I interjected, "what do you mean by *support the voice?*"

"You must lean, or rest, on the voice. It is ugly to sing in the nose . . ."

"You say *not* to sing in the nose," I said, "but very often when you are demonstrating a scale, you bunch your fingers together and hold them right in front of your nose."

"Certainly, because you can feel them vibrating when the tone is forward."

"Well, isn't that in the nose? Aren't you thinking nasal?"

"*Certo* [of course]," he responded. "I do scales almost nasally to keep the sound forward—with much *point*—very forward. You don't sing this way, of course. Never on the stage. But it is the *route*. Don't call it nasal, it is actually in the mask. Jussi Björling taught me this trick of the fingers in front of the nose. That helps you put the voice in the mask.

"Generally, Americans sing with a darker sound, as Warren did. It's their nature and it's a mistake to try to copy that sound unless it is natural to you. We Italians sing more brightly in the mask . . . But you have to be careful about that famous *maschera*—because it can bring you problems. Too much in the mask and you tend to be sharp, just as too dark brings the tendency to be flat."

"All right," I said, "now let's back up a bit and return to *appoggia,* or support."

"Well, you must breathe deeply and *lean* the *voice into the breath.* The diaphragm must be in a downward position, then when you push in with the lower abdomen, the air is compressed from below and above. The pressure must not go up to the vocal cords."

"Do you also feel that the larynx is lowered?" I asked.

"Of course."

"All right, now let's just talk a bit about singing high notes, after you've gone up past the *passaggio*."

"I have never exaggerated on high notes. When I had the honor to get to know the great conductor Serafin, he said that a singer should *not* touch continually on the high notes when practicing. One should vocalize in his normal middle range. If one insists too much on the high notes, the middle begins to wobble, because the muscles have been fatigued from pulling the voice up. I have very much admired Robert Merrill, and at his age the voice is still fresh and beautiful. This is a man who never exaggerated with the high notes. His voice is always stupendous."

"But in the actual singing of the high notes, how do they differ from the middle and low?"

"Basically the same throat position but with a little more space in the throat as you go up."

"Now," I said, "in conclusion, do you have any general advice for young students?"

"Yes, you must put this down! If all students would only realize how easy it really is to sing, how many great voices there would be around. Unfortunately, most of them never come to this understanding. They shouldn't exaggerate too much in research on the voice. They don't have to sing or vocalize *every* day, and they should try to lead a simple life, without exaggerated sacrifice. But they should attend the theater often and hear the others, especially those who have endured on the opera stage for twenty years or more. There has to be some reason why they have been so successful for so long. Be intelligent in choosing your repertoire, know your limitations. And . . . record everything you do.

"And, finally, singers should practice yoga. It teaches you great concentration."

"Did you actually study yoga?" I asked.

"Oh yes! For breathing and concentration. When you sing on the stages of all the great theaters of the world, including those giant halls on the Met tour up to ten thousand in capacity, you have to have nerves of steel.

"But again, keep the singing simple."

And thus our interview came to an end. As I left, my opinion had been reconfirmed as to Mario's open, inquiring mind. But add to that a healthy appreciation of the good points of his colleagues and competitors as well as a very sound appraisal of his own resources. A successful opera career is based on possessing a great voice, but there are many more essential contributing factors, including a good tape recorder.

Rita Shane

Rita Shane was born in New York. Her training was American and she made her debut as Olympia in TALES OF HOFFMANN *at the Chattanooga Opera in 1964. Her coloratura soprano has graced several roles at the Metropolitan Opera since her debut there as the Queen of the Night in 1973. Other roles in her Met repertoire include Berthe in* LE PROPHÈTE, *Oscar in* UN BALLO IN MASCHERA, *and Violetta in* LA TRAVIATA. ⁊

"RITA," I said, "I am going to have my editor print a blank page in the book with your name at the top of it."

"Oh, Jerry! All right, give me another chance."

Rita Shane and I were standing behind the portable stage in the Sheep Meadow during a performance of *Rigoletto* with "The Met in the Parks." She had been my first interviewee for this book, and I as yet had had no experience in drawing information from my reluctant subjects. Almost every one of Rita's answers was either "I don't know" or "I don't remember." Now I had over a year's experience in doing interviews and I wanted to try again, and so did Rita. We agreed to meet after the summer was over.

Five months later she warmly welcomed me into her West Side apartment. I was given a quick introduction to a nine-year-old whirlwind answering to the name of Michael. He and a neighborhood pal were requested to take their antics out to the patio so we could have as peaceful an interview as possible. With this accomplished, we went to work on bypassing Rita's "I don't knows" and "I don't remembers."

Rita was born and raised in New York City, and attended the Bronx High School of Science. She then graduated from Barnard as a student of musicology. Three years after marrying Daniel F. Tritter she began formally studying voice. The next summer she was accepted as an apprentice in Santa Fe. Two and a half years after she took her first lesson she made her professional debut in Chattanooga as Olympia in *Tales of Hoffmann*. Subsequently there came a long series of important theaters including the New York City Opera, La Scala, the Munich Opera, the Vienna Staatsoper, and Salzburg. Her Metropolitan Opera debut was in the fall of 1973 as the Queen of the Night in *The Magic Flute*.

"Rita," I said, "let's talk about vocal technique."

"I *cannot* talk about *my* specific technique, because I think I'm a different person every day. It depends on how I feel, on whether or not the weather is affecting me . . . I cannot specifically say that *this* is the way I do it."

"But Rita," I protested, "this is a book on vocal technique. We have to come up with something . . . Are you saying you have a different technique every day?"

"No," she said. "I don't have a different technique. But something that might work for me one day does not necessarily work for me the next day.

"I don't mean to sound vague, Jerry, I very much know what I'm doing when I do it. It's very difficult for me to put these things into words."

"But words it must be," I insisted. "Let's talk about breathing and support. How do you take a breath?"

"I don't take a dancer's breath. A dancer breathes very high and very shallow. They don't get anything involved below."

"For singers, should there be any involvement of the chest?" I asked.

"The chest . . . no, I think the ribs . . . I can only demonstrate. This is very difficult for me," she said in an aside, putting her hands on the lower part of her ribs, expanding them. "You can also push in here," she added, pointing below her armpits, "but below, the back is involved too. The most correct way is if you bend over . . ." She bent way down from the hips and said, "For me to get into specifics this way . . . I'm not sure that I want to."

I leaned down to look at her reddening face. "Do it anyway!"

"Then you're going to quote me," she sputtered, "and I'm going to say, 'Wait a minute, I didn't mean to say that . . .'"

"*Rita!*"

"Okay," she conceded, laughing upside down. "The way that I know I'm taking a correct breath is to bend over. If you bend over you cannot take an incorrect breath."

"First of all," I said, "you cannot use the chest and shoulders, and it causes expansion of the ribs all around. That's excellent, only I don't recall you singing the Queen of the Night in that position."

"You *can* do it standing up," she chided laughingly.

"I'm relieved to hear it. Now, what does support mean to you?"

"It's going to sound absolutely crazy," she warned.

"By now I'm ready for it. It's par for the course."

"If you put one hand on top of the other," she said, extending both arms in front of her, one wrist on top of the other one, with a bouncing up-and-down motion, "to me, this is a voice resting on support: there's always a cushion. If this upper hand were not supported, it would collapse. It's strong, but not rigid."

"This strength you're speaking of, Rita, is from the underneath hand . . ."

"Yes, I would say . . ."

"What, then, in our anatomy corresponds to the hand on top?"

"The voice . . . the sound."

"With this cushion," I asked, "is there a pushing up against the vocal cords, or is there a holding away . . ."

"I have never mentioned *pushing*," she corrected me. "I believe you *let* breath come in, you *let* things happen. You don't force them to happen."

"Is support used, then, to keep you from shoving against the cords so they can stay relaxed?"

"Nothing must push against the larynx," Rita said firmly.

"Then this strength you spoke of has nothing to do with the larynx . . . ?"

"I don't feel anything in my larynx. I have no sensation of gripping . . . none."

"What do you think of the term *open throat?*" I asked.

"I don't think in terms of open throat."

"Some singers maintain that since the sound originates in the larynx, it is the important focus of attention," I observed.

"I agree, the voice does originate in the larynx, but I believe in letting things happen. When the air comes through, the cords very gently go together, not ramming together."

"Granted the muscular action of the cords must be gentle," I conceded, "but there are muscles being used nonetheless."

"And there are muscles all around the larynx," she added, "in the neck . . . If all this collapses, if everything pushes against the larynx . . . these great muscles, which essentially when you sing go out . . ."

"Wait," I interrupted. "Which muscles go out?"

She then indicated the large muscles going down the sides of the neck from below the ears.

"I think," she went on, "these side muscles, they ought to get out of the way."

"Do you think there's a kind of widening feeling there?"

"Yes, I do."

"Would you call *that* an open throat?"

"Perhaps that's what somebody else would call an open throat," she said, evading me again.

"Is there a sensation of opening?" I insisted.

"I don't have a sensation of opening. I might have had when I was starting. I do know that when I'm singing well, everything is open, awake. If you consider that an open throat . . . *maybe* that's an open throat."

"*Maybe*," I echoed in frustration. Courage! Try again! "Some people liken an open throat to the beginning of a yawn."

"It might be," she said noncommittally. "Some people could feel that. I, anatomically, am very large and wide open. I have a tremendous opening."

"Would you feel that, as you take your breath, there is simultaneously a sort of opening in your throat?"

"Yes, I do. I think if you take a proper breath, everything opens itself."

"Would you associate this opening with a slight pulling down of the larynx?" I asked.

"I don't feel a pulling down of the larynx. I can only use my hands and . . ." She demonstrated by cupping her hands side by side in front of her stomach. Then, as she took a breath, her elbow rose out from her sides, giving a bellows effect. There was the effect of opening and expansion down and out away from the larynx. This was most expressive in itself. I began to feel we were getting somewhere.

"Now, let's go to *placement*," I suggested.

"I don't necessarily think of placement. Sometimes I feel the sound almost against my top teeth . . . or I feel the sound going up into the soft palate. One day I feel that, and the next day I might feel the sound coming right out underneath my nose . . . not *through* my nose! There's a difference between nasality and nasal resonance. The difference is . . . one goes through the nose, and one . . ."

"Uses both the nose and the mouth," I supplied.

"Yes," she said. "If I go *aaongh* [a nasal sound] or I go *ah* . . . one goes through my nose, the other does not. I do feel a terrific strength almost against my upper teeth."

"Isn't that placement?" I prompted.

"Perhaps."

"Do you keep the sound *focused?*"

"Yes, I suppose it is focused. I guess I feel it up in my cheekbones."

"Placement," I concluded enthusiastically.

"Yes, I suppose."

"Rita," I said, "everyone knows you have an extraordinarily high voice. I am curious if part of this might be attributed to what you do, rather than what you are. When we did *The Magic Flute* at Wolftrap with the Met, I was just next to your dressing room, and you did something I had not heard before, an incredibly high and fast glissando . . . up and down . . . up and down, like lightning. Do you do these glissandos often?"

"I do them all the time."

"Do you start your day with these sounds?"

"No. When I wake up in the morning, I go almost like a puppy dog . . . *eeyou, eeyou* . . . to get my muscles going before I get out of bed. I do stretches with my mouth . . . *nyang, nyang, nyang* [this she did with an exaggerated opening of the mouth]. Everything an athlete would do . . . warming stretches . . . breathing exercises to get my body awake . . . to get my circulation going."

"Describe these glissandos you do," I said.

"I do them on nine notes [up and down] . . . a nine-note glissando followed by a nine-note scale. I do it sometimes to a high D flat above C [above high C]. I can do a fast one, I can do a slow one."

"I suppose the slow one helps keep the voice even," I said.

"I don't go through all kinds of contortions," Rita said. "I sing my low voice the same way I sing my high voice. I don't think of switching gears. Other very high voices switch. They go into some other kind of sound, which I don't do."

"Does the glissando help you with that?"

"I think it does. We talk about switches. I think there are certain natural turnovers, but I can sing a good three octaves with absolutely no switches. I basically always had that."

"Do you start early in your exercises with the glissando?"

"Yes."

"I feel that's a very important factor," I observed, "in the achievement of your unusual high notes and also in the evenness of your voice . . . Do you ever use your lips when you make vowels?"

"When you speak, do you make faces?" she retorted.

"No."

"No, I don't make faces to sing particular vowel sounds."

"Sing for me an *ah* vowel and go to *oo*," I said. As she did it, I observed, "You seem to be just closing your jaw, without puckering the lips."

"Yes, basically. There may be times when for effect . . ."

"Of course," I cut in, "but I'm talking about a classical technique."

Rita said, "We didn't talk about speaking. I have heard some singers speak one way and sing another way, which is something I find really—"

"I know," I broke in, "deadly. I'm one of those offenders, and since I am a rather compulsive talker, it brought me much trouble some years ago. Fortunately, at one point I consulted an expert in the field of speech problems, Dr. Morton Cooper, who incidentally is also doing a chapter for this book. I think a lot of the problems I had ten years back were largely due to improper speech habits."

"Do you speak differently than you sing?" she said, surprised.

"Yes, but not nearly as much as I originally did. I still have to be very careful about it."

"I speak the same way as I sing," she said. "I can go from speech right into singing. There's no difference. When I sing I don't collapse. Collapsing is *not* relaxing. They are two different things. When I say I keep my voice up, I don't mean I keep it up in any particular place. I just don't let it go on no breath and collapse. I'm one of those people who vocalize every day, like brushing my teeth. It makes my speaking voice feel better."

"I wonder if some of the major vocal collapses that do occasionally occur among great singers may sometimes be instigated by this basic problem," I said. "After all, the things we do every day, like sleeping, exercising, talking, eating . . ."

"*We want food!*"

This fifty-decibel shout came from the healthy lungs of nine-year-old Michael, who should never suffer from speaking with unsupported, collapsed tones. He stomped in with his playmate, and I concluded that the interview was over.

Why not? I had garnered a good fistful of information.

The interview seemed to have gone well. *Apparently* I have developed a better technique of interviewing, I *think* . . . *perhaps* . . . I *suppose* . . . *maybe* . . . Wait a minute, *I didn't mean to say that* . . . It's very *difficult* for me to put these things into words.

Golly, it must be contagious.

But so is Rita's beautiful singing . . . that I know for sure!

Beverly Sills

Beverly Sills has become familiar to millions of Americans through the medium of television. She has been featured in many TV opera performances and has also served as host of several TV talk shows. Born in Brooklyn, she has been involved in show business since the age of three. Her operatic debut was in Philadelphia as Frasquita in CARMEN. *For many years she sang leading roles with the New York City Opera. When the City Opera moved to Lincoln Center in 1966, Miss Sills' Cleopatra in* GIULIO CESARE *made her the most talked-about soprano in America and pushed her into superstardom. Among her greatest roles were Queen Elizabeth in* ROBERTO DEVEREUX, *Manon, and Lucia di Lammermoor. Her long-awaited Metropolitan Opera debut came in 1975 as Pamira in* THE SIEGE OF CORINTH. *Miss Sills recently retired from the stage and is currently General Director of the New York City Opera.* 🎵

MY editor, Ken McCormick, suggested that I include an interview with an opera impresario. When I interviewed Beverly Sills, our superstar of American opera (and international opera) had become the general director of the New York City Opera, so my editor's request was automatically granted, and a happy occasion it was, because it would be very hard to find someone more charming and enthusiastic than Beverly. Our interview in her Lincoln Center office went like this:

"Beverly," I began, "you are the busiest girl I have ever seen, and since your time is precious and limited, let us skip the biographical material, which everyone knows anyhow, and plunge right in to vocal technique. What are your observations on the use of the breath?"

"My mother took me to Estelle Liebling's studio when I was

seven, and I stayed with her for thirty-five years, until she died nine years ago. I was such a young child, it was very hard for a teacher to teach me breathing technique. She used to keep her hands on my diaphragm . . . the area right under the rib cage . . . and made me push against it to show what kind of support she wanted. When I was twelve or thirteen I didn't understand that I was using a breathing technique. Later I realized that her entire basis of technique was breath control. It stood me in very good stead, because one of the most successful things about my career was my ability to sing very long legato lines in the *bel canto* repertoire."

"Did you use any special exercises to help you sing long phrases?" I asked.

"Yes! It was inhalation . . . then exhalation on a *psss* noise, which went . . . [she demonstrated a hissing sound interrupted by suddenly closing her lips, giving a definite *p* sound] very gently exhaling a small amount of breath . . . cutting it off . . . and exhaling more, and cutting it off, and gradually lengthening the exhalation before the cutoff, and seeing how many we could get in the span.

"I started out as a child with two or three, and then I would run out. But as I progressed I could do six or seven very long exhalations without taking another breath."

"How long could you hold this?"

"I don't know," she replied, "but there are several pirated recordings of *Maria Stuarda* where there is a high B flat or B, which is sustained over the chorus in the prayer. I don't know how long that goes on, but it was one I had to go back and train for, because it starts pianissimo and then goes into a great crescendo, at the end of which you need as much steam as you had when you started. I actually worked on my breath control consciously for the first time in maybe fifteen years. I went back to doing exercises so that I could carry that note. It was quite interesting, because on nights when I was very tired I could not . . . no matter how I tried, when I pulled out every trick that I could think of . . . I could not sustain that note. So sometimes even the technique lets you down if you're exhausted."

"There's a real lesson in that," I observed. "It is of prime importance that a singer be in top physical condition and well rested.

Now, let's be more specific about the breath. When you breathe in before singing a phrase, do you think deeply?"

"No, I think of the rib cage . . . but never the upper chest. It's like filling a balloon that's inside where the diaphragm is, to see if I can make the balloon expand to fill out my rib cage."

"After you have begun to sing a phrase, do you constantly have the feeling of maintaining this outward expansion even though the ribs are continually moving in?"

"Yes, sure," she answered emphatically. "It's sitting on it."

"What's the purpose of this continuing outward pressure with regard to the whole picture?" I asked. "Do you have any ideas about that?"

"No. You see, I was never an intellectual singer. Liebling gave me whatever technique I had at a very early age, and from that point on I simply sang. It was like second nature. The first half hour when I vocalized, we worked on consciously doing things to support the voice, to open the throat, to put head tones, but once I began to perform I never consciously did anything."

"Let's discuss some of those terms you just used," I suggested. "First, let us tackle *support,* or its Italian counterpart, *appoggio.* Now, *appoggio* in Italian means 'leaning upon' something, reminiscent of your description a few moments ago of 'sitting on it.' But some singers apply this concept in two distinctly different ways. Almost all singers conceive of leaning upon this balloon, of which you spoke. However, some singers apply this concept of *appoggio* as 'leaning' the vocal cords into the breath a little bit."

"But isn't that a combination?" she countered. "How does one exist without the other?"

"Yet there are many singers who insist that they must feel absolutely nothing in the throat," I added.

"That's not me," she said. "No, it's a combination. I use that 'sitting on the diaphragm' to produce the feeling that I want in my throat."

"Can you describe that sensation or feeling in your throat?" I prompted. "What does open throat, for example, mean to you?"

"It's something I tried to avoid for most of my career . . . until I went into the heavier repertoire, because a voice that is basically lightly textured, the way mine was, is first of all a head voice."

"Then you didn't use chest voice?"

"I didn't begin to use it," she continued, "until I sang Constanza in *The Abduction* and had to go to G below middle C. It didn't bother me, because it was only touched, and wasn't used for dramatic purposes. It was simply part of a scale that Mozart had written. When I went into the *bel canto* repertoire, I began to use my chest voice higher than I had ever used it before, up to an F or F sharp, which is very dangerous for a voice like mine, and probably shortened its life, but it was a deliberate choice: I wanted to make a dramatic effect, and I made it, period! I opted for the shorter career, though when people say fifty-one is young to retire, it may be, but I've been singing since I was seven, so for me it's forever!

"However, the open throat came when I wanted to make my voice heavier and darker."

"What sensation do you have in the throat when you employ this open feeling?"

"Well," she mused, "I thought of keeping it out of the head as much as I was able. I *placed everything in the mouth and on the hard palate. When I go for the head tones, I go for the soft palate.* When I used to sing Zerbinetta I went to the soft palate. I looked in the mirror when I was singing, just to see what was going on. When I went to the very high tones I found that my soft palate was going higher . . . for the high E's and F's. But when I wanted to produce more sound and get a darker quality, I put it into my hard palate; it went into the front of my mask, so to speak."

"Have you ever used the imagery of the yawning position," I asked, "to produce the open throat?"

"No. For me it's more the sound of the vowel. If I want to go into head tones it becomes an *awe*, almost with an *oo* sound in it that pushes it into the head. If I want an open throat, it's a real *aah*, and that's a very dangerous way of singing for my taste. But sometimes you can make a great dramatic effect with it . . . and I used it!"

"Now, you feel the chest voice is produced by using *ah* instead of *awe?*" I asked.

"Yes, it's a real *aah*. As soon as I went into *awe* or *oo*, it went out of the chest; it went into my head. But if I really wanted to get a meaty chest tone, it was a wide open *ah*."

"Let us go back," I suggested, "to the use of the breath. Male singers seem to have a greater tendency to push downward in supporting, than women do, who usually speak of expanding the ribs in the back as well."

"I never did that," she said thoughtfully. "I know Marilyn Horne and I talked about that . . ."

"How about the use of the breath on the attack?" I asked. "Some singers insist that all attacks must begin light as a feather . . ."

"It depends on the kind of attack that it is. If you start 'Un bel dì,' yeah, it's a feather. But you take the cabaletta in *Attila*," and she sang its opening phrase, "try that like a feather," she laughed. "It depends on the effect you want to make, on how you use the diaphragm. It's like staccati: the first thing a coloratura learns is that all of the staccati don't come from the throat here, but come from the support of the diaphragm. Lots of times, when coloraturas do the Bell Song, you see . . ." Beverly demonstrated by popping her diaphragm area in and out.

"On the other hand," she continued, "there is an attack in *Roberto Devereux* which went right up to a high D, and it was a real *wham* on that. It can't be a feather. You know, the way I got that D out, it was not a feather, it was like a *hammer!* I really had to push."

"One more thing on breathing," I interjected. "Some singers advocate breathing through the nose."

"I never breathe through the nose, not when I'm singing. In the opera you don't have so much time. That's fine at the beginning of an opera, or after somebody else has been doing an aria and you want to get a good fresh start."

"Do you think vocal placement is different for every singer?" I asked.

"Well, I think it's very dangerous to listen to other singers' placements, just because it's successful with them. I'll give you an example.

"When I was twenty-four years old, I went to live with Rosa

Ponselle. We became intimate friends, and you have to realize that twenty-six years ago Rosa was a woman in her late fifties. To hear her, with that voice, walk around at eleven o'clock at night, with a glass of red wine in her hand, singing Isolde, singing anything she pleased . . . it was overwhelming.

"I tell you, for a young girl to hear this voice that was completely in the mask . . . I've never heard anything like it. It went up to the high C and it was still in the mask, never in the back of the throat, never the top of the head. It was all here . . ." She indicated the cheeks.

"It was an inspiration to me, and of course, little Beverly had to have it in the mask also. 'If Rosa can sound like that in the mask, Beverly's going to put it there too.'

"A little problem. First of all, Rosa's face was like five inches broader than mine. Second of all, Rosa had what I think was the creamiest, richest, Italianate sound that I've ever heard. Mine has always been, at its best, a French voice. For the French repertoire you couldn't touch me. There I was, walking around with my hands on my cheeks, trying to get the voice into the mask. And I would call Miss Liebling, and Miss Liebling would talk to Rosa and say, 'With that little face she's never going to get it in the mask.' And I never got it in the mask, although Rosa would say:

"'Stop it, stop it! Get it in the mask, get it in the head.'

"But you can't imitate; all our faces are constructed differently . . . and the vocal cords, otherwise we'd all sound alike. I don't think anybody should ever teach by imitating."

"Well," I observed, "especially since your voice and Rosa's were so entirely different by nature—yours light, and hers heavy."

"I think I got away with a lot of repertoire that was basically heavy for my voice, because I've always been a very text-conscious singer, and words have always meant a great deal to me. But by using those vowels, I was able to give intent and intention to the music without necessarily giving the weight."

"This is one of the subtle sort of things about singing that is hard to teach, even if one has a fine teacher," I added.

"One of the reasons that there are so many charlatans teaching today is because you can't see the vocal cords," she said emphatically.

"I can."

"Really?" she said, surprised. "How?"

"I strap a dental mirror onto a pencil flashlight, run hot water over the mirror, pull out my tongue, stick this homespun apparatus past my uvula, and look at my cords via the bathroom mirror. And still you can't watch the cords as you are singing, so singing is not a tangible thing; it leaves a lot of mystery."

"Exactly!" was her response.

"With a pianist, you can watch the fingers."

"Exactly. And that singing teacher, sitting at the piano, can't see the cords when you're singing either."

"The only advantage I can find in seeing my vocal cords is the impression I have that they keep on good behavior when they know you are watching them." This observation drew a laugh from Beverly, who continued with, "We're all different artists. I don't think my breath control would work for everybody. I don't think where I put my voice would work for everybody. But breath control was hammered into me, and it was the whole base of my training.

"I have kept my flexibility throughout the years, and that is the one thing that is untouched by the ravages of time. I can still sing runs and trills almost in an unimpaired fashion. But what has deserted me is my breath control . . . and for various reasons: I had a terrible illness, and my age . . . I am young for a woman . . . I am not a young singer!"

"What was your training like under Miss Liebling?"

"She was the last surviving student of Marchesi, and I did nothing but Marchesi exercises . . . nothing *but*. She came to hear me do Marguerite once, in this house, and called me up the next morning at half-past six, to tell me that the trill was lousy, and the trill was heavy, and the trill was not clean. We went back in the studio at nine o'clock the same morning, and I could hardly see straight, I was so tired. As you know, *Faust* is a very long opera. For one hour we did trills and trills until I thought I was going gaga, but when I walked out I had my trill back.

"I still have my scale book which she wrote out for me, and they are all Marchesi scales."

"What kind of scales were they?" I asked.

"Very fast arpeggios . . . scales . . . very fast. The last two scales of the Costanza aria . . . I didn't realize, until I learned the role of Costanza, that that was what she had been giving me. When I did *Anna Bolena,* I did a series of twelve consecutive trills, in the last cabaletta . . . it comes in the last minutes of the opera . . . and I never missed them, never, not in all the *Bolenas,* and that's a long, tedious role. That was her teaching of how to do those trills, and they were consecutive, a third apart, and rising. That was technique! Those were the things she taught me. I could trill on high D's, and never realized I was doing anything special, because that was part of my training."

"And in your voice lessons?" I prompted. "You did . . ."

"Primarily a half hour of exercises. They were all light, fast scales. She never worked on sustained tones with me. By the time a half hour had passed, I was completely warmed up. Then we went to sustained singing with things like 'Addio del passato,' which was one of her favorite things to keep me from getting lazy. She felt that the light scales buttered up the voice."

"Did you continue your studies all through your career?"

"Yes, I was with her six weeks before she died. I was still seeing her every morning, and she was in her nineties. As she got older, she couldn't see, or play the piano well. But for me the most valuable thing was the vocalization period; that was all I really wanted from her.

"In 1962 I met Roland Gagnon, who really became my vocal mentor. Every morning, from nine o'clock to twelve o'clock, we worked in my apartment on repertoire. And when I traveled and did opera, many times he joined me in the cities where I was singing, and we continued to work. I was never without him for more than a week. He was my one luxury that I couldn't afford to do without . . . Just last year he tragically went to sleep one night and never woke up. So, I guess that when I decided not to sing anymore, he decided he wasn't going to be around to criticize me anymore. I miss him a lot."

"Then you believe a singer must have another ear . . . someone else to keep us on the track?" I asked.

"Oh, sure. I was lucky to have a very observant mother who has grown up with me and my voice, and probably knows it only second to my own intimate knowledge of its limitations and potentials. But I think it actually takes another singer to be able to assist you if you're in trouble.

"In your case, your wife was a wonderful singer. If she has something to say, she has lived through it, and therefore the validity of what she says is enormous.

"It's the way I feel now in this company. At the beginning, I thought, 'Oh, I can't criticize a singer who's doing a role that I adored . . . even a role I didn't do.' And then I thought, 'The heck with that! Thirty years of experience . . . Ask the girl who did it!' And I feel that if they're not willing to take what I have to say, that's fine! But I'm going to say it. So I do offer suggestions now. I do suggest, 'Try the B flat on a head tone and you'll make it.'

"'Use the text.' I think in this way I'm extremely valuable and compassionate to the singer, because I have lived through it. I listen to Micaela; I know that B is coming: you can see the singer tense for it. Ah, there's the attack on it . . . I once sang Micaela sixty-three consecutive nights. Is there anyone who knows Micaela better than I? So I feel whatever help I can give is important.

"When a certain singer came to do Anna Bolena, I could tell her where to conserve, because the last twenty minutes of *Anna Bolena* is the most difficult part of the entire evening. I pointed out to her it was not necessary to give all the time, but to use the text. Sometimes the most intense moments are those that you barely . . . I mean, a good pianissimo will get that audience hushed up just as much as a rousing high C. And in this case, I was able to be very helpful."

"What do you think are the most important factors that made you what you are?" I asked. "I perceive a certain candid honesty about you regarding yourself, and I feel that's most important."

"Yes. Two things, I think. I found singing such a joyous experience that I couldn't wait to get on the stage. I never had to pull out a lot of trinkets to make my dressing room attractive to me; my dressing room was a stepping-stone, and the sooner I got that makeup on, the better. I couldn't wait to get on the stage, and I think when you see a performer who is obviously enjoying herself like that, you are prepared to go along with her. That's one thing.

"Second of all, as I said before, I was a communicator. The words meant as much to me as the music. I wanted the people to have an emotional experience, which is why I never could be content with the 'stand up and sing' roles.

"This joyfulness that I felt when I sang, and this need to communicate with people, these are my two strongest points. I've always been a people person, I love people, I like to be with people, and when I got on stage, I was home free."

"Beverly, I only heard you once in person. It was when you sang Norma with the New Jersey State Opera. That night your singing was flawless, but what impressed me even more was the way you came out and faced your audience. Just your attitude toward us out there was remarkably captivating, and I never forgot it. You are truly born for the stage, a complete artist."

"They say that we have to be schizophrenic, split personalities, in order to exist as humans *and* artists, and there was definitely that split. I am a Gemini, and they are definitely two people: there's the one that goes home and prepares dinner at night, because I enjoy doing that . . . I want my husband and children to taste my cooking . . . and there's the person who just couldn't wait to get to the theater and become somebody else. When I woke up in the morning, and *Manon* was on that night, it was the longest day in my life. That's why I'm always the . . ." Beverly halted reflectively. "It's so hard for me to talk of myself in the past tense . . .

"I was always the first person in the theater all the time. If it was an eight-o'clock curtain, I was here at five-thirty, and it wasn't that I needed to vocalize, because I was all warmed up. I couldn't wait for it to begin."

With that, Beverly had to dash. I accompanied her out of the inner recesses of the theater into the bright, cold sunlight. As I watched her quickly cutting her way through pedestrians and traffic, enthusiastically heading for her next appointment, I decided she must be more than just the twins of Gemini, it would take quintuplets to successfully race through the path of her life.

Beverly: No one will ever be able to think of you in the past tense. You're always with it, no matter what *it* may be.

Godspeed.

Risë Stevens

Risë Stevens is one of the most well-known of American singers. The mezzo-soprano's interpretation of Carmen was for many years the standard by which others were measured. In addition, she appeared in several films in the 1940s which introduced her to a wide audience unacquainted with opera. Miss Stevens was born in New York City. Her debut was in Prague in 1936, as Thomas's Mignon. Two years later she made her Met debut in the same role. Another role she was closely associated with was Octavian in DER ROSENKAVALIER. Since her retirement from the stage she has held several managerial positions. 🎵

RISË STEVENS . . . superstar? She easily places in that category, but I prefer to regard her as superachiever. Risë Stevens, née Risë Steenberg, began singing professionally at the age of ten on Milton Cross's Sunday-morning radio show "The Children's Hour." She already had a large contralto sound, seemingly impossible for one so young. After graduating from high school she entered Juilliard on a scholarship, studying with Anna Schoen-René. At her teacher's behest she sailed for Europe on the *Deutschland,* destination Salzburg, at the age of nineteen. All that summer she studied with Marie Gutheil-Schoder, a famous Rosenkavalier, a role that soon turned out to be tailor-made for Risë. Her heart was set on Broadway, a natural choice for as good-looking a girl, but Schoen-René had other plans for her and, after her graduation from Juilliard, managed to steer her into serious operatic studies. Before long Risë was singing Rosenkavalier in major companies, and her subsequent debut at the Metropolitan was in *Mignon* on a Texaco broadcast with Milton Cross presiding.

Risë's natural beauty, combined with her star-quality voice, quickly brought her to the attention of Hollywood, where she made three films, *The Chocolate Soldier,* with Nelson Eddy, *Going My Way,* with Bing Crosby, and *Carnegie Hall.* During her illustrious international career Risë vowed that when she turned fifty she would retire. Many singers had made similar, but vain, promises. However, she meant it and when that day arrived Risë notified Rudolf Bing that she would accept no further contracts. Bing was dismayed and begged her to reconsider, but to no avail.

Singing only proved to be one facet of Risë's accomplishments as this superachiever took over the task of heading the Metropolitan Opera's National Company and later the Mannes College of Music as president.

My memories of Risë were performing with her in countless operas such as *Khovanchina, Mignon,* and *Boris,* and now here we were dealing with each other on an entirely different level.

Risë's apartment reflected what was always evident in her career: everything was first-class. Anticipating the same from our interview, I was not disappointed. We began speaking about attitudes that mold or destroy a career.

"I think it has to do with everything," she said, "your personality, your technique, the will to want that kind of a life, because it is very difficult, Jerry, let's face it . . . You live a certain kind of regimented life, you try to eat the right things. I was always wrapped up in the cold and very careful in the summer . . . drafts and windows open and windows closed . . . all kinds of idiosyncrasies."

"Of course, it all has to do with the fact that the vocal cords are so sensitive to moods and physical condition," I added.

"It's a physical instrument," she continued. "Your vocal cords are your life."

"Emotion alone is so critical," I said. "I remember I got angry with someone on the telephone once and before I hung up I was so hoarse I could hardly speak."

Risë picked up on this. "If I were teaching classes, which I did, and I tried to emphasize certain things, I'd get myself to such a pitch that I found myself getting hoarse trying to get through to these people. And it's strange because I speak correctly."

"Yes," I said, "but the emotional strain shows through."

"And yet you don't do that when you sing," she cut in. "If you have an emotional scene, you're very conscious of controlling that emotion, of how you produce the voice, even in those moments. Look at Callas . . . for me, the most thrilling thing one could hear—you always felt this was the last performance she could ever possibly do. She gave everything. That's very exciting to listen to. I think there is a danger to that. You pay in the end, and the majority of people want that kind of thing. They couldn't care less whether it was your last performance or not.

"Jerry, I don't know if you'll go along with me, but I really have the feeling today that the singers on the whole are much better, technically, than we were. They've gone into a much more extensive kind of training. In those days it didn't matter whether you sight-read or not. But a Caruso . . . a Pinza. They had an incredible instinct . . . There were all those people there who taught them by rote and, mind you, they were better than half the musicians in many instances, because they learned them [their roles] so, they were almost indelible in their minds."

"In my experience," I agreed, "the roles I learned early in my career I learned by rote . . . including the fact that I did not know languages. Oh, I played the piano a bit, but my teacher, Curci, pounded the notes and words into me five times a week for three months on any important score. I never tried to memorize a score in those days, I just sang it until I knew it. Those roles I never have to relearn; they're always with me. Later on in a full career, there is not as much time and I learn a role by sight-reading it on airplanes, or wherever, cramming it into my memory. Six months after the production I hardly remember the score. There's something to be said for rote. However, there are certain things a singer must be taught technically."

"When I started out," Risë reflected, "as a youngster, it was unusual to have that deep a voice. At fourteen I never could go beyond an E [the second E above middle C] because I didn't know where to put it. It was an area where the voice was unnatural [above the E]. Now came the process of learning, so that when I came to Anna Schoen-René . . . although I had already learned to sing F, F sharp, and G, and above that . . . I made myself *not* know what I was singing . . . Do I make myself clear when I say that? I said to myself, 'That's not a G, that's not an F sharp' . . . so that I wouldn't think about it, because I *knew* that I never could go beyond an E. My training was not such that I could say to myself, 'Aha, today I hit a high A.'

"But in Juilliard I learned . . . ear training, so sharp you know where you are. But in those days I didn't know, so that I was being fooled all of the time. This wonderful woman, Schoen-René at Juilliard, emphasized the studies I had to have . . . sight reading, ear training. There's no doubt that I would have been highly lacking had I not gone . . . I don't know, I question it sometimes, because when you come back to the Pinzas and Carusos—Pinza had that natural quality, it was voluptuous. There wasn't anything he couldn't do with it, *piano, forte* . . ."

"And after an illustrious opera career he conquered Broadway and went on to films," I said. "A film career must be quite different from an opera career."

"Everyone asked me if I enjoyed making films. In essence," she said, grimacing, "no! I didn't like what they called *routine*. The continuity was never there. I felt an enormous lack of reaction from the audience. I used to look at Bing Crosby and say, 'You know, you're remarkable, because you put on a performance for the cameraman and everyone who's in the studio, and very seldom you get a reaction from them,' because they were so involved in moving cameras and lights . . . it was just routine with them. But he did a number as though there were an audience and they were going to respond. I could not do that. I felt this terrible lack, and the fact that you repeated and repeated. The film is put in incorrectly, or technically the light didn't work. By the time they shoot the thing you're exhausted."

"Risë," I said, "I'm enjoying our Hollywood excursion, but I think we had better get to vocal technique. You mentioned that you couldn't sing above an E natural, by nature. How did you acquire the necessary notes above it?"

"It was a real struggle," she answered, hesitating thoughtfully, "a constant going at it and technically getting to know where those tones should sit. I found that . . . when I relaxed more in trying to get the high tones."

"What did the relaxing?"

"Your larynx, your tongue, your jaw, and when you open your mouth, it's a relaxed feeling rather than a forced feeling. I almost used to *set* my jaw for high notes. It was rigidity that I was forming in the jaw, which, of course, will also affect the vocal cords, and the whole throat . . . What I mean by relaxed is . . . not having the feeling that I was pushing the tone with the breath to get up there. The most important thing is breath control."

"What do you mean by breath control?"

Risë frowned in concentration. "If I were to take a balloon . . . I would take a deep breath and I would slowly blow that balloon up, until I got it to the size I wanted it. I think singing is very similar to this. You cannot sing . . . *haaaa* . . ." She sang a very breathy, noisy, and flat sound, obviously with no control, placement, or support. "That's breath, too, but you cannot shove the breath into the tone. The tone has to sit on the breath. Breath is like a *buffer*." She simultaneously demonstrated by holding one hand with the palm up and the other hand above it, palm down, pressing one against the other.

"By the analogy of your hands, are you indicating that *buffer* is like a force and a counterforce?" I asked.

"Right! The breath acts like a buffer and the higher you go, the more buffer you need . . . the more breath you need to control that tone."

"Do you mean more strength between these counterforces, or with the breath against the larynx?"

"I think it's very dangerous to say, 'against the larynx,' if that means you're *pressing* on the larynx. A lot of singers make a terrible mistake: they're always thinking about larynx. When I did not know about the larynx I was singing better. The easiest way to sing is when it flows easily. Some people think so much about all of these technical things that they really mess themselves up."

"Like the centipede which was asked which foot it lifted first," I said. "It became so confused it couldn't walk."

"Right! I've seen so many singers get into trouble because they're so busy thinking of the tongue, the jaw, the chest, the diaphragm . . . It's too much!"

"Yet at one time," I countered, "you had to think technically to acquire those high notes. But obviously, after you learned how, that information was relegated to your subconscious, and you didn't think about it anymore when you sang."

"Right! It becomes automatic."

"But for students who have like problems, this verbalizing of technique is important. However, it must eventually become a subconscious activity. There's too much to do in an opera to be concentrating on technique all the time."

"What they are trying to do is conquer tone," she said, "and that's important, but don't let it become such a rigid kind of tone that it's not saying anything . . . I don't believe in something, Jerry," she said emphatically. "Many singing teachers with whom I have spoken, they have *made* a voice! That is *bull!* You cannot *make* a voice. You can help it technically. You can make singers conscious in order to overcome certain difficulties. But you cannot make a voice. I think a person only makes a vocal career if he has a natural instrument . . . I'm very blunt. I just tell them they don't have the voice; they're throwing their money away."

"You're actually doing them a favor. Well, back to technique, Risë. Was there anything special that helped you acquire your high notes?"

"Anna Schoen-René always thought of me as a mezzo rather than a contralto. She started lightening the voice; she gave it a quality that was not always that heavy sound. She knew, technically, I was not going to lose that. But she was after something that was not so—I'm going to use a bad word—'forced' in sound. It was not a forcing, but it was always a big tone. So now she was after the piano . . . the crescendos . . . decrescendos. In other words, the finesse singing, which is very important. It was a struggle because it was unknown to me. And then the voice got more and more even . . . easy on the top. It began to flow more. I had no difficulty in hitting a high G, or A."

"Now let us talk about terms like head voice and chest voice," I said.

"I think there are three areas in a voice," she said. "There is a chest voice, and there's a middle register, which goes into the high voice . . . the head voice. As a mezzo, if you have the easiness in that passageway between the chest and the middle voice, it makes it easier for the high."

"Where is your passage from the chest voice to the middle?"

"E or F [the first above middle C]. I worked very hard on it. My thinking was to make the sounds as close to one another as possible within the passage."

"What sensation did you find in the throat when you were mastering this part of your voice?"

"I never felt it in the throat."

"Another approach, then," I said. "Some people feel that exaggerating the nasality a bit in the _passaggio_ notes helps. Would you say that's your experience?"

"Very close. I've never thought of it in terms of nasal. I always thought of it in terms of the mask. In a way it's right. That's exactly the sound that's produced there . . ."

"Is there any special way that you thought of it?"

"No, not really."

"It was just the case of the teacher saying yes, or no, better, or worse . . ."

"Right! And my getting used to what that sound sounded like, how it reverberated within me. I think singers always have to have a mirror . . . someone to say, 'Ah, ah, ah . . . you're doing something, Risë . . . you don't hear it because you're in performance. Watch when you sing that phrase."

"Someone like your teacher, Schoen-René," I said.

"But she died when I was quite a young student. For a long time I didn't have a teacher, and then I started studying with Vera Schwarz, a very famous singer and teacher from Vienna. I was at a place where I needed help again."

"Going back a bit, can you verbalize the difference between head voice and chest voice?"

"The difference is that one feels as though it's coming from down below in the chest, and the other feels as if it's hitting up in the

mask." She indicated a point above her eyebrows. "Above the nose
. . . the whole facial mask."

"You don't feel it as much in the mask when you use chest
voice?"

"No, although actually everything is in the mask, really."

"What about high notes?" I asked. "How do they feel different?"

"I don't think they all sit in the throat in the same way. There
are certain singers who can sing without hardly opening their
mouths, and get out the most fantastic high notes I've ever heard in
my life. I was not one of those. I had to really open up and let go.
It's very individual."

"Well, most singers," I observed, "say that as they go up they
think deeper and with more spacing in the throat."

"My feeling," she answered, "always was that when I went to hit
a high note, that everything opened up, the larynx, the throat, the
mouth, the top of your mask, the sinuses . . . I would take a huge
breath and let that breath soar the tone."

"Would that be equivalent to the expression I've often heard,
'feed air'?"

"No," she said, "it's very dangerous to say 'feed air,' because then
they start pushing . . . it becomes *airy*." With that Risë sang a very
overblown blatant note. "That's not what we mean. You must support it. Vera Schwarz used an example which I find hits the nail on
the head. You know this thing that kids play with . . . there's a little ball on the top of it. As you blow into it the ball keeps popping
up and down. If you blow too hard the ball will fly off it. The thing
is to keep the ball sitting on that all the time with just enough
breath to keep it bobbing. But if you blow too hard the ball's gone.
I think the word buffering conveys that to me."

"How do you think breath should be trained?" I asked.

"You can do it with a candle." Risë held an imaginary candle
about eight inches in front of her lips. "I can go 'whhhh' and blow
it out, right? But I can take that candle and . . ." She pursed her
lips and blew out very gently, just enough to make a candle barely
flicker. "And very often I will time myself to see how long I can
blow that breath out . . . You can also do it against the palm of

your hand." She held her hand eight inches in front of her lips. "You do that with a tone," she continued, "you're on the right track. That's a buffer!"

"How do you breathe?"

"I'm a big breather. The actual proof of breath control is: sing as many phrases in one breath as you possibly can, and you time yourself . . . But with young singers you can't do that too soon . . . there's no more breath there and they start straining . . . then they're singing on the vocal cords. That's very dangerous!"

"But the actual taking of the breath . . . how about that?"

"I used to feel it very much in the back, and right here in the top part of my stomach. No chest! And none of this business . . ." She demonstrated heaving the chest.

"What does *open throat* mean to you?"

"I find it a terrible term," she grimaced. "Everybody's got a different explanation for it."

"Most singers concur with the beginning of the yawn," I said.

"Correct," she said. "I go with that."

"In general, Risë, what sort of discipline were you subjected to as a student?"

"For one year I didn't sing anything but scales."

"Did you use books of scales?"

"Not books, because in those days I did not read music. Schoen-René would start with very slow scales." She sang:

"In other words, try to find the focus of the voice, and then she'd go higher, and when the change started from the middle voice to the high voice she would say, 'Now, you hear that change . . . that has to be branched over. It must not sound different. But it must sound as if it's easily going into that.'

"Then it would be the high, full scale:

And several months later she started to do the same scale three times. Then she would give me grace notes to do:

Now she was trying other things with the voice, to give it flexibility, different styles:

The *ah* vowel was hard for me," she said. "Strangely enough, after years the *ah* was no difficulty for me."

"Well, Risë, I think I have taken enough of your time," I concluded, not wishing to stand in the way of any superachievements she had on the agenda for the rest of the day.

With that, Risë promptly escorted me to the dining room and insisted I partake of a lovely lunch which she had cooked with her own capable hands. Chalk up one more superachievement for which my bottomless stomach was deeply grateful.

Joan Sutherland

Dame Joan Sutherland is one of the outstanding singers currently active. Her phenomenal soprano voice and dazzling technical ability have made her the exponent of bel canto singing in her generation. Born in Australia, Dame Joan debuted in London in a small role in THE MAGIC FLUTE *in 1952. It was her performance as Lucia di Lammermoor at Covent Garden in 1959 that catapulted her to worldwide fame. She also sang Lucia at her Met debut in 1961, which was acclaimed by the public and critics alike. Dame Joan has concentrated on (though not limited herself to) the bel canto operas of Bellini and Donizetti, and has won praise for her portrayals of Norma, Marie in* DAUGHTER OF THE REGIMENT, *and Elvira in* I PURITANI, *as well as for the other roles in her large repertoire.* ℘

IT is not the purpose of this book to compose paeans of adulation for great singers, and surely Joan Sutherland does not need any superlatives from my pen, having already received enough of them to suffice for a dozen successful careers. Thus my purpose in this chapter will be to try to find at least one factor in Joan's vocal development that is not simply a gift from God, but rather some tangible idea, or practice, that can profit other singers, both students and professionals alike.

Our diva has been hailed as one of the finest singers of her kind since the days of Melba and Tetrazzini, and it would be criminal negligence to fail to search out some of the secrets of this phenomenal talent.

But where do these secrets lie? In the fertile mind of her conductor-pianist husband, Richard Bonynge? Before she married him they were both students at the Royal College of Music. He usually sat in on her lessons with Clive Carey and also accompanied her on the piano, always deeply concerned with her vocal development.

These were the days when Maria Callas reigned as the queen of *bel canto,* and it was then that Richard decided that if Callas could do it so could Joan Sutherland. Was he the mastermind behind this glorious career? Certainly this could have been a major factor. Such husband-and-wife teams have scored impressively in today's opera arena.

But might not the secrets of her career equally be found buried in those formative years of early childhood, when Joan, from the age of three, would sit hours on end listening to the rich mezzo-soprano voice of her mother, a voice she describes as being like that of the late Ebe Stignani. As a little child she would sit on the piano bench and imitate her mother's singing. Mrs. Sutherland constantly corrected her daughter's mistakes and gave her special breathing exercises, but she would neither teach her voice nor have her take lessons, maintaining that a youngster should not be formally taught until the age of eighteen. Her mother felt instead that she should learn to play an instrument and had her take up piano. Joan learned to play well enough to accompany herself when singing and studying, but to this day wishes she had taken it more seriously, since the piano is the most important instrument for a singer to master. Joan's mother had studied with a pupil of Marchesi and sang at least twenty minutes every day of her life up to the time of her death at the age of seventy-four.

Joan's childhood must be taken seriously, since almost all successful opera singers have sung extensively as children.

We must yet seriously consider that Joan's secrets might well lie buried deep in the very genes that were fortuitously assembled at the time of her conception.

In our desire to find out how Joan Sutherland does it, we must not forget her unusual physical endowment. She is a tall woman of almost heroic size, with a voice to match. It is not impossible, but certainly highly unusual, to find a large, dramatic voice housed in a small frame. One would expect a woman of such proportions to have larger than normal vocal cords.

Indeed, when Joan was eight years old she was taken to two nose and throat specialists, because she suffered terribly from sinus problems. Both doctors were astonished when they saw her amazing vocal cords. They knew of her mother's prodigious singing voice, and they both predicted that Joan might well develop into an extraordinary vocalist. Ordinarily they would have advised a fenestration and scraping operation on the girl's sinuses, but under the circumstances they felt she should bear with this painful physical condition until she was an adult, for fear that side reactions to their procedures might mar a potentially great career. So, indeed, Joan's greatest secret might well lie in heredity. Most likely, however, it is a judicious mixture of all three possibilities.

I had first tried to contact Joan in 1978 regarding an interview for this book. We had not worked together often enough to have more than a pleasant speaking acquaintance. After my first call Joan phoned back, but I was out of town. Upon my return she had left for Australia. In September of 1980 I had completed my manuscript and it was in the hands of my editor when I was finally able to contact Joan in San Diego, California, where she quickly consented to do an interview with me on the phone, calling from coast to coast. It was not easy having no tape recorder to work with. I had to copy everything she said in my laborious longhand for the next forty minutes, so if this all-important interview is not as detailed as some others, that's unfortunate, but it's better than no interview at all. That we got as much in as we did is a tribute to our diva's enormous patience and clear, concise thinking.

"Hi, Joan, you're a sweetheart to give me all this time on such short notice." In twenty-four hours she would be singing her final performance in San Diego with Beverly Sills, and the next morning it would be a grueling flight to Sydney, Australia.

"Since we have limited time, let us get right down to a discussion of your vocal technique," I said.

"Well," she began, "I've always said singing was very simple. Everybody tries to make it seem more complicated than it is, and that is terrible. Singing is basically breathing, supporting, and projecting. It's that simple."

"Okay," I said. "Now, you speak of breathing and supporting as being two different things."

"But they are!"

"Fine," I said, "let's begin with breathing. How do you take a breath?"

"Originally I was taught to breathe through the nose. But because of my repertoire it just cannot be done. When I have to sing that florid type of music, I don't have time to close my mouth. I have to breathe through my mouth most of the time. I also had another thing that forced me to learn to breathe through my mouth . . . I had very bad sinus trouble from the age of eight and I developed mouth breathing at that time to compensate for it."

"It's amazing how many singers suffered from nose and throat problems as children. I, for one, had bad asthma," I said.

"And learning to sing probably helped your condition," she suggested.

"I also had terrible frontal sinus headaches," I said, "that would force me to bed for a week at a time. That was cured in my twenty-eighth year when my nose and throat doctor discovered I had a polyp by the duct of my right frontal sinus. In three little minutes it was removed and I've never had an attack since."

"You're very fortunate," she said. "In my case I had to suffer with it for years. Finally, just before my critical debut in *Lucia* at Covent Garden, my doctor insisted I couldn't go through another winter in that condition. But with my commitments . . . and the rehearsals for *Lucia* . . . there was no way I could have the operation at that time. So I had to say no."

"And you made that tremendous debut under such painful and trying circumstances," I commiserated. "People think singing's easy. Just open your mouth and sing . . . Well, back to simple—not easy—basics."

"I was taught to breathe deeply through the thorax with . . . let's say, the diaphragm, as everyone does—but it feels like the pit of the stomach, or the abdomen, really. It's deeper than the stomach, it's the pit of the abdomen. Many singers breathe much too high," she said.

"Is the rib cage involved in this deep breath?" I asked.

"You can't help but expand the rib cage if you breathe deeply," she replied.

"Of course," I agreed. "Now, let's discuss support. Some singers describe it as a sensation of pushing down . . . like giving birth to a baby. Others say there must instead be a tightening of the lowest abdominal muscles, providing a sort of floor beneath. And yet others liken it to a feeling of having a balloon in the region of the diaphragm which you push in from all sides."

"It *is* like a floor. It *is* like a balloon," she exclaimed. "It's like a floor holding an air-filled balloon . . . without tying the top of the balloon, though."

"Hold it, Joan," I protested. "You're going too fast for me to write all this down. Forgive me for being so infernally slow."

"You poor thing," she sympathized. "How will you ever be able to put this all together and make sense out of it? I am skipping all over the place."

"On the contrary," I said, "you are being quite methodical and clear . . . Now, you were speaking of support being like a balloon . . ."

"Yes," she continued, "you must control the passage of the air. You control it so it deflates slowly. That way you prevent the air from escaping too rapidly. And then you sing *on* the breath, not with it."

"Yes," I said, "I have often heard that expression, usually in conjunction with the ball bouncing on top of the fountain . . . If that covers your thoughts on support, let's move on to what 'open throat' means to you."

"I think you should feel nothing in the throat," she said emphatically. "If I feel anything in the throat, I know I'm singing badly. Open throat means to me a feeling of complete relaxation in the throat. The most I would feel would be that the chin was dropped."

"Then you don't think in terms of any kind of throat setting, or . . ."

"You pitch the sound in the mind," she said, "and . . . project!"

"Now, are you using the word 'project' in the sense of vocal projection . . . placement?" I asked.

"Yes, of course."

"Then, what are your thoughts on placement?"

"I was taught that iniquitous forward production," was her response.

For a moment I was unsure of her meaning. Had she been taught that way and subsequently decided it was bad, or was she ironically maintaining she believed in it, while many others held it to be very bad? When I voiced my perplexity, she explained, and irony prevailed.

"I believe in it. Yes!"

"Then placement . . ."

". . . is projecting into the correct sinus cavities. One feels as if the sound were being projected against the front of the hard palate . . . the dome of the palate . . . the front of the dome," she amended. "It's basically very simple, that's really all there is to it. In actual practice it takes a while to overcome the pitfalls."

"Can we take a few moments to discuss the registers of the voice?" I suggested.

"Some people believe there should be no registers," she said. "But you can't get away from the fact that there are low, middle, and high registers. Through technique we have to disguise or blend the three so there appears to be an unbroken line of sound."

"Do you use chest voice?" I asked.

"I feel the chest voice should be used sparingly," she said. "In a way, my chest voice has been underdeveloped."

"Because it is not necessary in your kind of repertoire?" I asked.

"Oh no! A dramatic soprano needs it in *Trovatore, Norma,* and also *Fledermaus.* It is also necessary in some of the Handel operas, which have such a great range. But I really have left it rather underdeveloped."

"How about the second register, the middle voice?" I prompted.

"The basis of training any voice," she said, "is to develop a solid middle. I like a solid middle, a fat sound."

"And going from the chest, if one uses it extensively, to the middle is problematic for many," I said. "It can cause a real hole in the middle voice, which I agree is the foundation."

"Once you get a hole in the middle of the voice," she said, "forget it!"

"Most sopranos I've spoken with are cautious about using much chest voice just because of a fear of aggravating that sort of problem," I said. "As we said before, although singing should be simple, it's not easy."

"Well, a very important thing," she said, "is that not everybody can sing. I don't believe you can just fabricate a great voice out of nothing. I think that lasting voices are the gift of God."

"But what a singer does with that gift is also so important," I interjected. "All right, when I first opened my mouth at the age of sixteen I had a big, impressive sound. Doctors looking at my vocal cords are always so surprised how large and open the throat is and how unusually easy it is to see the cords, which are quite long as you would expect from a person who is six and a half feet tall. I was born with that. But I had no high voice at all. That means I simply didn't know how. But I learned how. I have seen some singers with extraordinary voices who never find the way to sing high notes and end up as comprimarios because of this one defect."

"In my case," Joan said, "when I was a child I used to sing with a mezzo voice at the piano, because all of my mother's music was in low keys. But when I sang around the house I used a higher voice. But nobody would have realized I could sing repertoire such as *Lucia* then. My voice had not been trained in that area."

"You know, Joan," I mused, "everything you have said thus far is completely mainstream good vocalism. Every good singer says the same things. But you're not just a good singer, you're an extraordinary singer. Is the difference simply that you were born that way? Or do you do anything different in technique that sets you apart? Granted, you were born with a superior instrument, but let's zero in a moment on something you had to develop, such as that extraordinary high voice. Apparently you didn't always have that."

"When I went to England to study with Clive Carey, I was frightened of my top."

"Now, that's the sort of thing I'm looking for," I said. "When you sing a high E, it is not the typical thin, squeaky coloratura sound, it is a dramatic sound that knocks one off his feet. What did you and Clive Carey do to achieve that?"

"Clive always said the middle voice should be taken up as high as possible to preserve the quality, the fatness of the voice. As a result, the break between my middle and high voices comes higher than for most sopranos: it's around A or B [just below high C]. In the middle voice you mustn't let the sound get too high in placement too soon. Otherwise if it gets too high-sounding and if you 'think high prematurely,' you can't reach the D's and E's [above high C]. So you preserve that fat sound until you get to the *acuti* [high notes], and then you should sort of flip back . . . Well, you should feel that the sound projection flips to the back of the soft palate and the sound travels out through the back of the top of the head."

"When you reach the real high range, your feeling of placement in the front of the dome of the hard palate flips back to the rear of the soft palate, and then I assume the forward projection of the voice is now diverted up and back a bit," I said. "Anything else to add to this?"

"You anchor the high voice to the middle. Don't let the middle voice creep into that higher area, that higher placement. Well, will that do it?"

I glanced at my watch and realized we had been at it for over forty minutes. I would have liked to go on for a couple of hours, but Joan had certainly been more than gracious, so I thanked her and wished her well on her journey home.

Then my mind went back to the original question, "Where do the secrets lie?" Surely the last part of our discussion on high notes came up with something different, unique. It was such a tangible idea, or practice, that I was seeking for this book, but it was far from the whole picture.

Where do the secrets lie? By fortuitous circumstance Joan Sutherland came under the excellent influence of Clive Carey and Richard Bonynge. By fortuitous circumstance Joan Sutherland was raised in an unusual and stimulating musical environment. By fortuitous circumstance Joan Sutherland was born with a unique vocal instrument, but also with a mind more than capable of meeting a career's challenges. And just who arranged all these fortuitous circumstances? In the final analysis I think Joan is right. It is all a gift of God.

Martti Talvela

Martti Talvela is universally recognized as one of the front-rank bassos in the world today. Born in Finland, he made his debut in 1960 in Helsinki as Sparafucile in RIGOLETTO. He became known for his Wagner roles at the Bayreuth Festival, where he appeared beginning in 1962, especially the part of King Marke in TRISTAN UND ISOLDE. Mr. Talvela made his Metropolitan Opera debut in 1968 as the Grand Inquisitor in DON CARLOS, and later was enthusiastically received in the title role of the Met's new production of the original version of Mussorgsky's BORIS GODUNOV. 𝄢

"DID it bother you that I was taller than you?" Martti Talvela's inscrutable eyes fixed themselves on me. Until the Finnish bass came to the Met, I was incontestably the tallest member of the company, towering over all at six foot six and a half. Now this ex-amateur boxer and schoolteacher, six foot seven and apparently three hundred pounds plus, had replaced me as the reigning skyscraper.

Did it bother me that he was taller than I? I adapt quickly to all challenges.

"Certainly not," I coolly riposted. "Why do you think I bought these shoes with three-inch heels?" I now stood at an impressive six foot nine and a half, carrying, I admit, a mere bantam weight of two hundred forty pounds. Martti and I were sparring in a friendly competitive spirit, as he had just very successfully performed in *Boris Godunov,* a role in which he stands unique on the Continent, and I was soon to replace him in the last four performances.

Since this incident, about five years had passed and he was doing his first Gurnemanz at the Met. I came in to interview him during the second act while Klingsor was holding forth with his Flower Maidens.

We began speaking about his childhood on a farm by Lake Ladoga in Finland. He showed a good talent for business as well as singing when he was five. A visitor at his home asked if he could sing and he replied, "Yes, but it will cost five marks!"

And so his professional career was launched. Martti sang all the time in choirs and about the house. He and his father and brothers brought firewood out of the forest by horse and cart. Martti was the driver, and they clearly knew when he was ready to drive home, because he would begin singing. There was always music in his family; his father sang and played the violin.

"My people are very friendly, optimistic, singing, dancing all the time," he said. "We have some kind of mixed temperament. The normal Finnish man, he is very quiet . . . before the first bottle of vodka," he laughed.

"I went to pedagogic high school to be a teacher," he continued. "I taught only three years at a high school in the city where I now have my festival. In high school we had a lot of music. I had this teacher's background and I had three languages. I made my high school without my own money, because we lost everything when the Russians took Karelia. We lost our farm, but my father and mother built it up again."

"When did you start learning opera?" I asked.

"I visited an opera house for the first time in my life when I was twenty-five. I learned from recordings by Ezio Pinza, Cesare Siepi . . . your records I didn't have at that time. Pinza had a gold voice. I only heard recordings, but so much that my wife, who was pregnant for our first child, she couldn't any more stand the voice, because even years after that, when Pinza sang from the recording, she got . . . what is that sickness when you get in the morning?"

"Morning sickness," I said.

"Yes, and she had some kind of association with . . ."

"You mean she heard his records so often during her pregnancy that afterward she always got morning sickness when she heard his voice?"

"Yes! But not anymore, because she loved it too."

"When did you seriously start studying?" I asked.

"My real start was after I won a national competition for recital singers in Finland. I was already twenty-seven years old. When I

Martti Talvela

began to study opera I was twenty-eight. I never believed that anyone can teach you until I met Carl Martin Oehman. He was very
famous . . . sang at the Met. He was my first teacher.

"And then the trip to Stockholm. The Royal Opera . . . Fantastic
company! Fantastic colleagues. I worked there for one year. I met
Göran Gentele and we worked on *Midsummer Night's Dream* . . .
until four and five in the morning. Nobody thought it was too
much. I sang about twelve roles in Stockholm. After one year I
debuted in Bayreuth and Berlin. Berlin became my first home. I
sing today almost only at the Met and Berlin. This is enough, it's
about forty performances a year and you know how heavy that can
be . . . Filippo, Gurnemanz, Boris . . . And then I try to sing recitals.

"People here, they ask me for recitals, but they always ask me to
do programs with Chaliapiniade. I am not going to ever do this
kind of program. I sing Moussorgsky, of course, but I do not sing
Russian folk songs . . . Why? I'm not Russian, I'm Finnish. I do
songs like Schubert . . . songs that are too big for baritone . . .
'Prometheus,' 'An Schwäger Kronos,' 'Doppelgänger' . . . maybe
'Aufenthalt.' I like those dramatic songs . . . and Rachmaninoff. I
have done the *Winterreise* . . .

"If anybody asks me to give a classical program and it is not interesting, I am ready to give the money back, because singing is not
a job, it is a profession. You have to express what you feel."

"When you studied voice with Oehman, did you use scales and
arpeggios?" I asked.

"Not really. We immediately went to songs . . . some Swedish
songs, some Mendelssohn songs and Schubert . . . immediately.
The voice was in pretty good shape. Oehman always told me, 'You
have to find yourself.' One thing that came to me was breathing. My
muscles on my stomach, they have always been in perfect shape,
because I was a boxer. The breathing was too much, too strong, but
it has to be relaxed at the same time. The breathing is important
that it goes to the whole body.

"We have only very few truths in singing. Many teachers will
make it more complicated. One truth is, in my opinion, you have to
learn by yourself. Try and try it again. But you have to know, for

example, that the tongue has to be down, because this makes relaxation for you . . ."

"Let's go back to breathing," I interrupted, "and come back to the tongue afterward. When you take a breath, is it a deep breath? Do you use the chest at all?"

"I'd rather use the whole body," he responded. "Then when I have parts which are more difficult, I take it very high breath, and without any pressure, and I keep it a little bit down . . . back down." He demonstrated what he meant.

"Oh," I observed, "after you take the breath high, you sort of fix or lock the chest in position, and start exhaling from below."

"Yes, yes!"

"But you feel the pressure should be held away from . . ."

"The *gola*," he said, "down here . . . how do you call it in English?"

"The larynx," I said, "or the throat."

"Throat! If the throat is under pressure, the singing is off. You have to feel a total relaxation. It must be down and relaxed." He demonstrated again.

"Ah," I said, watching his massive frame closely, "you take the breath with the chest and all the rest of the body, and then you lower the chest a bit . . ."

"About one inch," he said.

"So the pressure goes away from the throat?"

"Yes. I don't use it very often."

"Only for a long phrase?"

"Or maybe when the music, the line, goes very much down." He then sang a low phrase from the end of the aria "In diesen heil'gen Hallen" from *The Magic Flute*.

"Of course, you need a greater quantity of breath when you sing low," I said.

"And you need more relaxation."

"Some singers," I said, "describe support as a feeling of pushing down . . . like giving birth to a baby. How do you feel about this?"

"I don't push down. I fill my whole body . . . like breathing a rose . . . a beautiful wild rose . . ."

"Smelling a rose," I corrected.

Martti Talvela

"Smelling a rose. I do help the breathing with my hands when I am training." He held his hands and arms out a bit to the side, raising them as he inhaled, and lowering them as he exhaled. "I think the whole body has to be full of air . . . but not pressure."

"Do you feel any compression in the diaphragm?"

"Not really. It's only full. Just stop before there's pressure. Your body has to have some kind of elegance . . . straight."

"Not a low, collapsed chest," I said.

"No, because artistically it collapses then. I don't think it's a matter if the breathing goes here or elsewhere. I worked years with only my stomach. My breathing was this . . . [he took a breath without moving his chest and, as a consequence, his stomach protruded] but this is wrong, because then your chest is empty. This is something I learned from Maestro Marzollo in New York, so I can say he is my second teacher."

"Before, you mentioned the tongue has to be down," I said.

"Yes."

"What does *open throat* mean to you?"

"It means that situation just before a yawn. My own mistake is that my tongue doesn't believe me," he laughed. "It goes up, and this is very bad."

"Do *head* and *chest voice* mean anything to you?"

"No," was his firm reply. "The formation of the voice has to be all the time the same. You make a complicated game of your singing . . . you think, 'Now the phrase is down in my chest voice,'" he said, with a deep, rumbling sound, "and then, 'my head voice . . .'" he continued in a light, falsetto sound, ending in a spontaneous burst of laughter that shook the dressing-room walls.

"I would say," he went on, "you sing a recital program, you would use a little bit more your head."

"What do you mean by 'your head'?" I asked.

"The chest voice is heavier. But the voice should be in one position. The color comes immediately when your voice is in good shape, and you *think* what you sing. The sound is your servant. Many times I do a heavy sound on purpose, because the sound is only a servant, and we have to tell people something of what we intend. What they do not see, they can find out only when we mean something with our singing. You shouldn't be an empty bell. The sound should be there too."

"The soul must show through," I observed. "Now, how about placement?"

"Here in the throat you shouldn't feel it, but it's got to come up." He indicated his face and sinuses. "I don't know what it should be, because it's all so individual. It *has* to come *up* . . . you have to find training up . . . because if it's relaxed up . . ."

"Relaxed up," I said. "You mean not forced up into position . . . not driven there . . . relaxed?"

"Yes."

"As you go from low to high range, do you feel any change in space in the throat?" I asked.

"I feel, if it is extremely high . . . like in the Ninth Symphony . . . [he sang the difficult opening phrase] I have to push a little. Sometimes when I am in very good shape, I don't feel any change, even to the F sharp, but it's not very often. Like Caruso said, 'The day I'm in perfect shape, nobody sings.'" This too ended in a big laugh.

"Do you feel as you go up like that into the high range that there's a little more spacing in your throat?" I continued.

"You don't have high notes and low notes; the voice has to be in the same position. When I'm working, learning, not cold, there's no movement here in the throat. The position is the same and you can go to D, E, even F. Higher I cannot go."

"When you warm up on the day of a performance, do you use scales, or sing the role you are performing?"

"I sang today, Gurnemanz. In a tiny voice, of course."

"You sang it lightly . . . marking?"

"No! I sang it with pianissimo . . . not marking. It's so difficult . . . so long [Gurnemanz], and I sang it yesterday."

"Lightly, or full voice?" I asked.

"I am in the hotel, I cannot sing it! Small voice . . . I sang it, looking at the score. You have to see the notes, also. When you need, you have to find the picture in your mind."

"Do you do any singing with the full voice on the day of a performance?" I asked.

"Yes, in the theater, maybe ten or fifteen minutes, but that day I have been singing almost two hours."

"But quietly . . . pianissimo," I added.

"Yes."

"When you sing pianissimo for two hours, do you still use the diaphragm in the same way as when you sing forte?"

"Yes, the breathing has to be the same. The resonance on that pianissimo should be also rich."

"The third act will begin in twenty minutes." It was the voice of Stanley Levine, our assistant stage manager, coming over the intercom, and it was time to wind up the interview and let Martti get back to the old Gurnemanz.

"Do you have any further observations on singing technique?" I asked.

Martti reflected a moment. "If you can explain how the Lord looks . . . He does not exist anymore. The same thing with singing technique. You cannot really describe it. But you have to give impulses [clues] for other people, for yourself, how to find it. There are always different models . . . Singing is a juggler's business. The juggler takes one more of those balls, and then one more, until he has twenty-five balls, at least . . ."

I must admit it has felt that way to me many times. And then there are those other times when the voice is very easy, and singing seems so simple. And, as Martti said, that's the day "nobody sings."

Shirley Verrett

Shirley Verrett was born in New Orleans and trained in America. Her debut occurred in Cologne, Germany, in a modern opera, THE DEATH OF RASPUTIN, by Nicolas Nabokov. She achieved success in Europe at several major opera houses before making her debut at the Metropolitan Opera as Carmen in 1968. Miss Verrett established her career as a mezzo-soprano, but more recently has sung soprano roles as well. At the Met in 1973, she sang both the soprano role of Cassandra and the mezzo-soprano role of Dido in the opening performance of the new production of Berlioz's LES TROYENS. TV audiences in America have seen her portrayal of Tosca in the "Live from the Met" series. Miss Verrett has also performed both Norma and Adalgisa in NORMA.

MY father, Ray Heinz, turned to the man seated next to him and proudly announced, "That's my son up there."

The black gentleman to whom he had spoken quietly smiled. "That's my daughter up there."

Shirley Verrett and I had just sung our first performance together in Beethoven's Ninth under the baton of Zubin Mehta. The occasion was the official opening of the Dorothy Chandler Pavilion in Los Angeles.

And then, over a decade later, there I was dashing through a torrential downpour from my cab to the door of Shirley's West Side apartment. Now she was a brilliant star of the Metropolitan and I had just recently witnessed her beautiful portrayal of Tosca on television with Luciano Pavarotti. Quite a success story for a young girl who had debuted at the Met as a mezzo-soprano and then switched to dramatic soprano!

We quickly began the interview, since she was on a tight schedule and had to leave in an hour. It soon became evident that the word *quick* was the keynote to the interview. *Quick* is the only way to describe the facile brain that I had come to pick. That racing mind could only be compared to a high-speed IBM computer as the words came tumbling out at record speed. Without a doubt I garnered more information in one hour than normally would have been possible in three. Space will allow me only a skeleton account of what transpired.

Certain phrases flew at me that began to give just an inkling of what made this young dynamo function.

"Sometimes I've read a book of three hundred pages and maybe I'll get one sentence I can use, but it's worth it.

"I had to stop with teachers because I knew there was something else I could get out of my own voice.

"I got interested in reading medical books because of a swayback.

"I was very curious and asked, 'Why certain scales?'

". . . working alone after the Juilliard days . . . experimenting right on the stage . . . always experimenting!

"I never used to take everything the teacher said.

"I said, 'Now I'm going to sing as if I never had a lesson in my life . . . in certain passages.' People used to say, 'You'll ruin your voice.' What do they think I am . . . stupid?"

A gestalt began to emerge of a determined, inquisitive, and unorthodox mind diligently applied to the conquest of the operatic voice.

Before delving into technical matters I extracted some biographical material from her. She was born in New Orleans and brought to Oxnard, California, at an early age. When she was four and a half her mother discovered she had a voice. It was a happy combination of a natural talent and a musical family. Her father was her first teacher and began by telling her things about the diaphragm, but she "didn't understand all that."

At the age of five Shirley made her public debut in church, singing, "Yes, Jesus Loves Me, the Bible Tells Me So."

Her first professional teacher was Arna Fitziu; and then she continued as a student at Juilliard in New York under Madame Freschel. From there it was a short step to the Met. Recently she has worked with Maestro Marzollo because she "wanted another pair of ears."

"Did Arna Fitziu begin teaching you with scales and arpeggios?" I asked.

"Of course," she responded. "And I was very curious and asked, 'Why certain scales?' Certain scales were for flexibility, and certain scales were for stretching the voice."

"Stretching the range, or what?" I asked.

"The range and many things," was her answer. "Not having to sing forte all the time."

"Did you have a natural pianissimo?"

"No. I had to teach myself. There were a couple of times I had to do it on my own, and I had to stop with teachers because I knew there was something else I could get out of my own voice."

"Can you give me an example of a scale you used to stretch the voice?" I asked.

"I liked the Great Scale—that's Lilli Lehmann's term—where you go up by steps on one note . . . crescendo-decrescendo . . . say, you start on *mah* . . . counting: one, two, three, four . . . then *meh, mee, moh, moo* . . . crescendo-decrescendo all the way up as far as you can go . . . then counting to eight eventually."

"Did you use the Great Scale as a warm-up?"

"That wasn't the first scale," she replied. "Usually the first kinds of scales you do are the short, fast ones . . . [she demonstrated]:

that kind of thing and:

If the notes aren't there you hit it and come down. It's easier than trying to sustain it. I still believe you should start off with the faster-moving things. Sometimes it's easier to go across notes that might be weak and then come back to them . . . Every voice seems to have a little weak spot, and mine—because I started singing as a mezzo and not as the voice it was supposed to have been—had a little break between the E and F above middle C. To bridge that I started doing:

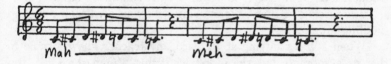

that kind of chromatic exercise throughout the voice, especially in that place where the little break, the transition, was."

"Some singers," I said, "feel that putting the voice more in the mask . . . or nose . . . helps in the transition."

"I don't believe in that," was her firm reply. "I found that as I've gone into this other repertoire [I understood this to mean changing from mezzo-soprano to soprano], these two or three notes . . . this passage has been bridged all by itself because the voice has *lifted*. Someone had told me about this lifting. I never thought of the voice lifting out of one area into another where it really belongs. And this is exactly what has happened to me.

"There is a vocalise I used to do going down to the second F below middle C . . . but you could never sing that in public. I used to have fun going down there. It was wrong for me to do that even though my voice was continually going up, so I began to lift, vocalizing from the G or F below middle C, going up as far as E flat and E natural full voice."

"Well," I recalled, "the first time I heard you after this 'uplifting' transition was in *Norma* in Boston."

"That was the first *Norma* I ever did," she interjected.

"I stood there with my mouth hanging open, and said, 'My gosh, she's a real soprano.'"

"I always was," she answered, "but I had to go the other route."

"But when you went down you still had that beautiful low voice . . ."

"But a dramatic soprano has to have that," she said. "You know, that's where the difficulty comes in. You get very angry a lot of times with people . . . When you're a mezzo-soprano . . . a soprano with a few notes missing, who can't really get that top . . . what they try to do is make those mezzo-sopranos sound more like what *they* think a mezzo is supposed to sound like. A mezzo's voice shouldn't be pounded, rounded off . . . It should be natural, clear . . . no forcing . . . no covering. Sing with your own color . . . stop fiddling around!

"When I was studying at Juilliard, my teacher knew I came to her as a soprano, but she didn't want this. When she said, 'You sound like a soprano,' I said, 'I feel free.' I used to fight back. I never used to take everything the teacher said. Then she'd say, 'Round it off . . . Put a little more of the umlaut instead of plain *ee.*'

"Starting as early as I did I got used to my own voice, and I always knew when I was trying to superimpose. If I have to do all kinds of covering, then something's wrong. The sound should come out very, very free . . . The sound that comes out without you doing anything about it. Then, as you learn, you have to modify the vowel a little bit when you go up . . . without doing all kinds of things inside . . . and with the mouth . . . A lot of people teach that the jaw has to come forward . . . or you drop the jaw from the hinge by the ear. It's true you can practice that way if it's not natural to you to open the throat.

"I was brought up with my father where everything was rounded lips, and it took me a long time to get out of that. But we've got long necks, we've got short necks, the cavity inside the mouth is different . . . In my race we have thicker lips, so how can a teacher who has a tiny little mouth say, 'Do the same thing?' We've got to work with each individual."

"Many singers," I said, "believe in opening the mouth naturally, but not in using the lips to form vowels like *oo* and *ee.*"

"At this point in my life I agree that lots of vowels should not be

Shirley Verrett

with the lips. If you are speaking you don't use the lips that much for *oo*. When you sing oftentimes you go like this . . . [she sang an *oo*, much overdoing it with the lips]. I think that's exaggerated. You must use the mouth and just as natural as possible, but it takes a lot of training to do that."

"You spoke of scales that stretch the voice and one to bridge the passage. Are there," I prompted, "other scales, say, for flexibility?"

"Of course," she said. "You do the fast arpeggio and Arna Fitziu taught me a scale that I use to this day for flexibility. That is:

all the way through the voice. It's a fantastic scale for me."

"What kind of vocalizing do you do now and how long?" I asked.

"About a half hour to forty-five minutes," she said. "Very rarely to an hour. But I'm working with English words for the first time in my life. I used to do just vowels. Now I'm beginning to work on things like *chocolate* . . ." She sang:

Shirley said she repeated this scale going down one note lower each time, sometimes ending on *kee* instead of *coh*. She then proceeded to do another scale, based on the word *apple* . . . sung as *ahpel*:

Ahpel, ahpel, ahpel, ahpel, ahpel, ahpel, ahpel, ahpel, coh. ✳

She again said she repeated it starting a note lower each time, sometimes ending on *kee*, until she reached the low G.

(I have subsequently tried the chocolate and apple scales myself and found they gave the tongue muscles a great workout. Try them for yourself.)

"Then," she continued, "I start working myself back up as high as the voice will go and at that point it absolutely feels to me, physically, as if the throat is stretching."

"Stretching open, or . . . ?" I was groping for her meaning.

"Stretching *open*. I know it's only the vocal cords that are doing something back there—you know, more taut—but it feels as if the throat is stretching. The tongue is doing something like coming out of the throat . . . even farther when I'm going up to the high E . . . Then I start down with another scale that sounds like NBC:

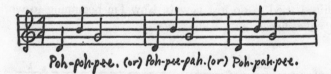

Poh-poh-pee. (or) Poh-pee-pah. (or) Poh-pah-pee.

That has a tendency to keep the voice very narrow . . . nice and rounded . . . and also bridges that transition point . . . very nicely. I go up as high as I can with that, usually not above B natural above the staff. Then I do the Great Scale: that is a great exercise for strengthening the elasticity in the voice. Then I do some fast passages for flexibility."

"Let's discuss technical concepts in an ordered fashion," I suggested, "starting with the breath."

"When I was at my best, a lot of people used to think my breath would go on forever," she began. "They didn't know I had worked for years trying to compensate for a swayback by taking difficult breathing exercises, reciting poetry . . . maybe a stanza or two in one breath to compensate . . . to train the muscles. It has helped me a lot going through this . . . I understand a bit more about my own instrument and I got interested in reading medical books because of my swayback. If you can't take a deep breath because the back is swayed, you start appreciating what the breath is all about in singing. Now I am free . . . the back is straight and it's just . . . Go! I've tried scapular breathing, with the shoulders raised . . . just to prove it to myself. I don't go into technical things like intercostal breathing, but when you take a breath the rib cage stretches out. The diaphragm descends and flattens out, giving room for the lungs to expand."

"Do you think of taking the breath deeply?" I asked.

"I do," she said. "At the beginning I always like to take a breath through the nose because I feel that it does warm the air. But you can't stop (sniff) every minute (sniff) and do like that. It's between the mouth and the nose that you're taking the breath . . . You can take up too much breath, and that's bad. If I take *that* kind of breath, I lose it too soon because more air comes out when you say the first word. I sing my best when I take a breath normally."

"Okay," I agreed. "Now, what about open throat?"

"For me," she said, "it all comes from the way that breath was taken."

"Some singers allude to the beginning of a yawn," I said, "or smelling a rose."

"Well, I don't go into that," she said. "But, you know, Jerry, to tell you the God's truth, I cannot think that an open throat is any more than the vowels being in the right place and breathing correctly."

"If the vowel sound is correct the throat is open?"

"The throat would be open," she agreed. "If it's impeded by the tongue something's wrong. You know, most people think you have to have a groove in the tongue and they groove it so much that it sits up against the uvula . . . against the walls of the throat. I don't know how the sound can come out that way."

"Some people talk about depressing the tongue in the back with the larynx down," I said.

"I don't like to fiddle with the larynx," was her reply.

"Do you think of the sound starting in the larynx?"

"I think so, but I don't like the pressing of it. When you start gripping, that's bad."

"Others say there should be no sensation in the throat," I said.

"That's right. Free . . ."

"What about placement?" I asked.

"One thing I will definitely say: I don't believe in singing forward! The sound goes forward and impinges on placement. I was taught that you place the voice forward in the mask. These things I don't believe in anymore. I believe that placing the voice forward is actually the breath that comes from these vocal cords . . . and they begin to radiate."

"As you go up the scale, say, on the vowel *ah,* do you find you need a little more spacing in the throat?" I asked.

"As I watch myself the mouth seems to drop all by itself. But as soon as I start to clutch and say, 'Oh, oh . . . I'm going up higher,' I'm in trouble."

"What do you feel about *coloring* the voice for effect? Should one always sing on the stage exactly as she does in the studio?" I asked.

"When I was singing *El Amor Brujo* I said, 'Let it all hang out' . . . open chest for days. But when I was in the studio, at my home before I finished that piece . . . knowing what I was going to do on stage . . . I would always vocalize all the lines . . . *keeping the line.* And then I changed my mind when I got on stage. I said, 'Now I am going to sing as if I never had a lesson in my life . . . in certain passages. But I could not vocalize that way, because if I did I would have a break in the voice a mile long. And people used to say, 'Oh, don't do too many of those . . . you'll ruin your voice.' I used to say to myself, 'What do they think I am . . . stupid, that I'm going to vocalize this way?' Of course you have to know how to change gears all of a sudden and say, 'Okay, now I'm going to go into blatant chest and see what happens,' but you're not doing this for your vocalise, you're only doing it for the moment."

As the interview ended and I left Shirley's apartment, I knew I had just encountered that exceptional kind of mind that knows how to change gears all of a sudden . . . experimenting . . . always experimenting . . . even "experimenting right on the stage!"

Would you have the courage to try that? If you are lucky enough to have inherited a *quick* mind like Shirley Verrett, you might just pull it off.

Bill Zakariasen

Bill Zakariasen was born in Minnesota. As a child, he sang in the church choir, but did not study voice until he was already in college. He developed his tenor voice and sang leading roles at the University of Michigan opera workshop. He sang in the choruses of the New York City Opera and the Metropolitan Opera, but eventually decided to devote his time to writing. Currently Mr. Zakariasen is music critic for the New York Daily News. 🎵

STOKIE: THE MAGNIFICENT PHONY

This arresting headline on the music page of the New York *Daily News* really grabbed me. Its audacity, combined with my own recent experience of doing *Boris Godunov* with Leopold Stokowski in Carnegie Hall, compelled me to read further.

". . . He was born a Cockney in the south of London, yet he manufactured an inimitable accent that resembled Pomeranian. He became one of the world's leading conductors, although his only previous musical job was that of church organist . . . When he conducted *Turandot* at the Met in 1961, he never learned the score . . .

"Yes, 'Stokie' was a phony. He was also a genius necessarily larger than life . . . he quickly turned the Cincinnati Symphony into one of the world's leading orchestras, and shortly later he did the same for the Philadelphia. How he did it is a secret that died with him . . .

"I sang in the chorus during those Met *Turandots*, and I remember he seldom gave the right cue. But I also remember the score never sounded so luxuriously romantic or as terrifyingly exciting under any other conductor . . ."

An unusual review, such as would only be possible from a critic who had had considerable experience as a performer. And his experience working with Stokie closely paralleled my own.

Bill Zakariasen

I vividly recalled doing *Boris Godunov* with Stokowski and the American Symphony in Carnegie Hall. It came as a great surprise to me that the Maestro seemed to have no conception of *Boris*, understanding nothing of the words and drama. I complained to my wife Lucia that Stokie simply did not know the opera.

"How can you say such a thing?" she cried indignantly. "I have never heard any orchestra play *Boris* with such beautiful dynamics and quality. You are wrong!"

So my experience seemed to closely parallel that of Bill Zakariasen, who had written the audacious critique of Stokie following his death.

When Ken McCormick, my Doubleday editor, suggested that I might include a Met chorister in this book, I immediately thought of Bill. The idea of interviewing a colleague who had sung in the Metropolitan Opera chorus for ten years, only to graduate to music critic for the New York *Daily News*, appealed to me. This promised to be an interesting interview of an interesting person.

We met in my dressing room at the Met, and Bill seemed very much at home in the theater where he had given ten years of service. I was curious about how those years had influenced his view as a music critic. First we discussed his background.

Born in Minnesota and raised in Flint, Michigan, Bill sang in the church choir as a boy soprano. He did not pursue music after that until his fourth year in college. Instead, he intended to be a biologist, but soon switched to a major in English. He joined the chapel choir but did not study voice. He did take courses in dance and joined some acting groups. For his fourth year of college he transferred to the University of Michigan, at which time he began to study voice, developing into a dramatic tenor. Joseph Blatt, head of the university opera workshop, soon had him singing Florestan in *Fidelio* and other dramatic tenor leads in their local productions. (According to reliable sources, he had an outstanding voice.)

After graduating from the University of Michigan, Bill came to New York seeking a career in opera. He immediately became involved in the church circuit and summer stock, doing both solo parts and choral work, a path followed by many young singers faced with the problems of survival in the big city. Then came a chorus-comprimario* contract with the New York City Opera, and for the small roles he sang he received an extra fifteen dollars a week. In 1960, after three years with the City Opera, Bill joined the Metropolitan Opera chorus, where he sang for the next ten years. This experience provided him with a unique insight into opera from a critic's point of view. For example, his attitude toward that capricious diva Maria Callas just borders on that of a fan.

One night when Bill was playing the part of one of the spies in *Tosca,* Miss Callas stepped into the title role without having a staging rehearsal with the full cast. In the first-act Church Scene she entered the stage, backing up without seeing Bill directly in her path. After a precarious collision, she whirled about and burned him down with her fiercest glare. Bill, rather shaken, came off stage only to be met in the wings by Stanley Levine, assistant stage manager, who cheerfully said, "You're in for it now."

Bill immediately sought out Callas to apologize.

"Oh," she said, "you're the one!"

With that, Bill prepared himself to go out and collect his severance pay.

"That was marvelous," she continued. "I've wanted to do it that way for years. Keep it in."

The next performance Bill deliberately placed himself in her path and the collision was reenacted, complete with the same fiery glare from the prima donna—followed by a sly wink.

"Now, that's a good sport," Bill said to me enthusiastically. "She never deserved her notorious reputation as a temperamental artist. She was a true professional."

Then our conversation was diverted into choral singing itself.

"Drawing on your thirteen years of experience as an opera chorister," I asked, "what would you say are the problems that a soloist would not experience?"

"Well, for one thing," he said, "a chorister's musicianship must be more polished. That's because mistakes stand out more strongly. If a chorister sings *forte* when everyone else is singing *piano,* his

* A comprimario is one who sings secondary parts in the opera, usually character roles.

error is very obvious to the listener. Also, a chorister must learn a lot more music than a soloist."

"What are the dangers to the voice of a chorister?"

"First of all," he continued, "you can't hear yourself when you sing in a chorus, and there is no way to know if the sound you are making is correct. Also, the choral director will often demand a certain type of tonal production that you can't agree with, but you must comply. These sorts of things get the voice off line.

"Also, the vigorous routine of three hours of rehearsal each day with performances at night is too much for any chorister with a poor vocal technique. Some people are always out with laryngitis and others never. Of course, one advantage is that, if you have a cold, you can take it easy. But one of the greatest hazards is a result of the repetitive routine which can cause one little by little to lose the desire to continue studying. In this process of degeneration, you arrive home tired from rehearsal. Facing the prospect of a performance that evening, you don't feel much like vocalizing or taking a voice lesson.

"After ten years in the Met chorus, I began to feel I didn't want to continue for the rest of my life in such a direction. Others like myself had left the Met chorus for bigger ambitions. Most wanted to be soloists and one even left to be a composer. About this time I had a fall on the ice and broke my leg, necessitating a leave of absence.

"After my recovery I almost went back, but I had returned to writing, doing some articles for both *Opera News* and a hi-fi magazine, and finally I decided to go into the literary field. I went to San Francisco, where I worked for the San Francisco *Examiner* off and on for three years as a replacement, reviewing everything from plays to movies. I also was music critic for the San Francisco *Progress*.

"After twice winning a grant from the Music Critics' Association, I returned to New York, where I began doing reviews for *The West Sider*, and finally, in October of 1974, I got a call from the *Daily News*. They had no regular music critic and needed a review of the opera *Death in Venice* at the Met. They liked my coverage of the work enough to hire me as a freelancer until August 1975, at which time I joined the staff on a permanent basis."

"Was there any significant incident in your choral career that turned your thoughts to becoming a music critic?" I asked. "Surely, just being on the stage night after night with all of the greatest artists does qualify one to make discriminating comparsions."

"There was one experience," he answered, "that perhaps influenced me. We were doing *Romeo and Juliet* at the Met with Franco Corelli. At one point in the opera Franco, each night, took a high B flat fortissimo with a diminuendo to pianissimo and it was beautiful. For some reason, Franco often singled me out of the crowd at the end of the scene and asked how the B flat was. But one night he tried to do it entirely pianissimo and it did not come off as well. When he came to me and asked how it sounded, I diplomatically said it was fine.

"'You lie! You lie!' he cried angrily. As he stalked off to his dressing room, I followed him and amended my statement.

"'All right, it is not for you. It's better the other way.'

"From then on Franco often came and asked my opinion. It was an unusual situation—the great Franco Corelli was coming to me, a chorister, for my opinion. Maybe I should become a critic."

"Which you did," I added. And now my ex-colleague from the Met chorus sits in judgment of all those with whom he rubbed shoulders for so many years on the New York opera stages, including, of course, yours truly, and I find comfort in the fact that those reviews come from the pen of an experienced veteran who has "trod the boards."

Glossary

The terms *appoggio,* support, head voice, middle voice, chest voice, and placement are not described here, for one of the purposes of this book is to determine what these terms mean to singers who have successfully employed these concepts.

Acuti: High (plural) used to denote high notes.

Bright sound: A clear, penetrating sound such as produced by, say, a trumpet.

Closed tones: An expression used almost exclusively in describing the transformed vowel sounds in the extreme upper part of the male voice, usually called the upper register. Some people object to the use of this expression, fearing it may influence the student to close his throat, but it is very commonly used.

Col fiato: "With the breath," in contrast to "on the breath," is used (in the bad sense) in reference to driving the tone (forcing) by applying too strong a pressure of breath against the vocal cords.

Color: It is a common practice in singing to use colors to represent different kinds of sounds.

Coloratura: Florid, fast types of scales. The kind of singing associated with the highest and lightest kind of soprano called the coloratura soprano.

Cupo: A cavernous and mysterious sound.

Dark sound: Usually associated with the bass voice and the contralto. A typically dark instrumental sound would be that of the contrabassoon.

Diaphragm: A sheet of muscles that separates the stomach and abdominal region from the thorax. It is used in inflating and deflating the lungs. Many singers erroneously speak of the area beneath the front of the rib cage (in front of the stomach) as being the diaphragm.

Diminuendo: An Italian musical term that denotes a lessening of the amount of sound one is producing.

Edema: A congestion of blood in tissues that produces swelling.

Focus: A term that generally denotes concentrating something such as a beam of light. The use of "focus" in singing is discussed with various singers in this book.

Girare: The Italian word meaning "to turn." Its usage in singing will vary in meaning from singer to singer.

Hard palate: The frontal part of the palate which forms the inflexible dome behind the upper teeth.

Hook: A term used by singers to describe an abrupt change in register when singing. It is principally employed in describing a sudden change from middle voice placement to high voice placement in the male voice. This change of register need not be abrupt, but it takes considerable practice and technique to make this change imperceptible.

Larynx: The voice-box, in the region of the Adam's apple, which houses the vocal cords.

Legato: The Italian word for "tied." In music its meaning varies according to whether one belongs to the Italian school or the German school. In the Italian school, to sing legato means "to join consecutive pitches together with minute portamentos." In the German school, to sing legato means "to go from one pitch to another as quickly as possible, but with no intervening tiny portamento."

Mask: In the singer's parlance, mask usually refers to the region of the nose and the cheeks, back up by the sinuses. It can also include the sinuses above the eyes. Singing in the mask generally indicates that the vocalist has a sensation of heightened vibration in the above region of the face.

Mezzo-soprano: The next lower voice category below soprano. Lower than mezzo-soprano is the contralto.

Open tones: The type of voice production used in the middle range of the male voice, in contrast to the closed tones used in the upper register.

Glossary

Passaggio: The Italian word for "passage." Very often the human voice seems to have two or three ranges (or registers) in which the voice is produced in a slightly different manner. There is then a transition to be made between these registers. Each of these transitions, which occurs at a more or less distinct part of the range, is called a passage. Eliminating this sensation of transition is the prime objective of many singers so that the voice will seem to be a homogeneous column of sound, instead of sounding like two or three different voices emanating from the same throat. Many famous singers have never conquered these passages, while others have never seemed, by nature, to have them.

Pharynx: The back of the throat, that region above the larynx. The upper part, extending up into the nasal passage is called the nasopharynx.

Ping: A voice is said to have ping when it has a brilliant, resonant, carrying sound.

Projection: A term designed to cause the singer to think of his voice reaching the back of the theater. It is a vague term, meaning different things to different people, and even an undesirable concept to some.

Register: Different ranges of a particular singer's voice may seem to be produced by somewhat different methods. There may be two, three, or even more such ranges, and they are called registers. (See *passaggio.*)

Scuro: Italian for "dark."

Sfumatura: From loud to soft; a diminuendo from a *forte* tone to a *piano* tone.

Slancio: An Italian word used commonly by singers to denote singing with abandon and energy.

Smorzato: Same as sfumatura.

Soft palate: The rear portion of the palate to which the uvula is attached. It is capable of being raised. Many vocalists feel it should be raised during singing.

Solar plexus: That region just in the divide in front of the rib cage.

Glossary

Squillo: A trumpet-like quality to a voice.

Stringere: Italian verb meaning to "tighten" or "squeeze."

Sul fiato: Italian for "on the breath," used in the sense of "floating" the tone on the breath as in the much-quoted example of the jet, or fountain, of water with the ball bouncing on top of it.

Ultrasonic: A piece of medical apparatus employing high-frequency sound to treat injuries, bruises, edema, etc.

Vocal coach: One who teaches music repertoire (concert songs, arias, operas, etc.) to singers. This is not the same as a vocal teacher who teaches vocal technique. Very often good vocal coaches also teach technique, thus mixing the two disciplines.

Vocalise: Some sort of vocal scale or arpeggio used in training the singing voice.

White sound: A vocal sound produced by singing with the mouth opened wide horizontally, accompanied by a spreading, also horizontally, of the back of the throat (called the nasopharynx). This causes the tongue to pull back and block the throat.